KNOWLEDGE, SKILLS AND COMPETENCE IN THE EUROPEAN LABOUR MARKET

What's in a vocational qualification?

Establishing transparency and comparability of qualifications across member states is vital for the free movement of labour in the European Union.

This book examines how qualifications, knowledge, skills and competences are understood transnationally and in different national contexts and reveals a complex picture of differences and similarities both within and between countries. Against the background of EU policy initiatives, and in particular the European Qualifications Framework, the central focus is on the prospects and difficulties of establishing cross-national recognition of qualifications.

Drawing on case studies of particular sectors and occupations in England, France, Germany and the Netherlands, this insightful and informative book, written by leading academics in the field, will be a vital resource for students and researchers involved with vocational education and training, continuing professional development, labour market studies, human resource management and European Union policy.

Michaela Brockmann is a Senior Research Fellow at the University of Westminster, UK.

Linda Clarke is Professor of European Industrial Relations at the University of Westminster, UK.

Christopher Winch is Professor of Educational Philosophy and Policy at King's College, London, UK.

KNOWLEDGE, SKILLS AND COMPETENCE IN THE EUROPEAN LABOUR MARKET

What's in a vocational qualification?

*Michaela Brockmann, Linda Clarke
and Christopher Winch with
Georg Hanf, Philippe Méhaut
and Anneke Westerhuis*

Routledge
Taylor & Francis Group

LONDON AND NEW YORK

First published 2011
by Routledge
2 Park Square, Milton Park, Abingdon, Oxon OX14 4RN

Simultaneously published in the USA and Canada
by Routledge
270 Madison Ave, New York, NY 10016

Routledge is an imprint of the Taylor & Francis Group, an informa business

British Library Cataloguing in Publication Data
A catalogue record for this book is available from the British Library

Library of Congress Cataloging in Publication Data
Brockmann, Michaela, 1964–.
  Knowledge skills and competence in the European labour market:
  what's in a vocational qualification?/Michaela Brockmann, Linda Clarke,
  and Christopher Winch.
      p. cm.
    Includes bibliographical references and index.
  1. Vocational qualifications – European Union countries.
  2. Vocational education – European Union countries.
  I. Clarke, Linda, 1947–. II. Winch, Christopher.   III. Title.
  HF5381.6.B76 2011
  331.11'42094 – dc22   2010049504

ISBN: 978–0–415–55690–3 (hbk)
ISBN: 978–0–415–55691–0 (pbk)
ISBN: 978–0–203–81479–6 (ebk)

Typeset in Bembo and Stone Sans by
Florence Production Ltd, Stoodleigh, Devon

Printed and bound in Great Britain by
TJ International Ltd, Padstow, Cornwall

CONTENTS

ILLUSTRATIONS

Figures

Tables

Boxes

CONTRIBUTORS

Michaela Brockmann is a Senior Research Fellow at the University of Westminster, UK. She has been working on major studies on vocational education and training across Europe and has published widely, including in the *Oxford Review of Education*. Her research interests include qualitative methods and biographical approaches to youth transition.

Linda Clarke is Professor of European Industrial Relations at the University of Westminster, UK, undertaking research on vocational education and training, skills and labour relations in Europe, particularly the construction sector. Her publications include *Vocational Education: International Approaches, Developments and Systems*, with Christopher Winch, Routledge 2007.

Georg Hanf is Head of the International Monitoring and Benchmarking/European Vocational Education and Training (VET) Policy section of the Federal Institute for VET (BIBB) in Bonn, Germany. His main area of interest is comparative research into the development of VET systems in Europe. He is the author of numerous articles on the history of VET, the impact of European Union (EU) policy on the German VET system, qualifications systems and frameworks.

Philippe Méhaut is senior researcher at the Institute of Labour Economics and Industrial Sociology (LEST), Aix Marseille University, France, and former Scientific Director of CEREQ (Centre of Research on Qualifications), with comparative research interests in VET, labour market segmentation and low-wage work in Europe.

Anneke Westerhuis is programme leader at the Centre for Expertise in Vocational Education and Training in the Netherlands. Her publications include: *The Role of* *the State in Vocational Education* (in Clarke and Winch 2007: Vocational Education: international approaches, developments and systems); and *VET Research in Relation to VET Policy, Planning and Practice* (in Rauner and Maclean 2009).

Christopher Winch is Professor of Educational Philosophy and Policy at King's College, London, UK, researching aspects of vocational education – including declarative and practical knowledge, and vocational agency. In addition to *Vocational Education* with Linda Clarke, his publications include *Dimensions of Expertise*, Continuum 2010.

FOREWORD

The community of researchers undertaking sophisticated comparisons of different nations' arrangements issue frequent warnings about 'policy borrowing' – the tendency of policymakers to extract single elements of other systems and assume that they can be imported into their own jurisdictions and have the same effect there. Policy borrowing – now associated with the 'educational tourism' which has arisen through the big international surveys of educational attainment – fails to recognize the extent to which all aspects of education and training in a nation exist in strong dependent relations – and this despite the rise of transnational economic and social forces. When policies migrate, they typically fall short of policymakers' and others' expectations. But increasingly, due to the European policy urge towards creation of a single European labour market and rising levels of trans-national movement of labour, it is not simply systems that need to be compared but individual workers. The complexity of comparison increasingly affects both individuals moving to another system context (and requesting entry, recognition and appropriate rates of remuneration), and those who are responsible for making decisions about the capabilities of those individuals. As with policy borrowing, any crudeness in these processes may bring problems both to systems and to individuals – including refusal of entry, inappropriate rates of pay, inappropriate return on personal investment in education and training, and poor utilization of capabilities.

Qualifications frameworks – particularly the European Qualifications Framework – are increasingly seen as making a contribution to the enhancement of trans-national mobility. But they are typically reductive, and must be checked against the reality of the portfolio of attainments that workers and trainees carry. This the book does, with original insight. The analysis presented in this book is, however, not narrowly focused on the form and operation of such frameworks. Rather, it looks both inwards into systems and outwards towards the characteristics of transnational mobility.

Prior comparative analyses, including the large international surveys of educational attainment, typically have focused on measuring different levels of skill and knowledge – an approach that has tended to encourage a focus on atomistic elements of skill and knowledge (thus allowing comparisons of differing 'quantities' in different systems), and a conception of rank order amongst nations, where a higher score is seen as superior. But transnational analysis has been in need of methods and tools that enable more incisive and explanatory approaches. The analysis of this book is oriented towards deep explanation of the organizing principles that lie behind profound differences in the composition of occupational roles which, superficially, carry the same nominal title in different national settings but, on examination, differ fundamentally.

Over the past two decades, modularization (unitization) of qualifications and 'outcomes-oriented' approaches to assessment have swept like an international wind of change through national qualification arrangements. Voices raising concerns frequently have been labelled regressive, such as the UK trades' unions anxiety, expressed during the 1980s, that modular training would reduce the amount of training available to workers and promote a culture of 'minimum competence'. Few outside Germany were aware of the caution with which modularization and outcomes-based methods were being approached there – and the reasons for that caution. In 1986, Jochen Reuling's comprehensive and insightful analysis of the pros and cons of modularization expressed sophisticated concerns that modularization and outcomes-based approaches could erode the potency of the key organizing principle of the German Dual System of apprenticeship – the concept of *Beruf* (profession) – and disturb the careful balance of checks and incentives which lay at the heart of a strong set of imperatives for both employers and young people to participate in employer-based initial vocational education and training.

In the Anglo-Saxon community, the importance of such organizing concepts was subordinated to considerations of the utility of modularization and outcomes-based approaches. The conceptual base here was oriented strongly towards empiricism – that modularization and outcomes-based approaches would respond to the actual content of 'modern' work and thus reform vocational qualifications into a more responsive and flexible system. Indeed, it would be less of a system and more of a 'catalogue' of content from which employers and training providers (. . . and young people? . . .) could select, according to their perception of need. Liberation politics drove many of the developers of the time – particularly widening access to training and reduction of the power of institutions in determining the shape and content of vocational qualifications. The consequences of the adoption of modularization and outcomes-based approaches drove arrangements towards liberal economic forms – particularly reduced restriction, higher determination of qualifications by the form of production, and high levels of 'flexibility' in learning arrangements. The value of the authors' analyses is the extent to which they highlight some of the potential losses incurred by treading this pathway. In particular, although UK reforms included considerations of 'occupational competence' within the analysis of the requirements of work, this was only a weak determinant of content, with all processes – the 'functional analysis' of job roles and the development of modules – tending to emphasize atomistic analysis of the content of work. This book lays down a challenge to these approaches.

The chapters present a new, sophisticated examination of the way in which different 'driving concepts' invoke crucial differences in the form of vocational education and training in different national settings and the way in which these affect the constellation of skills, knowledge and dispositions possessed by those learning and working in those settings. But the analysis then extends to how these differences affect transnational mobility and with what degree of fidelity the instruments and processes supporting mobility represent these differences. Within this are embedded critical issues of social justice and economic effectiveness.

The book is a major contribution both to empirical analysis of differing vocational education and training systems and to the methodological canon – and should hold the attention of both policymakers and researchers alike.

Tim Oates
Cambridge
November 2010

ACKNOWLEDGEMENTS

This book represents the results of a three-year project entitled 'Cross-national Equivalence of Vocational Qualifications and Skills'. We would like to thank the Nuffield Foundation for making the project, including this book, possible and in particular Catrin Roberts and Josh Hillman for their continued support throughout. A special thank you also goes to Professor Richard Pring as co-director of the Nuffield Review of Education 14–19 with which this project coincided and who promoted our work within the Review and beyond. We would like to take this opportunity to acknowledge the contributions of all those who attended the various events, a number of which we were able to host at the premises of the Nuffield Foundation. Their active participation and feedback has been invaluable.

Most of all, we would like to thank our project partners in Germany, France and the Netherlands – co-authors of this book. An international study like this one is always a major challenge and relies on the collaboration of national teams. We have been highly privileged to be able to draw on our long-standing working relationships with Anneke Westerhuis, Philippe Méhaut and Georg Hanf, without whose invaluable expertise and continuing and committed involvement neither the project nor this book would have been possible.

Similarly, we are grateful to the members of the Advisory Group – Annie Bouder, Philipp Grollmann, Ben Hövels, Ewart Keep, Tom Leney, Tim Oates and Richard Pring – for their constructive feedback on various draft reports and for their invaluable guidance and enthusiasm.

Finally, we are thankful to Cathy Winch for her French linguistic support with a number of the chapters.

Michaela Brockmann, Linda Clarke and Christopher Winch

ABBREVIATIONS

AITTS	Advanced IT Training System
ANKOM	Anrechnung beruflicher Kompetenzen auf Hochschulstudiengänge (Accreditation of vocational competences towards HE)
APEL	Accreditation of Prior Experiential Learning
APL	Accreditation of Prior Learning
BA	Bachelor of Arts
BEP	Brevet d'Etudes Professionelles
BIBB	Bundesinstitut für Berufsbildung (Federal Institute for Vocational Education and Training)
BMBF	Bundesministerium für Bildung und Forschung (Federal Ministry of Education and Research)
BTEC	Business and Technology Education Council
BTS	Brevet de technicien supérieur
CAP	Certificat d'aptitude professionnelle (French certificate of professional ability)
CBE	Competency Based Education
CEDEFOP	European Centre for the Development of Vocational Training
CEN	European Committee for Standardisation
CEREQ	Centre d'Etudes et des Recherches sur les Qualifications
CGP	Commissariat Général du Plan
CITB	Construction Industry Training Board
CPC	Certificate of Professional Competence
CQP	Certificat de Qualification Professionnelle
CSCS	Construction Skills Certification Scheme
CVET	Continuing Vocational Education and Training
DECVET	German Credit System for Vocational Education and Training

DQR	Deutscher Qualifikationsrahmen (German Qualifications Framework)
DUT	Diplôme Universitaire de Technologie
EC	European Commission
ECTS	European Credit Transfer and Accumulation System
ECVET	European Credit System for Vocational Education and Training
EQF	European Qualifications Framework
EU	European Union
European CV	European Curriculum Vitae
FE	Further Education
FIMO	Formation Initiale Minimale Obligatoire (French lorry driving compulsory mode)
FQ-EHEA	Framework for Qualifications of the European Higher Education Area
GP	General Practitioner
HE	Higher Education
HGV	Heavy Goods Vehicle
HR	Human Resources
HRD	Human Resource Development
HRM	Human Resource Management
IAB	Institut für Arbeitsmarkt-und Berufsforschung
ICT	Information and communications technology
IFSI	Institut de Formation en Soins Infirmiers
I–E–O	Input–Environment–Outcome
IKBB	Innovationskreis Berufliche Bildung (Innovation Circle Vocational Education and Training)
ILM	Internal Labour Market
ILO	International Labour Organization
ISCED	International Standard Classification of Education
IT	Information Technology
IVET	Initial Vocational Education and Training
KMK	Ständige Konferenz der Kultusminster der Länder der Bundesrepublik Deutschland (Standing Committee of Education Ministers of the Länder of the Federal Republic of Germany)
LGV	Large Goods Vehicle
MA	Master of Arts
NARIC	National Recognition Information Centre
NHS	National Health Service
NMC	Nursing and Midwifery Council
NQF	National Qualifications Framework
NVQ	National Vocational Qualification
OECD	Organisation for Economic Cooperation and Development
OLM	Occupational Labour Market
OMC	Open Method of Co-ordination

OQF	Occupational Qualifications Framework
PhD	Doctor of Philosophy
QCF	Qualifications and Credit Framework
RCN	Royal College of Nursing
SEDOC	System for Education and Occupations
SFIA	Skills Framework for the Information Age
SME	Small- and medium-sized enterprise
SOEP	(German) Socio-economic Panel
SQF	Sectoral Qualifications Framework
SSC	Sector Skills Council
TDA	Training and Development Agency for Schools
UCATT	Union of Construction and Allied Technical Trades
UK	United Kingdom
UKCG	UK Contractors Group
USA	United States of America
VAE	Validation des acquis de l'expérience
VET	Vocational Education and Training
ZMT	Zone of Mutual Trust

1

INTRODUCTION: CROSS-NATIONAL EQUIVALENCE OF SKILLS AND QUALIFICATIONS ACROSS EUROPE?

Michaela Brockmann, Linda Clarke,
Christopher Winch, Georg Hanf,
Philippe Méhaut and Anneke Westerhuis

What this book is about

Moves to create a competitive European economy and a unified European Union (EU) labour market set out at the Lisbon Conference in 2000 have set in train a steady stream of subsequent initiatives in education and training. Notable among these has been the official adoption of the European Qualification Framework (EQF) in 2008, to be followed by an EU-wide credit accumulation and transfer system (ECVET). The operation of EQF envisaged is through voluntary arrangements between member states, thereby establishing multilateral 'Zones of Mutual Trust' (ZMTs). These zones will – it is assumed – be based on similarities and mutual understanding of differences between national vocational education and training (VET) systems and labour markets, on a certain convergence in sectoral, occupational and enterprise education and training needs, and above all on mutual appreciation of the aims, conceptual basis and approach towards VET and qualifications (Coles and Oates 2005). EQF and ECVET depend, therefore, on shared assumptions and ways of working between the economies and educational systems of the EU member states and on developing a common framework of understanding.

By exploring similarities and differences between VET systems, qualifications and skills across Europe and at the same time seeking to go beyond this by identifying concepts and categories that might be regarded as transnational, the book represents more than a comparative text. Whilst our focus is on particular countries with distinct VET systems – namely England, France, Germany and the Netherlands – each also exemplifies particular conceptions and approaches. Thus, key to the German system is the notion of *Beruf,* denoting a person's occupational identity, status and capacity. For the French system in contrast, still very much school-based and state regulated, *savoir* (most closely translated as knowledge) is critical. The

Dutch system, with its more utilitarian approach is built around the notion of *competence*. And, for England, VET remains dependent on the notion of *skills,* a peculiarly Anglo-Saxon concept, tied to the workplace and even devoid of educational content. Though these four notions – *Beruf, savoir, competence* and *skills* – are by no means unique to the countries that exemplify them, with competence becoming especially important to each, they do have a particular significance, largely associated with the differing labour market and institutional contexts on which each VET system is constructed.

Through pinpointing difficulties in establishing equivalence of vocational qualifications – posing problems for mobility – and the reasons for these, ways to overcome them are also suggested. In this respect the book is intended to contribute to current policy debates and key initiatives, such as the EQF and ECVET, aimed at facilitating cross-national recognition of qualifications and hence the mobility of labour. It seeks to:

- describe the various EU initiatives in VET and qualifications, the assumptions on which they are based, and their economic, social and political background;
- elucidate concepts critical to the construction of particular European VET systems – *Beruf, savoir, skills* and *competence,* showing why this is so and the relevance of these to other countries' VET systems;
- identify the ways in which certain occupational qualifications (nursing, software engineering, bricklaying and lorry driving) are converging and/or diverging, the underlying reasons for this, and the possibilities for establishing equivalence;
- assess what these developments mean for the development of ZMTs and for the implementation of EU VET initiatives; and
- provide an interpretive dictionary of key concepts related to VET and qualifications, describing how each is understood in different countries/ languages.

Our research study

The book draws on research conducted by the authors from 2006 to 2009, funded by the Nuffield Foundation and adding an enhanced international dimension to the Nuffield Review of 14–19 Education in England and Wales (Brockmann *et al.* 2009a). The purpose of our research was to analyse how key concepts related to VET are understood and applied within different national contexts, in particular England, the Netherlands, Germany and France, through case studies drawn from four sectors (information technology (IT), construction, health and logistics) and qualifications (software engineering, bricklaying, nursing and lorry driving). A critical focus was to assess the value and difficulties of applying the EQF, making it a particularly timely research in the light of EU initiatives aimed at enhancing the transferability and comparability of qualifications in Europe. Given the distinct traditions of VET systems and labour processes in European countries, the EQF raises important questions regarding the validity of comparators and thus the feasibility of such a framework. Our findings suggest important obstacles to and opportunities for the development of common understandings of qualifications and skills.

The research aimed in particular to:

* describe the significance of different terminology such as 'training', 'occupation', 'vocational education', 'competence', 'practical or industrial knowledge', 'applied theoretical knowledge', 'skill', 'labour', 'job', 'trade' and 'skilled worker';
* develop and apply transnational categories for analysing 'skills and qualifications';
* examine, compare and contrast differences in particular 'skills and qualifications' in France, Germany, England and the Netherlands in terms of the way they are imparted through the VET system and deployed in practice in the workplace;
* identify the problems such differences pose to integration within an EU framework; and
* explore the difficulties entailed in assessing skills and qualifications in crossnational contexts in and between our four countries and the means by which these are overcome, and propose criteria for evaluating them cross-nationally.

The countries chosen, all located in North West Europe, each represent distinct approaches to VET. Thus the English system is heavily committed to a dominant stake by employers, state intervention on the supply rather than the demand side, an outcomes-based approach to qualifications and the organizing central concept of *skill*. France represents a system heavily oriented towards the education system, characterized by a considerable degree of state planning together with social partner involvement, in which the salience of knowledge is recognized through the organizing concept of *savoir*. Germany represents a strong social partnership model, known as the Dual System, embodying the principle of education or employment and citizenship, with a high degree of planning of both the qualification and the VET systems and an organizing principle based on the Germanic conception of an occupation, the *Beruf*. The Netherlands is again a social partnership-based system but differs from France and Germany in respect of the comprehensive nature of its qualification system and a very high degree of licence to practise regulations for labour market entry. The integration of theory, practice and attitude (*houding*) is emphasized and is encapsulated in the peculiarly Dutch conception of *competences* which recognizes the role of personal character and judgement in operating in complex situations.

The occupations and sectors were selected as ones associated with labour migration across national boundaries and as sometimes subject to skill shortages in a number of countries (EC 2008a; MAC 2008). They also provide important contrasts, constituting a mix of traditional and modern, manual and non-manual, highly regulated and lightly regulated, and narrowness and breadth in scope. Thus, nursing in the health sector represents a qualification subject to a high degree of EU regulation and (increasingly) initial qualification within higher education (HE). Software engineering within the IT sector is a qualification with flexible entry requirements, considerable cross-national activity and a strong orientation towards HE for initial qualifications combined with work-based learning. Bricklaying within the construction industry represents a traditional occupation, configured in widely differing ways across the four countries. Finally, lorry driving in the logistics sector represents an occupation that is highly regulated at the level of a basic licence to practise but has a varied pattern of non-mandatory qualifications across the four countries.

The methodology of our research project is distinctive in that, although planned and carried out as an empirical investigation into policy implementation, it primarily involved a linguistic and conceptual examination of variations in the usage and salience of particular terminology in different European countries and in a variety of policy-relevant contexts – European, national, firm and workplace. The first phase, concerned with the development of a transnationally applicable conceptual framework, was conducted in liaison with outside advisers and on the basis of documentary evidence. The framework consisted of seven dimensions through which we explored the institutional and conceptual basis of the VET and labour market systems related to the four occupational qualifications:

- *Governance* – the regulatory framework of VET qualifications.
- *Education* – the structure and content of relevant VET provision.
- *Qualification* – the nature of qualifications.
- *Knowledge* – the understandings of knowledge underpinning VET.
- *Competence* – the prevalent notions of competence structuring VET.
- *Use of labour* – the ways in which labour is deployed in the labour market.
- *Exchange of labour* – the currency of qualifications in the labour market.

On the basis of this framework a macro-level inquiry was conducted of major stakeholders in the VET systems in each country and at the European level to look at the use of these concepts. Representatives from bodies responsible for VET in each occupation, together with training providers, employers' organizations and trade unions were interviewed, with a view to gaining an understanding of how the concepts are understood and operationalized at different levels in each of the VET systems. This phase included research partners from one country being involved in interviews in another in order to facilitate the development of transnational categories of analysis. In addition, investigations were undertaken at EU level, including with the European Commission (EC), trade unions and employers' associations, and with organizations that exemplified alternative ways of comparing qualifications, such as the United Kingdom's (UK) National Recognition Informa-tion Centre (NARIC). The subsequent micro-level phase of the research principally concerned data collection in workplaces employing those from our selected occupations, interviewing individuals directly connected with the use and exchange of the associated occupational qualification. Employers and employees in different companies were interviewed, again using the interview schedule structured around our analytical categories. The final phase of our research was concerned with analysing, evaluating and interpreting our data, an important feature being the constant iteration of our findings with our research partners from the different countries and the project steering group.

Occupational qualifications that constitute typical or common entry routes into the occupations in the countries concerned were chosen for our case studies, though these are not the only routes, nor necessarily representative of the respective national VET system (Table 1.1). It is important to distinguish between qualifications and occupations. Qualifications are awarded on the basis of particular knowledge or know-how and may or may not be congruent with occupations, which are associated with a particular division of labour within a sector of any given society. In this respect, qualifications refer to the VET system, whilst occupations refer to the labour market. Our study is concerned to investigate the ways in which the respective occupational qualification is produced, understood and valued and how it corresponds with the different occupational divisions of labour, qualifying labour to work in that particular occupation in one or the other country. As such the study represents a dialogue between occupations in the labour market and the particular qualifications stemming from the VET system which are associated with these, as shown in Table 1.1.

TABLE 1.1 Case study occupational qualifications in each country

	Software engineering	Nursing	Bricklaying	Lorry driving
England	Higher Apprenticeship, BA	Diploma, BA	NVQ Level 2	NVQ Level 2
France	DUT	Diplôme, BA	CAP	Titre
Netherlands	Secondary VET	Secondary VET	Secondary VET	Secondary VET
Germany	Software developer (CVET)	Vocational school	Dual system	Dual system

Dominant VET typologies

Two features stand out from the literature over the past decade comparing national VET systems: the complexity and interwoven nature of the multiple factors underpinning them; and their fluid nature and openness to pressures stemming from economic and political developments both at the national and supranational levels. Together, these features make for a complex dynamic of divergent and convergent tendencies. Thus, Brown et al. (2001) demonstrate that, while subject to the same global pressures for economic competitiveness, countries' approaches to skill formation vary according to their respective culture and political economy.

Germany's 'high skills society model', Japan's 'high skills manufacturing model' and the UK's 'high skills/low skills model' all constitute different approaches to economic development (ibid.). Similarly, Green *et al.* (1999) distinguish between, on the one hand, common trends affecting EU countries, including economic (restructuring, changes in work organization), demographic and social factors, and, on the other, what they refer to as 'sources of divergence' in VET systems (1999: 23). The authors convincingly show that, while common trends induce common policy orientations, convergence is tempered by the embeddedness of each individual country's education and labour market traditions. In a similar vein, others have argued that, rather than converging, differences between EU VET systems have become more marked with the expansion of post-war education as countries have built on their traditional institutional structures (Müller and Gangl 2003).

While these studies elucidate the complex interplay of factors influencing VET systems, they tend to focus on comparisons of national systems as a whole, thereby potentially obscuring a more nuanced picture of similarities and differences, both within and across countries. For example, Müller and Wolbers (2003) distinguish between occupation-oriented systems (e.g. Germany, Austria and the Netherlands) and those that are focused on general, school-based education (e.g. the UK and France). An exception is Bosch and Charest's (2008) study of VET in ten countries, which differentiates between VET and HE and suggests variation *within* countries as well as between them. Examining VET systems in the context of economic change, and building on Hall and Soskice's (2001) distinction between liberal and co-ordinated market economies, Bosch and Charest (2008) point to the continued divergence of VET systems as a result of differences in industrial relations, welfare systems and product markets. Countries with co-ordinated market economies, characterized by a high level of social partner involvement in VET, have been able to reform their VET systems in line with new economic challenges and as a strategy for innovation. By contrast, initial VET in liberal market economies has been marginalized and increased emphasis placed on general and higher education, albeit often of a vocational nature. On the other hand, at the level of HE there appears to be a degree of convergence in terms of provision, the structure of qualifications and the relationship between qualifications and the labour market. This trend has been underpinned by the general expansion in HE in countries across Europe (and worldwide) and by the Bologna Process, aimed at facilitating a common degree structure (Prokou 2008).

The neglect of conceptual complexity: outcomes and inputs

It is perhaps inevitable that a cross-national project such as the EQF seems to ignore subtle national variations in the way that VET systems and the concepts underpinning them manifest themselves. However, such homogenizing tendencies bring their own dangers, particularly if the process of simplification means that valuable elements of the VET systems of some countries are neglected to the benefit of dubious ones originating in some others. This can happen despite the apparently benign intentions of the designers of instruments such as EQF. We will focus on two areas of oversimplification that are in danger of making EQF less acceptable and more problematic than it might otherwise be in some countries.

Different conceptions of competence

The scale of the challenge involved in working with a common understanding of competence across the EU is even more complex given the requirement that each EU member state has to develop and then relate its own national qualification framework (NQF) to the EQF by 2010, 'in accordance with national legislation and practice' (EC 2008b: 10). The EQF concept of *competence* is illustrated through a slightly adapted extract from the grid of level descriptors relating to level (3) and therefore including descriptors of knowledge, skills and competence. In Table 1.2, we use the terms 'Competence' and 'Competency' to distinguish particular conceptions of competence though the EC uses the same word 'competence' to apply to different senses of the term. Thus, Competence in the overall sense is defined as:

> the proven ability to use knowledge, skills and personal, social and/or methodological abilities, in work or study situations and in professional and personal development.
>
> (EC 2008b: 13)

What we have termed 'Competency' in the Table is, in the context of the EQF, described in terms of responsibility and autonomy (ibid). The phrase 'responsibility and autonomy' encapsulates both the German notion of the autonomous and responsible individual worker and the English notion of a managerial hierarchy. However, it can be argued that the descriptors under this heading tend to favour the English conception rather than the German one, thus sidelining the vital role

TABLE 1.2 EQF level (3) Competence

	Knowledge *Knowledge is described* *as either theoretical or* *factual*	*Skills* *These are described as* *either cognitive or practical*	*Competency* *This is described as* *responsibility and autonomy*
Level 3	Knowledge of facts, principles, processes and general concepts, in a field of work or study	A range of cognitive and practical skills required to accomplish tasks and to solve problems by applying basic tools, methods, materials and information	Take responsibility for completion of task in work or study. Adapt own behaviour to circumstances in solving problems

Source: Brockmann *et al.* (2009b: 789).

that self-management rather than subordination plays in the German workplace. In the German context Competence is understood as *berufliche Handlungsfähigkeit,* referring to the ability or capacity of the individual to act within the labour process of a defined *Beruf* or occupation.

One key element that is not explicitly included in the EQF is that of 'occupational capacity' within an integrated labour process, an element intrinsic to VET systems such as the German and referring to the scope of activities encompassed within an occupation and the depth of knowledge implied. It is an element associated with the (often broad) potential of labour itself to perform particular activities and is arguably implicit in the EQF model through the presence of the overriding category of Competence (see Table 1.3 below). This notion of occupational capacity is however foreign to the English NQF (now QCF – Qualifications and Credit Framework), where qualifications do not refer to clearly defined occupations in the sense of *Beruf*. Indeed, the English framework is based not on occupational capacities but rather on work activities and on task-based skills.

Responsibility and autonomy are intrinsic elements of Competence through the third EQF category of competence, which we have termed 'Competency' (see Table 1.2) and which describes the degree to which they are present. The problem is that the English conception of competence does not recognize them as intrinsic to itself except as a supervisory or managerial function at higher levels of the NQF. This means that what we have termed the 'Competency' category in the EQF is interpreted in the English context as the degree to which the individual controls or is controlled by others, rather than as a category of independent agency. It thus refers to the degree to which a worker is supervising or being supervised in the workplace and, in terms of EQF, to the degree to which labour itself is able to act autonomously and takes responsibility. The English understanding relates in particular to the distinction between its own National Vocational Qualification (NVQ) Levels 3 and 4, whereby Level 4 is assumed to contain an element of supervision. A critical point of interpretation for the QCF will, therefore, be the way in which the 'Competency' category is interpreted, at these levels. This problem is finessed where occupations are regulated by the EU, as in the case of nursing, but not all are; with these, there is a real problem in incorporating 'Competency' in the EQF sense into English qualifications or, worse, incorporating the English sense into the EQF one.

The problem of oversimplification of conceptual complexity and the way in which conceptions that are crucial to the VET systems of some countries are marginalized is illustrated in Table 1.3 in relation to competence. The EQF conception of competence has a tendency to marginalize both the integrative and personal nature of competence as conceived in France, Germany and the Netherlands and to play down its self-managing aspect.

Sultana observes that:

> While there is no single, authoritative definition of the word competence, there seems to be an increasing consensus that the term should not be used

in a narrowly technicist manner to refer to just skills, precisely because of the implications this has for education and training.

(2009: 20)

The EQF competence definition, however, does not make allowances for learning processes and learning environments:

> competence means the proven ability to use knowledge, skills and personal, social and/or methodological abilities, in work or study situations and in professional and personal development.

(EC 2008b: 11)

TABLE 1.3 What is meant by 'competence'?

Competence as framing concept
Covers different, and often contested, conceptions of competence

Conceptions of competence
These are often incompatible and relate to each other on a continuum from occupationally based rich descriptions of action capacity to restricted task-based descriptions of operational adequacy

	Integrated concepts of competence	*Discrete conceptions of competence (1)*	*Discrete conceptions of competence (2)*
National conceptions of competence	The German *Handlungskompetenz*, includes a social, moral and civic dimension and integrates various aspects of competence within an occupational context	French and Dutch conceptions, although task-based, assume a holistic integration of knowledge, skill and attitude in practice	'English' competence, entails task performance to an acceptable standard, which may, but need not, involve the application of underpinning knowledge
EQF conceptions of competence	The EQF competence framework implicitly integrates knowledge, skill, responsibility and autonomy, but excludes the moral and civic dimensions. It can also be described as a 'learning outcomes' framework	The EQF third column 'competence' (in this chapter referred to as 'Competency') involves responsibility and autonomy as separate categories from knowledge and skill and is therefore potentially non-integrative (e.g. refers just to seniority in the workplace)	

Source: Brockmann *et al.* (2009b: 793).

Organized learning and daily life are distinct environments, having different effects on learning outcomes whose quality is conditioned by environmental factors, including the programme, personnel, curricula, instructor, facilities, institutional climate, courses, teaching style, friends, room-mates, extra-curricular activities and organizational affiliation (see, for instance, Reynolds and Cuttance 1992). The question of whether the creation of ZMTs is able to compensate for apparent differences in types of competences and in *in situ* understanding of the concept is yet to be answered.

Learning outcomes

Our second example relates to the overall design feature of the EQF characterized as a 'learning outcomes' approach. Once again, very important distinctions are passed over without comment in the use of this phrase. There is a clear and uncontroversial sense in which the aims of any educational or training process are described as 'learning outcomes'. For example, the English BTEC[1] National Level 3 qualification in Construction within Unit 1 covers Health, Safety and Welfare and is prefaced by a number of learning outcomes, whose content includes *Accident Prevention*:

> *Risk assessments*: items to be assessed, principal hazards, likely injury outcomes. *Use of Control Measures*: use of procedures, substances, lifting assessments and manual handling assessments, inspection, personal responsibility for health, safety and welfare.
>
> (EdExcel 2003: 1)

Such learning outcomes are part of a programme of study in a given area and indicate content that may then be assessed through the use of instruments, such as practical activities or examinations, which may be referenced against *standards* as the levels of expected performance within a given curriculum. For example, National Curriculum English (Reading) at level 5 requires that students:

> show understanding of a range of texts, selecting essential points and using inference and deduction where appropriate. In their responses, they identify key features, themes and characters and select sentences, phrases and relevant information to support their views. They retrieve and collate information from a range of sources.
>
> (QCA 2005: 58)

Assessment instruments are devised to ascertain whether and how well the standard has been reached, exactly the same as is done for learning outcomes (see EdExcel 2005). There is thus an internal or conceptual relationship between the *prescribed content* (which aims to satisfy the learning outcome descriptor) and the *assessment* of whether the learning outcome has been achieved.

This approach to assessment is not, however, what is intended in the EQF methodology. Indeed, the EQF approach is to draw a conceptual separation between learning process and learning outcome in the same way as is done with NVQs, so that one may satisfy a set of EQF descriptors without having had to follow a prescribed curricular and pedagogic path. There is thus no internal or conceptual link between assessment of the learning outcome and any prescribed path of study (curriculum and pedagogy). Ability to deliver an *in situ* performance which satisfies the descriptors is all that should matter in order to achieve a learning outcome (although this possibility cannot be ignored). The danger is not so much that continental systems of assessment and qualification will migrate to the English conception of learning outcome, but that the English approach will not be understood because of its ambiguous terminology, leading to confusion when the equivalence of qualifications is assessed.

Comparative VET policy

VET as object of EU policymaking

The EU economic development agenda is a major driver for European policy making in VET. With the 2000–2010 programme launched in the Lisbon declaration, the EU defined its competitors in strong and emerging economies, only to be competed with under the condition of European cooperation, coordinated by the EC. One of the instruments targeted to meet these aims is VET, valued for producing the highly educated labour force needed to raise production levels, to produce capital-intensive products and to facilitate labour market flexibility (Leney and Green 2005; Heyes and Rainbird 2009).

This was the situation in 2010. However, VET has been an instrument for labour European market policies since the very beginning of the European Community[2]. As Cort points out, the European Coal and Steel Community, the predecessor of the subsequent European Economic Community and EU, already identified the mobility of workers and the transnational recognition of vocational qualifications as conditional for the establishment of a common market for coal and steel (Cort 2008a). This VET policy was continued in the European Economic Community era, when the Community policy domain was extended to include the agriculture and transportation sectors. For instance, Article 41 of the original Treaty of Rome stipulates that:

> provision may be made within the framework of the common agricultural policy for measures such as: an effective co-ordination of efforts in the spheres of vocational training, of research and of the dissemination of agricultural knowledge; this may include joint financing of projects or institutions.
>
> (Treaty of Rome 1957: 17)

But the ambition was also higher, aiming to define a policy covering all economic sectors, as VET was framed as an appropriate tool for common labour market policies (Heyes and Rainbird 2009). This can be deduced from another Article (128) in the original Treaty of Rome:

> The Council shall, . . . lay down general principles for implementing a common vocational training policy capable of contributing to the harmonious development of both the national economies and of the common market.
>
> (1957: 28)

Although the right to use this tool for policymaking at supranational communal European level has long been disputed between the Commission and the member states, in 1963 the principles for implementing a common vocational training policy, as announced in the Treaty, were agreed. These included the expansion of the policy area to general education, preparing the ground for expanding from vocational training to the wider field of VET (Pépin 2006). But it took youth unemployment stemming from the economic (oil) crisis at the beginning of the 1970s for the need to be felt to develop a European policy. Before then, as Ertl (2006: 7) puts it: 'most Member States did not consider the ten principles of 1963 legally binding, joint action in VET was very limited'. Justified by the need for economic cooperation in the mid 1970s, the Community did initiate some activities. These were, however, mostly small and lacking in cohesion, though the need was felt at community level to define a supranational education policy to include VET as well as general education.

European VET policymaking found a new impulse in the Treaty of Maastricht of 1992, stating in Article 127 that:

> The community shall implement a vocational training policy which shall support and supplement the action of the Member States (29).

This Article encouraged the Commission, under the flag of ongoing economic integration, to initiate more ambitious and comprehensive programmes for the co-ordination of national policies in education and training. Still, the member states did not follow unconditionally, invoking the principle of subsidiarity to guard their autonomy and, in doing so, limiting the impact of newly extended and more integrated EU activities (Ertl 2006; Cort 2008a). However, the movement could be delayed but not stopped. The Rubicon was passed with the Bologna declaration of 1999, heralding the Framework for Qualifications of the European Higher Education Area (FQ-EHEA) and EU-wide acceptance of the Dublin Descriptors (2001–4) expressing the agreement of all member states to implementing a supranational education (HE) framework. Earlier initiatives on the recognition of VET qualifications – including a general system for the recognition of qualifications in regulated professions, the System for Education and Occupations (SEDOC) classification system, and the CEDEFOP (European Centre for the Development of Vocational Training) comparison of occupations and qualifications – had had little impact. Now, however, the initiatives in HE opened the way to a more promising initiative in the field of VET (Ertl and Philips 2003; Cort 2008b).

For Cort (2008b) the Copenhagen process, launched in 2002 and defining the aims and means for VET to be developed within the framework of the EU strategy agreed in Lisbon two years earlier, marks the slide from a 'bottom-up, voluntary process' discourse to a 'top-down centralised steering discourse' (116). This might sound like an act of conspiracy, but the fact is that nowadays the Open Method of Co-ordination (OMC) is reframed as 'too soft'. In the new *Europe 2020 Initiative* the EC warns that:

> country-specific recommendations will be addressed to Member States. Policy warnings could be issued in case of inadequate response.
>
> (EC 2010: 4)

The Lisbon agenda did indeed not succeed in changing the economic output of member states and low performing ones 'were insufficient to implement the necessary structural reforms in order to increase and enhance their competitiveness and welfare levels' (Karagiannis 2008: 201).

In his analyses of the history of the European Community, van Middelaar (2009: 426) quotes François Mitterrand's '*il faut laisser le temps au temps*'. Time is essential in European policymaking; the building of Europe is an ongoing process of permanently setting and resetting targets, of framing and reframing ends and means. The EU's dealing with VET is a perfect illustration of this seasoned policy approach.

VET's contribution to the EU agenda

VET is an important tool for European competitive strategy; for Heyes and Rainbird it is even its core strategy (2009). But where, precisely, does its contribution lie? In the literature on this subject, two policy aims – not necessarily mutually exclusive – can be identified. The first is that VET – or more precisely high-quality VET and better access to VET – is instrumental in producing a higher qualified labour force all over Europe. This is needed if Europe's future on a global market is not in the production of cheap, low value-added mass products (Ertl 2006; Pépin 2006; Hofheinz 2010). The other aim is the creation of an open European market for qualifications and the free movement of labour (Bohlinger 2008; Cort 2008b). For Cort, the push for transparency, harmonization, recognition and transnational transfer of vocational qualifications finds its basis in Europe's ambition to create an internal market 'where goods, capital, services and labour can flow freely' (2008b: 109).

The identification of these two aims opens up an interesting perspective for assessing the added value of the EQF. Will it contribute to enhancing the qualification levels of Europe's workforce or will its merit be in serving as a reference table for assessing the currency rate of national qualifications? For the former aim, the minimum condition is that the EQF defines horizontal and vertical (international) progression routes. For the latter aim, besides a common European qualification vocabulary, qualification currency rates have to be tested on the market and not just be announced in national fora. The aim of this book is not to assess the EQF's contribution to Europe's economic policies – it is far too early for that – but to point to differences in the national routes for obtaining qualifications and their impact on understanding what qualifications are. By acknowledging these differences, the launching of EQF is not the end of a policy process, but merely its beginning!

Labour market policy

Unlike employment and occupational health and safety policies, the EU has been reluctant to regulate VET, symbolized in the tendency to regard it as a 'no-competence' issue and in CEDEFOP (set up in 1975) coming under the Council of Ministers. Indeed VET has for long been one of the few areas in which governments have been able to subsidise producers without infringing competition policy (Rainbird 1993). And, though the soft law introduced into the area through the OMC may appear hard compared to what has gone before, it is nevertheless voluntary and has nowhere like the impact of regulation, whether in the form of Directives or Regulations. This does not, of course, mean that VET has been immune from regulation as part of labour market policy. For instance, as Hantrais (2007) points out, since 1964 over 60 sectoral directives have been adopted, ensuring the mutual recognition of conditions for access to particular occupations, many enabling recognition of work experience acquired in another state. At the HE level, mutual recognition directives cover many of the professions, including doctors, nurses, dentists, midwives, pharmacists, veterinary surgeons, accountants and architects. These were supplemented by more global directives, culminating in the 2005 (36/EC) Directive on the recognition of professional qualifications, generally understood as in all the other cases to refer to programmes of study and comparability between levels of education and training.

This process raises two questions: first, why has regulation on VET remained largely restricted to HE professions; and, second, why is attention now being directed to VET? In addressing the first, it is perhaps all the more surprising that regulation has been so restricted, given the development of the European Social Dialogue between the social partners (trade unions and employers) and the Protocol Procedure introduced under the Maastricht Treaty, enabling them to request the EC to formulate proposal items for regulation and since refashioned as the Social Agreement under the Treaty of Amsterdam. Social Dialogue committees, with working groups specifically on vocational training and on health and safety, exist for almost all sectors, as well as at EU level. And a spate of Directives were introduced from the 1990s through the Protocol Procedure, including Directives on Parental

Leave, Equality between Full and Part Time Workers, Fixed Term Work, Temporary work, and Teleworking, and played a critical role in shaping European labour legislation (Keller and Sörries 1999). With the changed political composition of the Council of Ministers and the European Parliament, however, combined with the aversion to 'hard' regulation, this has been reduced to a trickle.

The question remains, nevertheless, why has VET been relatively immune from regulation? Or has it? An interesting exception is the regulation concerning Heavy Goods Vehicle (HGV) drivers who come under the Directive on Certification of Professional Competence of 2003 (59), requiring a minimum of 35 hours of additional training every five years and designed to improve safety and the knowledge and skills of drivers throughout their working lives. If such legislation can be introduced concerning the training of lorry drivers, then why not for many more occupations, especially those where there are very obvious health and safety risks, such as electricians and many other construction workers, including bricklayers? A promising sign of openness to new policy at least in the area of Continuing VET (CVET) is, however, given by the EC in the context of the Lisbon Strategy for Growth and Jobs in order to:

> guarantee that workers with relatively low educational attainment have the skills required to participate effectively in the new production process that prevails in today's economy.
>
> (EC 2007a: 28)

The reasons given for this are to:

- reduce social exclusion and income inequality;
- sustain social protection by keeping older workers active;
- support 'flexicurity policies by making internal labour markets more dynamic and by enhancing job-to-job mobility'; and
- increase the 'innovation capacity of European firms by allowing workers to continually upgrade their skills' (ibid.).

These reasons provide a clue to the more difficult question of why attention is now being directed at EU level to VET and, especially, to establishing equivalence or comparability of qualifications through the EQF. One of the key problems affecting work-based learning and the acquisition of qualifications is the transformation in the labour market and the employment relation. Not only is the definition of an employee unclear, but – through subcontracting, outsourcing and the increasing fluidity of ownership – so too is that of an employer (Deakin 2007; EC 2007b). The increasing use of agencies, temporary workers and the self-employed has meant that employee status is no longer necessarily identifiable with the individual permanent contract of employment (Clarke *et al.* 2007). Throughout Europe, and particularly in certain sectors, such changes are evident, varying according to the particular employment regime and posing a threat to VET arrangements which continue to be premised on clear and individual employer and employee relations, on internal labour markets and – in many countries – on social partnership (Gallie 2007; Marsden 2007). They have also meant increased reliance on qualifications – rather than, for example personal reference or experience with a particular firm – as a means to recognize a person's abilities, placing an added onus on improving their comparability and transferability and, perhaps, on developing occupational labour markets.

Introducing the chapters

Whilst divided into separate chapters, the book has coherence as a whole, intended to guide the reader through distinct themes and to follow a thread from the European policy perspective (Chapter 2), through the education- and knowledge-based approach of France (Chapter 3) to the dual-based systems integrating both educational and work-based elements in Germany (Chapter 4), built on the rock of the *Beruf*, and in the Netherlands (Chapter 5), constructed around notions of competence. With the English 'skill'-based system (Chapter 6), mimicking labour market realities, comes a jolt and contrast, which is reinforced and brought to life in the portrayal (Chapter 7) of the different occupational qualifications of both bricklayers and lorry drivers in the four countries, revealing at the same time the continued trade- and even job-based character of the English labour market compared to that in the other countries, where occupational qualifications have gained greater currency. Only with nursing and software engineering (Chapter 8), where HE plays a significant role, is the English situation retrieved and the respective occupational qualifications more comparable to those in the other countries. Finally the book concludes (Chapter 9) by considering possible ways forward to establish equivalence of vocational qualifications, before providing a detailed and considered interpretive dictionary (Chapter 10) of key terms applied in VET, outlining the often marked differences in the meanings attached to each. The following section details the contents of each chapter in turn.

Chapter 2 begins by providing a historical overview of the EU's attempts, since the Treaty of Rome in 1957, to influence VET policy within the member countries. These attempts culminated in the EQF, whose aims, implementation strategy and main design characteristics are explained. The aim of the EQF as a 'meta-framework' is to promote transparency and comparability of national qualifications. The means by which this is to be done is through the OMC, a voluntary activity on the part of interested countries, which is, in turn, facilitated through the development of ZMTs (Coles and Oates 2005). Controversial aspects of the EQF are identified and analysed. These include: the concept of *learning outcomes* (see discussion above); the capacity of the EQF to act as a 'translation device' for qualifications from two or more countries; the lack of a 'scope' dimension whereby the breadth of an occupation can be specified; and, finally, the various potential translation difficulties in rendering terms like 'competence', 'skill' and 'knowledge' into other languages (a particular preoccupation of Chapter 10 of this book). Attention is also given to the need to *reference* national qualifications to the EQF. This process involves determining the cognitive level of a national qualification with a point within the EQF and this too is a process in which trust between the different governments participating in the EQF on the one hand, and labour market actors on the other, is of paramount importance. Closely associated with this requirement is the need to develop the detail of EQF at the sectoral and occupational level if it is to serve as a useful device within labour markets.

Chapter 2 goes on to look at further developments beyond the EQF, in particular the development of ECVET, the credit accumulation and transfer framework, which is designed to allow elements of a national qualification to receive recognition and be integrated into the national VET systems of member countries. The chapter concludes with an assessment of the progress of implementation of the EQF.

Chapter 3 introduces the French qualification system, which, as in the Netherlands, is more and more built on a framework of competences, representing a huge shift from a traditional input-based to an output-based model, and an opening to the Accreditation of Prior Learning (APL). However this shift does not affect one of the key characteristic of the French model, which is a rather broad and holistic concept of competence, one not synonymous with performance but a mixture of knowledge, know-how and behaviour (in French, *savoir*, *savoir-faire* and *savoir-être*) linked to broad occupational profiles. The definition of competence is also not only attuned to the direct (short-term) transition into the labour market but – similar to the German and Dutch competence – to the long-term perspective of the individual worker (mobility, lifelong learning), as well as to the individual citizen (citizenship, behaviour as a consumer . . .). On the one hand, the three dimensions of competence are highly interlinked and, on the other, cannot be encapsulated in performance at the work place. This feature is in line with the historical (and socio-economic) approach of the French VET system, whereby, following the 'encyclopaedist' tradition, knowledge is a strong component of self- and humanbeing, in part reinforced by the process of embedding of the VET system in the whole education system. The parity of esteem of general and vocational qualifications (in theory, not in practice . . .) is embodied in French rhetoric concerning 'meritocracy' and in the fact that every pupil should be able to move from a VET track to a general one (and vice versa). So, VET qualifications cannot be analysed without taking into account their dual currency, both within the education system and on the labour market, a duality that produces many tensions and raises questions with regard to the EQF process. Referencing to the EQF is not only a technical matter of how national concepts fit but also a socio–economic question concerning the relationship between levels in the general and vocational education systems. It could also have consequences for the relationship between qualifications and the educational structure as well as for occupational positions in collective agreements. In this respect, the question of ZMTs is not only one of concepts, even certified by a quality insurance process, but a social process including all the stakeholders of the VET system and the labour market.

Chapter 4 considers the changing relevance of the concept of *Beruf* in Germany. The Dual System is considered key to the generally highly qualified character of German society and the high productivity of its economy. However, it has long been debated as to whether the system can respond adequately to structural changes in the economy and in the organization of work, as well as to demographic developments, and whether the qualifications are able to meet emerging demands. Tensions arising from these changes have put the *Beruf* concept under pressure. Without abandoning it, recent reforms are intended to overcome certain rigidities. Here the qualifications framework approach may provide options to overcome certain limitations in the national and international context.

The chapter addresses the following questions: what is the significance of initial VET in the entire system? What is the meaning of *Beruf* as the organizing principle of German VET? What are the specific features of an *Ausbildungsberuf*, the main qualification type of the German qualifications system? How are the qualifications of the Dual System used in the labour market? What are the main challenges for the *Beruf* as the governing principle of VET from the labour market and from the educational points of view and how does the system react to these? Finally, what might be the impact of the EQF on national developments?

In Chapter 5, competence, the concept supposed to act as catalyst in the harmonization of the VET systems of the EU member states, is discussed. Far from acting as a new perspective for VET systems to strive for, the concept is shown to have already been absorbed and given meaning in national VET systems. This process demonstrates that educational concepts are embedded in national contexts such as the Dutch which, though only recently introducing the concept of competence into VET, gave it a meaning shaped by long-standing and recurrent debates on the position of VET within the education system. In this debate, multi-dimensional competences were seen as an alternative to narrow and task-based English NVQ-type learning aims, which had been experimented with in Dutch VET at one point, and embraced as more appropriate to achieving VET's long-standing mission of preparing individuals for life and providing them with knowledge sufficient to benefit from lifelong learning.

Beginning with an examination of the Dutch case, the chapter continues with an exploration of differences between the Dutch use of the concept and the English, French and German, showing how understanding is affected by contextual differences. For example, English competences are defined in terms of job-specific requirements, rather than nationally agreed and recognized occupations as in the Netherlands, France and Germany. And, whilst in the Netherlands and Germany competences form the basis of curriculum development, the link between competences and VET is less clear in France, although this is compensated for by an institutionalized process of curriculum development. In the assessment-led system of English NVQs, in contrast, competences form the basis for validation of *in situ* performance of prescribed tasks.

Chapter 6 is about the concept of *skill*, in particular that underlying the VET system in England and embedded in the labour market and the qualification system.

At the same time, it addresses the ways and the extent to which the English system is distinct from the French, German and Dutch in terms of the understanding of 'skill' and other concepts characterizing workplace practical knowledge. The concept of *skill* is most closely associated with narrowly defined tasks requiring manipulation and hand–eye co-ordination. It contrasts, therefore, with Continental conceptions of competence which are often broad, involve personal characteristics and imply the application of theory to practice. Nevertheless, the term 'skill' has come to be used in a variety of contexts, including in relation to activities with a substantial intellectual and social element. Terminology such as 'social skills', 'planning skills', 'thinking skills' and similar tends to lead people to think of practical workplace abilities in a fragmented rather than an integrated way, one which does, unfortunately, reflect much of the historical and contemporary reality of the English labour market – as illustrated through quotations from representatives of key stakeholder organizations within the sectors on which we have focused.

It is argued that the English output-related qualification system, such as the NVQ, rests on the certification of narrowly defined skills and reinforces the fragmented nature of the labour process, resulting in weak occupational identities and an obsession with managerial control. The emphasis on learning outcomes and the discounting of prior educational experience in the accreditation of practical workplace knowledge have been, to a considerable extent, adopted as design features of the EQF, reflecting the influence of 'Anglo-Saxon' conceptions of practical knowledge beyond British shores. Current English government VET policy too places much emphasis on skills immediately relevant to the workplace rather than on occupational capacity.

The following Chapter 7 represents a logical sequel to Chapter 6, as both bricklaying and lorry driving exemplify the English skill-based model which is especially evident for 'manual' occupations. The chapter brings out distinct differences between, on the one hand, the narrow English bricklaying qualification and, on the other, the broad, competence-based qualifications in France, Germany and the Netherlands. These are attributed to the persistence of bricklaying as a trade in the English case, where the bricklayer is rewarded for output and largely restricted to laying bricks and blocks, whereas in the other countries it can be regarded as a qualified occupation, especially in Germany and the Netherlands where the bricklaying qualification has high labour market currency. Differences are manifest in terms of governance, with the English qualification marked by weak, employer/trade-based regulation and that in the other three countries embedded within an industry framework and underpinned by social partnership and sector-wide collective agreements. In terms of VET too France, Germany and the Netherlands are characterized by comprehensive programmes, linked to curricula, part of the general education system, aimed at developing the person as an active citizen, and based on a multi-dimensional notion of competence integrating knowledge, practical know-how and personal and social abilities.

The example of lorry driving highlights further differences, above all in that, unlike bricklaying, it is an occupation governed by EU regulation. However, the currency of lorry driving qualifications beyond the compulsory driving licence is shown to be relatively low in England, France and Germany, though in the Netherlands it is important for labour market entry. This is despite the typically more extensive VET programme in Germany, framed around *Handlungskompetenz* and with a broad general education and knowledge base. In contrast to the Netherlands and Germany, too, the qualification in England and France is largely restricted to driving and opens up few possibilities for career progression. Indeed it provides a good example of the *titre* in France, a qualification under the Ministry of Labour rather than Education.

All in all, the chapter brings to life through actual labour market occupations the concepts elucidated in previous chapters: knowledge, competence, skill and *Beruf*. It shows the clear difference between skills-based qualifications and those which, whilst referring to activities in the labour market, are yet grounded in the education system through the curriculum, founded on a multi-dimensional concept of competence, and focused on developing the individual as a citizen as well as a worker.

Chapter 8 explores divergent and convergent tendencies in relation to the HE qualifications of software engineering and nursing and, in doing so, examines the prospects for EQF implementation. The fluid nature of VET systems is highlighted through recent developments in nursing and software engineering qualifications and through their response to a variety of other factors, including socio-economic change and technological advance, which have resulted in different labour market requirements and job profiles. The chapter identifies elements of convergence in relation to both nursing and software engineering, despite the very contrasting dynamics underlying these qualifications. In the case of nursing, convergence is based on common VET standards established through national and European legislation. By contrast, software engineering in all four countries is characterized by the notion of employability (i.e. individual responsibility for acquiring particular skill sets), albeit to a varying extent. In the converging labour market associated with this occupation, internationally recognized individual competences increasingly take priority over formal VET programmes. Nevertheless, as the chapter makes clear, there remain critical differences across countries between pathways and qualifications in relation to both occupations, reflecting the unique labour market and educational contexts in individual countries.

Chapter 9 explores the ways in which equivalence between qualifications across Europe can be established and, in particular, the basis for constructing ZMTs. Trust in the EQF process to make it possible to compare qualifications will depend on how national frameworks are referenced to it and whether these require qualifications to meet criteria which are strict, and hence exclusive, or loose and hence inclusive. ZMTs in turn will depend in the first place on what qualifications stand for and on the strength of involvement of the different stakeholders. Qualifications are of a very different nature according to whether they are grounded in the VET system – and more generally the education system – or in the labour market. This distinction impacts too on how learning outcomes are understood, on the one hand as standards and, on the other, as workplace performance descriptors. The labour market currency of qualifications is nevertheless also key to establishing equivalence between them; the stronger the currency, the more effective any framework is likely to be. The credibility of the system governing the recognition of occupational qualifications, the quality of VET systems, and the level and scope of the qualification itself all critically affect the validity of a qualification.

ZMTs may take a variety of different forms, being set up with the involvement of the social partners across sectors and cognate occupations and occupational families or between different countries. They may be underpinned by regulation, as in the case of lorry driving and nursing. Whatever the form, agreement will be necessary on what the qualification represents and on terminology. The chapter concludes by emphasizing the need to establish equivalence between VET-based rather than purely labour market-based qualifications.

Chapter 10 consists of an analytical and interpretive dictionary of central concepts in European VET, drawn from the four countries in the study. It is different from the other chapters in that it is designed for reference rather than for consecutive reading, although it can also be used for the latter. The intention in this chapter is to contrast the varying conceptions of different key terms in EU discourse, in official national discourses and in everyday usage in and around the workplace in the different countries. Wherever possible, examples of usage are illustrated, sometimes in great detail. In this chapter, therefore, will be found detailed accounts of particular concepts such as Apprenticeship, Knowledge or Skill, the official definitions given of them, their variable interpretation in VET and work contexts, national linguistic and conceptual variation and, last but not least, difficulties and ambiguities that may arise in the translation of terms that are apparently similar but in reality considerably different. The chapter also contains interpretive commentary on these ambiguities and on differences and similarities within and between key concepts. It thus forms a conclusion to the book as well as a useful source of reference.

Notes

1   BTEC refers to the Business and Technology Education Council which represents a form of educational qualification in the UK.
2   'European Community' is the umbrella term for the European Economic Community and the European Union.

2

EU INITIATIVES IN CROSS-NATIONAL RECOGNITION OF SKILLS AND QUALIFICATIONS

Philippe Méhaut and Christopher Winch

Introduction

In this chapter, current initiatives in European Union (EU) vocational education and training (VET) policy, above all the European Qualification Framework (EQF), are subject to detailed scrutiny. Unfamiliar educational concepts – such as modularity, credit, accumulation, transfer, learning outcome, accreditation of prior experiential learning (APEL) and qualification framework – are described in detail, their application to the EU outlined and key issues concerning their implementation set out. The chapter first outlines the main characteristics of the EQF and examines the political background to its development, before setting out and commenting on its key design features, indicating likely developments in implementation, and going on to look at dependent developments, in particular, the European Credit System for Vocational Education and Training (ECVET).

The basic idea of a Qualification Framework (QF) is to provide a common basis of comparison for all qualifications at the national level, NQF, or internationally, be they academic or vocational. This idea has been strongly promoted by the Organisation of Economic Cooperation and Development (OECD) and other international organizations, drawing particularly on the English and Australian examples. NQFs have also been developed, for example, in South Africa and Mexico. The growing transparency of qualifications is supposed to allow students to manage their course of study more smoothly and to increase mobility in the labour market. However, the example of Australia (where an NQF was implemented in 2000) has exposed numerous difficulties and has raised doubts concerning the effectiveness of such a framework. In that country, a new reform is in progress, this time drawing on the European model (for a critical analysis see Hampson and Junor 2010).

The aim of establishing possible equivalences in qualifications is therefore essential to such a project. The easiest way to conceptualize such a framework is

TABLE 2.1 Outline of the European Qualifications Framework: cognitive characteristics

Levels	Knowledge	Skill	Competence (autonomy and responsibility)
Level 1 (lowest)			
Level 2			
Level 3			
Level 4			
Level 5			
Level 6			
Level 7			
Level 8 (doctoral)			

as a two-dimensional grid, as illustrated in Table 2.1 in the case of the EQF. The rows on the grid represent levels of achievement from primary school to doctoral level. The vertical columns represent significant cognitive subdivisions: knowledge and skill are distinct categories and others, to do with, for example, managerial capacity, may constitute a third. Such is the case with the EQF. Crudely speaking, two qualifications, A and B, are equivalent if they lie at the same horizontal level in all three cognitive subdivisions on the grid; otherwise they are not equivalent. A QF takes two or more qualifications, and determines their equivalence in terms of their specification, usually as 'learning outcomes', a crucial term with more than one potential meaning. This brief description applies to both the EQF and to national qualification frameworks (NQFs), although, as we shall see, the EQF is not intended to provide a *direct* comparison of two or more qualifications.

From a Europe of worker mobility to a Europe of knowledge

The intervention of Europe (the Community, then the Union) in the field of VET is not new. But, since the Treaty of Rome, its objectives and modes of operation have significantly evolved. The Treaty of Maastricht and the Lisbon strategy each mark two important points in that evolution.

From the Treaty of Rome to the Treaty of Maastricht: the slow growth of European competence in the field of general and vocational education

At its inception, Europe had no competence in the field of education. As far as VET was concerned, the Treaty of Rome referred to 'general principles for putting into effect a common policy of vocational education' (Article 128). Nevertheless, as Bouder (2008) has pointed out in connection with the creation of the European social fund, the field of that common policy in fact only concerned the retraining of salaried employees.

However, and completely in accord with the principle of free circulation of goods and labour, the Treaty set out provisions for freedom of practice, mainly for non-salaried and/or regulated occupations. Thus, sometimes after interminable negotiations, a series of Directives came progressively to regulate the mutual recognition of qualifications for professions such as architecture, law and medicine. In the case of some occupations (for example, nursing), the European documents did not just organize mutual recognition; they also constructed standards for vocational education (number of years of study etc. . . .). More recently, two directives (1999 and 2005) have extended the system of mutual recognition to the near-totality of activities, again within the principle of free movement of labour.

Sometimes going beyond the principles of non-competence and of subsidiarity,[1] a certain number of initiatives were taken that contributed to the development of exchange and co-ordination within the field of VET (Sellin 1999; for a historical overview, Bouder and Kirsch 2008). Thus the Ministers of Labour at first, followed by the Ministers of Education (1974), began to meet in order to discuss vocational and, to a lesser degree, general education policy. The setting up of the CEDEFOP (the European Centre for the Development of Vocational Training, under the Council of Ministers) and the role that it came to play were also indicative of the progressively growing power of Europe within a field where, little by little, a degree of legitimacy was being constructed. This was despite the succession of abortive initiatives made for the construction of a system for judging the equivalence of occupations and qualifications (Bertrand and Merle 1993; Sellin 1999).

The 1995 White Paper on general and vocational education marked the acceleration of this process (d'Iribarne 1996). It set out a certain number of principles concerning the necessary evolution of VET systems in order to respond to the 'needs' of what came to be called the 'information' society, laying the foundations for a more active European intervention in the field of qualifications. This intervention more or less bypassed national systems of qualifications and led to the building of various European qualifications, based essentially on outputs or, in other words, on learning outcomes rather than on the curricula of VET programmes, and overseen by international validating authorities, with the help of, among other things, computerized systems of competence evaluation. Emblematic of this policy initiative was the creation of the European Passport, whose development – as stressed in the critical analysis of d'Iribarne (1996) – marked the triumph of liberal, largely Anglo-Saxon, policy.

The Lisbon strategy and the Bruges–Copenhagen process: the integration of VET in an economic and social strategy

The 1992 Treaty of Maastricht (gradually implemented from the end of 1993) and the Lisbon Summit marked two new important and complementary steps. The Treaty enlarged community competence by making reference to educational policy (Article 126), and vocational education (Article 127), without distinguishing between initial and continuing vocational education (IVET and CVET). It respected the principle of subsidiarity, which guaranteed the autonomy of the member states in their individual policies but at the same time justified community intervention when common objectives could not be reached through these means. This evolution of community competence was made concrete among other things by the publication in 1995 of a new Directive which included in its title the word 'education'.

The Lisbon Summit and, in the field of VET, its ramifications (often called 'the Bruges–Copenhagen process') (Bruges 2001, Copenhagen 2002, Bordeaux 2008) enlarged European intervention while significantly changing its overall context. The question of labour mobility remained, while general and vocational education policy were incorporated into a macro-economic and social strategy, often summed up in the phrase 'The Europe of Knowledge' (see Kuhn 2007 for a European and international review of the Knowledge and Learning Society). The contribution of general and vocational education was considered to be central to the development of an economic model founded on knowledge, as well as to social cohesion in Europe and the realization of a 'European social model' (European Commission 2002). With the rising influence of Life Long Learning, the borders between general and vocational education and between initial and continuing education were put into question (Verdier 2008). Active and co-ordinated policies, – which included but went beyond the question of qualifications – then developed with the help of a variety of old and new instruments.

Open Method of Co-ordination (OMC): voluntary co-ordinated action complementing subsidiarity

The gradual incorporation of VET in the OMC (Laffan and Shaw 2005; Guergoat-Larivière 2008) led to the development of shared objectives supported by benchmarking, reporting by states and policy peer reviews. Without going into the details of this process, we will simply note:

- That these indicators are wide-ranging (EC 2008c), covering for example the 2010 target of lowering the percentage of early school leavers, improving literacy results and increasing the numbers in upper secondary schooling. The scope is also wide, covering general, vocational, initial and continuing education.
- The approach concerns system performance well before the question of access to employment and labour mobility; it has a wide definition of this performance, using criteria to do with the Knowledge Economy (for example information and communication technology (ICT) skills) but also with social cohesion (for example civic skills).
- Although these indicators are founded on voluntary, co-ordinated action and respect the principle of subsidiarity, the very fact of their existence has a bearing on national policies and structures.
- Finally, there is a tension between certain indicators and the EQF.

The range of European instruments

Thus recent developments concerning the EQF must be placed in the context of the relative continuity of European policy (with the emphasis on qualification) but also integrated into the approach opened up by the Lisbon Summit. They must also be set alongside other instruments and initiatives.

The large European programmes, such as Comenius, Erasmus, Gruntvig and Leonardo, are well known. Suffice it to say that many Leonardo feasibility projects preceded, then supported, the implementation of the EQF.

Although existing at national and university level, the Bologna process is closely linked with the EQF. The construction of descriptors for higher education (HE) qualifications (the Dublin descriptors) and the wish to harmonize the structure of qualifications (Bachelor, Master, PhD) affect not only qualifications but also the structure of HE systems. Bologna was, in certain respects, a precursor of the EQF.

The European CV, the European computer driving licence and the Europass are also instruments for the transparency of qualifications and the promotion of labour market mobility that continue the initiatives of the past 50 years.

The EQF: a new instrument to promote transparency and co-ordination?

Adopted by the European Parliament in 2008, the EQF is described as a 'metaframework', designed to promote both a common terminology and a common reference point for the comparison of qualifications of the member countries of the EU. It can be seen as part of the general tendency, supported by international organizations (notably the OECD), to develop such frameworks at national and international level. The objectives for such frameworks are generally stated as a greater transparency and rationalization of qualifications, especially when national qualifications are so varied and numerous.

Multiple objectives

Without departing from these goals, the EQF seems however – at times explicitly, at others implicitly – to pursue other goals too (cf particularly Sellin 2008), hence the inevitable fuzziness of concepts and potential tensions between sometimes contradictory objectives.

The EQF appears first of all as a comprehensive framework aiming at transcending the borders between vocational and general education. In theory it also covers HE, drawing inspiration from and following the Bologna process and incorporating vocational Bachelor degrees, Masters and Doctorates. This further step goes together with the trend in most European countries towards raising levels of VET through a HE system which is becoming increasingly vocational. It is also consonant with one of the aims of European policy: parity of esteem between general and vocational education.

The EQF is fully engaged with the European policy of lifelong vocational and professional education, thus covering without distinction qualifications in both initial and continuing education. However, it goes further in – following European terminology and recommendations – aiming at qualifications that recognize learning acquired through 'formal', 'informal' and 'non-formal' processes. In order to do this, but also on account of the failure of previous European attempts to elaborate a system of equivalence between qualifications, it is founded on learning outcomes. It thus breaks with the 'input–output' approach (number of years of study, number of hours of VET (inputs) and, for example, an exam pass mark signifying a level of knowledge (outputs)). However, the interpretation of what is meant by 'learning outcomes' is a very strong one, with a parentage in Anglo-Saxon innovations in vocational qualifications and accreditation of practical experience. It is the result of pressure brought to bear by the OECD in favour of the 'piloting by implementation' of VET systems (Vinokur 1995), tending to turn the process of construction upside down and also to alter the degree of influence of actors centrally involved. One of the possible long term implications is a change in the financing of institutions to become more outcomes-based (see Felstead 1998, for a survey of this question).

The design features of the EQF are intended to achieve three distinct objectives. The first is 'horizontal' comparability of qualification levels between countries, supposedly necessary in the context of student mobility in Europe, and presented as a preliminary to ECVET. The second objective is 'vertical' comparability, more concerned with intra-national considerations in the context of lifelong VET and vertical pathways from one qualification to another (as in the French or Dutch systems). A third objective of the EQF, however, largely implicit, is that of position 'on the labour market', being presented as an instrument for the mobility of workers, facilitating comparison of qualifications and vocational abilities. 'Competences' are thereby formulated around a concept of autonomy which refers back to autonomy in learning but also to autonomy in the workplace. Markowitsch and Luomi-Messerer (2008: 60) identify three attributes of the EQF, as the hierarchy of tasks and functions, of educational systems, and of competence acquisition. In this respect, the EQF has not made a complete break with previous attempts at establishing equivalence based on an analysis of the labour process.

The framework is thus 'meta' in the sense that:

- different NQFs can be compared (which presupposes a certain flexibility in the use of language);
- all qualifications can be assimilated, whatever their nature, goals and origins;
- whereas its aim is first and foremost the development of general and vocational education policy, it in fact goes beyond this towards the old aspiration of 'the free movement of labour'.

The notions on which the framework is based are thereby fuzzy. It is an instrument of 'practical politics', characterized by 'a lack of theoretical underpinning and of a systematic foundation' (Markowitsch and Luomi-Messerer 2008: 61).

Controversial elements

The EQF and learning outcomes

As an instrument for the comparison of qualifications in both labour and educational markets, the EQF follows previous attempts by the CEDEFOP between 1985 and 1992 to establish a QF by developing common targets and linking these to 'inputs' through investigating commonalities in curricula, pedagogy and assessment. The aim was to define reference levels for certificates by combining the different functions these performed with entry conditions. However, the complexities that such an attempt revealed, in particular with respect to different divisions of labour in each country, led to the decision to focus instead on the classification of outcomes (Bjørnavåld and Coles 2008). Since it is anticipated that reversion to inputs would lead to the same difficulties that vitiated earlier attempts, the output-based approach selected for the EQF is *strongly* outcomes-based. It seeks to specify learning outcomes independently of any process which may have led to these, a feature not always fully understood.

England had, in the 1980s, developed an innovation, the National Vocational Qualification (NVQ) that suggested how this might be done. The accreditation of an NVQ is based on the idea that, if someone demonstrably has the ability to do something in workplace conditions, s/he should be accredited for that achievement, irrespective of how it was acquired – whether in the workplace, workshop or classroom. Crucial to this perspective is the *learning outcome*, which is the set of descriptors setting out the competence guaranteed by certification. This sense of 'learning outcome' is quite specific and does not correspond to the broader way in which this term is often used (Brockmann *et al.* 2008a).

EQF would not directly certify competences as its purpose is to act as a meta-framework, a comparator for qualifications in different countries. If certificated achievements can be specified in an NQF in terms of learning outcomes in the NVQ sense, then it should be possible to lay two or more qualifications alongside each other on the EQF grid to determine their degree of equivalence. If national qualifications are themselves based on learning outcomes and conform to the structure of the EQF, comparison becomes all the easier. There are in fact some grounds for supposing that the intention of the designers of the EQF was that it be used as a lever for encouraging EU member states to develop learning outcomes based on NQFs that correspond in structure to the EQF.

Both the EQF and NQFs are similar in the sense that they use a grid of vertical and horizontal classifications of qualifications in terms of cognitive characteristics (columns) and cognitive levels within an academic hierarchy (rows). Comparisons are affected by locating two or more qualifications in rows within the grid and, if the location of the row coincides, the qualifications or qualification classifications are deemed equivalent (see Table 2.1 for the EQF). This basic idea already existed within NQFs developed in different countries, for example South Africa, England and Ireland, prior to the setting up of the EQF. It should not be assumed that

NQFs correspond to the exact features of the EQF. There may, for example, be different numbers and types of academic level and fewer or more specified types of cognitive characteristic, but the basic idea of comparing qualifications or types of qualification is the same in both cases. Thus if the knowledge, skill and competence of two qualifications, A and B, at level 3 can be characterized in terms of their learning outcomes in each of the cognitive subdivisions, they are deemed to be equivalent to each other. NQFs generally compare individual national qualifications directly with each other.

Unlike NQFs, the EQF is not intended to compare individual qualifications directly, but takes two or more classifications of qualification from different NQFs and provides a judgement of equivalence or non-equivalence between them. Because it is designed primarily to be used with NQFs, the EQF is sometimes known as a 'translation device', because it 'translates' a classificatory judgement in the qualification system in country A to its equivalent in the qualification system of country B. It is thus not intended to be used as a direct method for determining the equivalence or non-equivalence of particular national qualifications. Because of this, the transposition process rests on different methods and authorities. For instance, in England it has been achieved through an 'administrative' process orchestrated by the Qualifications and Curriculum Development Authority (QCDA); in France it is carried out by the National Qualifications Commission, which brings together the different qualification awarding bodies and the social partners. The process has not yet begun in the Netherlands and Germany. The creation of a Zone of Mutual Trust (ZMT) (see Chapter 9) will depend on various factors including the way in which the transposition is carried out in each country and any conflicts it may give rise to, either at country or at European level.

Because of its strong learning outcome design feature the EQF also encompasses certified learning outcomes achieved through the APEL as well as through conventional pedagogic routes. Learning outcomes, as abilities that a candidate is said to possess, are completely distinct from any learning process that may have led to their acquisition. In this case common terminology may be highly misleading. The term 'learning outcome' is very often used in the sense of a 'standard', that is a set of criteria marking progress through a curriculum and serving as the basis for the design of assessment instruments. These instruments may determine the degree to which a candidate following the curriculum has or has not met the standard (Coles 2007). Learning outcomes, however, are either fulfilled or not fulfilled (Brockmann et al. 2008a).

A strong learning outcomes approach as suggested by the architects of the EQF (e.g. Coles 2007) has another potential problem. On the one hand, the horizontal levels of the grid are implicitly cumulative, even though EQF does not state that they are, since normally it is assumed that in order to pass from level 1 to level 8 one has to acquire knowledge, skills and competences at a lower level necessary to achievement at a higher level. On the other hand, learning outcomes are expected to be assessed irrespective of any other knowledge, skill or competence that the candidate may have acquired and are thus not cumulative. It is difficult to see how someone could be assessed, for example, through APEL at level 6 without having been previously assessed on those elements of knowledge, skill and competence which are presupposed for the award at level 6. One might argue that assessment of all the relevant learning outcomes, including at lower levels, would take care of this. However, the problem is that any ability is likely to be exercised in a variety of different situations and there is no guarantee that a learning outcome achieved in one context would be achieved in another (hypothetical) one. Indeed, one would assume that a learning outcome achieved at a relatively high level, such as 6 (equivalent to a Bachelor degree), would be exercised across a range of circumstances. However, APEL-type assessment, if it is conducted through the examination of a limited range of learning outcomes, cannot test this. This is not a problem for assessment through standards. For example, a standard in a literacy curriculum might be 'can make inferences beyond the literal in a text'. This criterion can in turn be used to construct a test instrument that samples this ability across a range of representative contexts, rather than just relying on one situation. Of course there is an inferential hazard in forming conclusions from a limited range of circumstances (Dearden 1979), but at least assessment based on standards has some control over the relevant variables, such as the range of learning experiences which the student has covered, whereas the assessment of a learning outcome through a small set of observed performances does not.

A multilingual construct – what may be lost in translation

The multilingual nature of the EQF introduces a further element of complexity into the trans-European comparison of qualifications. The cognitive subdivisions of 'knowledge', 'skill' and 'competence' are culturally specific English terms and there is a danger that important differences in the concepts in different languages are not properly appreciated:

> *Knowledge*: English does not distinguish explicitly between systematic and non-systematic knowledge in the way that, for example, German does through the distinction between '*Wissen*' (systematic knowledge) and '*Kenntnis*' (non-systematic knowledge). However, the German version of EQF renders 'Knowledge' as '*Kenntnis*' which may be no mere accident of translation but the expression of a political will about how the characteristics of qualifications are to be prioritized.

> *Skill*: the English term is notoriously elastic (see Chapter 6), rooted in the idea of ability to carry out a type of task. It does not encompass any idea of occupational capacity, for example, as German does through the specification of '*berufliche Handlungsfähigkeit*' or 'occupational action capacity'. German makes the distinction between a broad ability, which is rendered as a '*Fähigkeit*' and task-related knacks or skills, called '*Fertigkeiten*'. It is remarkable that, although the aim of the German initial VET system is to develop an individual's *berufliche Handlungsfähigkeit* (Hanf 2009), the EQF rendering of

'skill' is '*Fertigkeit*'. Once again, this is probably not a careless translation, but a deliberate (and political) act. This is all the more surprising since the *Berufsbildungsgesetz* (Vocational Training Act), which regulates the major part of the German system, and the *Ausbildungsordnungen* (training ordinances) which regulate the company part of Dual System apprenticeships, refer to *Fertigkeiten, Kenntnisse* and (since 2005) *Fähigkeiten*, whilst *Wissen* is applied to the framework curricula (*Rahmenlehrpläne*) for vocational schools.

Competence: this is perhaps the term that embodies the most complexity and potential for confusion. The EQF has itself sometimes been described as a 'competence framework' although the preferred terminology is now a 'learning outcomes' framework (EU 2010b). However, the holder of a qualification will be expected to show attributes, more or less integrated, across all three of the columns in Table 2.1 and will, in this sense, have attained learning outcomes that involve knowledge, skill, autonomy and responsibility. The English term 'competence' and its associated terms in other languages, such as '*Kompetenz*' in German and '*compétence*' in French have particular meanings in the vocational context which make each difficult to translate without losing important distinctions. Thus the English term 'competence' tends to refer to attainment of a skill at a threshold level or, alternatively, possession of a related bundle of skills (see Chapter 6). The idea of personal independence or of the bringing to bear of judgement informed by systematic knowledge does not belong with the English term in the way that it does, for example, in Dutch, French and German (Brockmann *et al.* 2008b, 2008c).

More worryingly, the idea of autonomous workers who can plan, control, co-ordinate and evaluate their own work is not apparently allowed for within the EQF, being something different from position within a managerial hierarchy, which is what 'autonomy and responsibility' in the third column of the EQF grid signify (see Table 2.1). This is a significant omission – one likely to prove an issue when detailed mappings are made to the EQF framework for particular sectoral and occupational qualifications – not just because autonomy in the sense of self-direction is, in varying degrees, a central attribute of skilled workers but because it is implicitly devalued as an attribute recognized in a qualification.

A further omission that is likely to cause problems when mappings are carried out is that of *scope*. To understand this, one needs to consider that occupations in different countries that are nominally the same (for instance, bricklayer, *maçon*, *Maurer*) may actually involve work in different areas within construction. Thus in some countries (e.g. England) bricklayers do little more than lay bricks, but in others they do a great deal more. To take the example of France, a qualified *maçon* is expected to be able to construct a house with some assistance from other occu-pations and the specific competences include: preparation of the work; organization of the workplace; installation of a structure; dealing with site waste; scaffolding; shell construction in blocks and bricks; masonry; reinforcements; formwork;

concrete; components; rendering and waterproofing; piping and conduits; keeping equipment in good condition; exchanging information (Méhaut and Hervy-Guillaume 2009; Brockmann *et al.* 2009c). These variations in scope, which are considerable between countries, are not taken account of in the EQF framework. Concretely this implies, for instance, that the skills column of an EQF-related occupational grid would need to determine the scope of the qualification in order to establish equivalence between two national qualifications. This cannot be done without modification which, at the occupational level, would require detailed negotiations between the corresponding interested parties in each country involved in establishing an occupational implementation within the overall framework of the EQF. The EQF cannot, therefore, do more than provide an – incomplete – outline of the terrain that needs to be mapped out at occupational level.

The second stage of implementation of the EQF, namely the alignment or reconciliation ('referencing' in official language) of national qualifications or NQFs with the EQF, is necessary in order that there is at least a nominal equivalence between the status (level) of a national qualification and an EQF level. If the EQF is to serve as the medium of translation between a qualification belonging to country A and a qualification belonging to country B, then it needs to be consistent and trustworthy. The very process of referencing puts pressure on individual countries to produce an NQF if this does not already exist, as referencing of individual qualifications to the EQF would otherwise be involved and thus become too burdensome. Once this referencing exercise has been carried out in each country then, in theory at least, it should be possible to determine equivalence by aligning any qualification in any country with a potential equivalent in any other country party to the EQF. This exercise is crucial to making the EQF work. However, the lack of a standard procedure for referencing or of a mandatory international peer review of national referencing exercises brings the danger that the process will not be trusted, particularly as there is a potential conflict of interest between impartial referencing and the political and economic imperatives of individual countries. A particular national referencing process may also not command international confidence if it is not sufficiently rigorous and thorough.

The process is further complicated by the needs of economic sectors and occupations for an accurate referencing process, which commands confidence in the labour market and not just within official circles and which determines the *scope* of a particular occupation, together with the expected level of standard qualifications. This sectoral qualification exercise is voluntary, but supported by EU Leonardo funding for pilot work. There is no procedure as yet for aligning the findings of sectoral and occupational working parties with the national referencing exercises and potential for conflict between these two processes. Sectoral and occupational qualification frameworks, operating within the overall EQF template, will be a necessary condition for the use of the EQF within the labour market. In this way, recognition of the EQF will operate at two levels. The first is through inter-governmental, mutual recognition of individual national referencing exercises, which is important for the development of national bilateral and multilateral relationships within the EU, particularly in relation to the nominal currency of qualifications within different national education systems. However, such recognition will be inadequate for the second level, which is the exchange and recognition of qualifications within the labour market. Neither will it be adequate for the *de facto* recognition of qualifications by individual educational institutions. Yet, the probity of referencing exercises is of critical importance for the acceptance and use of the EQF at institutional and labour market levels.

Beyond the EQF: the broader picture

The EQF by itself is meant to enable the recognition of qualifications across the EU but is part of a larger design for the recognition and accumulation of qualifications across Europe. The ECVET is intended to allow for the accumulation of vocational qualifications across the EU and is similar to but more ambitious than the European Credit Transfer and Accumulation System (ECTS) which operates in HE. The intention is that, for example, someone might accumulate credits towards a bricklaying qualification in England and subsequently use these towards the accumulation of further credits in bricklaying in, for example, Germany. The EQF is a necessary instrument for ECVET as it provides the basis for recognition of credits accumulated in one country prior to their being used in another. It is, however, like the EQF, an enabling instrument and thus voluntary and likely to be more difficult to implement, though the current target date for this is 2012. Units will be characterized as learning outcomes and credits will be awarded at any given level on the basis of notional hours of study; for example, a year of full time VET will count towards 60 credits (EU 2010a).

ECVET thus relies on the following educational concepts: *modularization* and *credit transfer* and *credit accumulation*, in addition to *learning outcomes*. A module in this sense is a self-contained unit of study which can be transferred to another – larger – programme of study composed of largely self-contained units. Once completed and accredited, its holder can enter another programme and use the achieved credit points, together with the ones subsequently achieved, to accumulate a larger number of credits, ultimately leading to a recognized exit qualification such as a Bachelor degree. Although ECVET is designed to take account of modular structures at national level, it does not presuppose their use in order to operate effectively, although it may well encourage the national development of modularized VET qualifications.

The problems with ECVET relate to its specific design features. Modularization in the sense in which it is employed in ECVET means that a sub-qualification at the unit level is self-contained, can be detached from the programme of study to which it originally applied and used as a preliminary to another programme of study. But ECVET is not appropriate for those qualifications, like the diplomas that issue from the German Dual System, which are holistic rather than modular (Ertl 2002). These presuppose the successful completion of the whole programme of study and thus exclude the assimilation of modules from other systems, though they can be packaged into modules themselves and used for credit accumulation and transfer into other programmes within the Dual System. However, they are not themselves merely the end result of a process of credit accumulation and transfer but also presuppose the successful integration of all the unit components of the qualification in an assessment taken at the exit point from the programme. This has given rise to serious reservations about ECVET on the part of some of the interested parties, such as the trade unions in Germany.

A device like ECVET, although its implementation requires a framework like the EQF for it to work, nevertheless causes tension with the EQF. The EQF was designed as an output-based translation device so that how its descriptors are satisfied by any qualification is supposed to be independent of how that qualification was achieved. The case is not so clear with ECVET. In one sense, the outcomes of a module may be realized irrespective of what, if any, pedagogic process was involved. But there is a quantitative element to a credit-bearing qualification that is difficult to account for in other than input terms. To take the example of a bricklaying module in country A and another in country B, classed at level 3 on the EQF grid, with one bearing 120 credits and the other 180 credits because the *scope* of the qualification is different in each case. Even though both may be achievable through some kind of APEL process, there is nevertheless an implication that a certain number of hours of learning are needed to achieve a certain number of credits. In the ECVET framework, this would be the equivalent of two, as opposed to three, years of study within a structured VET programme. The most reliable method of computing that learning time is to assess tuition and practice time in a learning environment, as APEL routes are, by their nature, too heterogeneous to provide a basis for doing this. ECVET does, then, appear to introduce input-based considerations back into the qualification framework in a way that was not intended by the designers of the emerging qualification structure. It will thus be misleading to speak of 'learning outcomes' in the ECVET methodology as if the same is meant as 'learning outcomes' in the EQF methodology.

We find, therefore, that another tension is introduced into the framework through the hidden, although unavoidable intrusion of an input element into qualification recognition. This, together with the tension associated with learning outcomes, is likely to lead to a modification of the purity of the output-based design over time.

Conclusion

We have described an ambitious, even audacious, attempt on the part of the EU to provide a qualification structure that will achieve the primary objective of introducing transparent information about qualifications into the European labour market. A secondary objective is to make individual transfer between education systems easier. A third (and unstated) objective may be to tilt the balance of power in constructing labour market relevant information away from educational institutions towards the labour market itself (Young 2009). Young also identifies the weakening of curricular boundaries and the promotion of 'learning how to learn' as other instruments in this broader, but largely covert, project. Consideration of these is, however, beyond our scope. This third objective would also be achieved through the development of output-based measures, such as learning outcomes satisfied by APEL and by credit accumulation and transfer, which weaken the hold of any particular educational institution in the awarding of a qualification. All three of these objectives are highly ambitious and depend to a significant degree on internal reforms in the constituent countries, such as the development of outcome-based NQFs. The success of this enterprise is by no means guaranteed and the remainder of this book is, to no small degree, an assessment of its chances.

Note

1   The principle of subsidiarity is invoked when European-level intervention is considered unnecessary as the policy would be best pursued at national level.

3

SAVOIR – THE ORGANIZING PRINCIPLE OF FRENCH VET

Philippe Méhaut

Introduction

In a memorandum written in 1920, the French Minister of Education, Edouard Herriot, set out to define the education of the worker:

> By law, the worker is also a citizen and an individual. As such, he is not a means but an end; he must have the ability, not only to produce, but also to think; he is entitled to the culture which makes one an individual, that is to say, a free being.
>
> (cited by Brucy 2008: 37)

This generous conception of the worker's vocational education, concretized the previous year through the creation of the Certificate of Professional Ability (CAP) and the obligation to complete three years of study before one could be examined for this certificate, has been sustained through the years, amid multiple tensions and battles between the actors in the French vocational education and training (VET) system. The trilogy of producer, individual and citizen, even when implicit, still lies at the heart of the conception of the main VET qualifications and is spelled out most notably in the concepts of *savoir, savoir-faire* and *savoir-être*. As we shall see in this chapter, French VET is thus grounded on a very different conceptual basis from the English 'skills'-based system. At the same time, as in the Netherlands, the French system is witnessing the growth in influence of the concept of competence which underlies the design of qualifications and the criteria for the assessment of students. In effect, every qualification should, nowadays, be capable of being awarded independently of how the learning took place (whether through VET, prior experiential learning, etc.). Nevertheless, in this instance again, the concept of competence appears quite different from its use in the Anglo-Saxon world. The 'kernels of competence' are larger, they are articulated in a more holistic perspective and 'competence' is not synonymous with 'performance'.

In order to situate the French system of qualifications in relation to the three other countries examined in this book – England, Germany and the Netherlands – and in order to understand it as an evolving system, we will first of all present the principal notions and/or concepts that underpin the conception of qualifications and their mode of construction. We will then see that these notions are very dependent on the one hand on the mode of articulation between academic and vocational education and on the other on the labour market. In conclusion, we will formulate, following on from this analysis, some hypotheses concerning the relationship between the national and the European frameworks for qualifications.

Key concepts underpinning qualifications

French terminology tends often to distinguish between three basic categories, as follows:

*   Knowledge (*savoir*) that is normally based on a body of scientific and/or technological knowledge, usually coded and shaped by a particular (scientific and/or technical) discipline that can be acquired by teaching or by self-directed learning.
*   *Savoir-faire* based on the implementation in a concrete situation of both knowledge and experience (such as the blue-collar worker's manual dexterity, the skilled worker's ability to deal with breakdowns or malfunctions). This 'empirical' *savoir-faire* may be acquired both through learning and through professional practice.
*   *Savoir-être* relates more to inter-personal relationships than to technical matters and may also relate to communication (for example with peers or clients), to problem-solving capacity (*aptitudes or capacités*) within a team, or to autonomy within the context of a hierarchy. These aptitudes or 'knowing how to behave' are not considered as innate attributes of the student but as the result of the learning process.

Unlike in the other languages, each of these three words includes the idea of knowledge (*savoir*) – hence the emphasis that is placed in France on '*savoir*'. This emphasis goes back in part to the century of the Enlightenment and the encyclopaedist tradition, but its persistence is also explained by tensions which have existed and which continue to exist in vocational education. For reasons of space, a historical approach is not possible here. Let us simply note that, from the beginning of the twentieth century to the post-war years, vocational education has progressively been attached to the general education system (passing more and more under the control of the Ministry of Education). During this period the influence of pedagogues and of a scholarly conception of vocational education has increased, assisted by the perception that, after the rise of Taylorism, work was often destructive of, rather than a creator of, competences. It was only gradually, at the turn of the 1980s, that the perception of work evolved, so that experience, regard for knowledge informally acquired, became recognized. In the same period VET which used 'alternance', mixing classroom work with assignments in the workplace, developed. More recently, interest in apprenticeship is being rekindled.

However, the distinction between knowledge and know-how is often criticized for its lack of a scientific basis. Some theoreticians of vocational learning emphasize knowledge in action (*savoir d'action*), concepts realized in action (*concepts en actes*). Effective action, often assimilated to know-how, in fact rests on a conceptual representation forged in experience. Such 'quasi-concepts' connect to the notion of knowledge (Boreham *et al.* 2002; Samurçay and Pastré 2004). Similarly, a lively controversy surrounds the concept of 'knowing how to behave' (*savoir-être*) which tends to occupy an increasingly large place in the reference grids (*référentiels*) and is criticized for its imposition of behavioural norms and for even introducing a certain degree of arbitrariness.

The word '*connaissance*' is also sometimes used with different meanings. It could be a global heading for all that an individual knows (i.e. including *savoir* and *savoir-faire* . . . one could speak of '*connaissances théoriques*' (theoretical knowledge) and '*connaissances pratiques*' (practical knowledge)). But sometimes, *connaissances* is a synonym of *savoir* (*on testera les 'connaissances' dans un domaine académique, en mathématiques, en français* . . . (testing knowledge in an academic subject, mathematics, French . . .)).

Although these notions lack a clear definition, they provide an important organizing role in the discourse of the different actors (employers, trade unions, representatives of the teaching profession) whom we have met in the course of our analysis of the four qualifications studied in this book. The trilogy *savoir/savoir-faire/savoir-être* is very often invoked, the partners all insisting on the inseparable character of these three dimensions. However, two important semantic and conceptual shifts have taken place that represent, at least in the field of VET, a quite profound change in relation to what is often presented, in international comparisons, as an overly theoretical and school-based model.

The first shift is the increasing prevalence of the concept of *formation* at the expense of that of education. According to Lucy Tanguy (2008), this movement started in the 1960s, mainly in the field of adult *formation,* and later gained ground in the academic education community. The term 'initial vocational *formation*' is gradually taking the place of the term 'technical and/or vocational education'. This could be explained by a tension between a holistic conception of education, principally stemming from the post-war educational reforms, and a more utilitarian conception focused on the relationship *formation*–employment. Such a tension, discernible in the structure of the qualifications we are studying, does not imply – at least as far as 'initial *formation*' is concerned – a dismissal of the trilogy, as, unlike in the UK, initial *formation* remains largely integrated into the education system.

Box 3.1 The variety of qualifications

As in other countries, there is a growing diversity of certificates (Maillard 2008a), accepted by all actors (Labruyère and Teissier 2008). Being constructed by different actors and targeted at different constituencies, these certificates have each different shares of *savoir*, *savoir-faire* and *savoir-être*. However, because of its history and the numbers involved, the *diplôme* remains the principal point of reference.

A *diplôme* (even if a strict legal definition does not exist) is a national qualification, academic or vocational, awarded by a public body (a Ministry). It is recognized nationally and valid for all time. The main provider of vocational diplomas is the Ministry of Education (about 900,000 candidates a year) but other Ministries, for example, Health and Agriculture, also provide about 130,000 a year. In contrast to Britain, the state does not delegate the award of diplomas to private bodies; training and awarding bodies are not separate although examination boards are made up of professionals (employers and employees) as well as teachers or trainers belonging to the training providers. This does not mean, however, that preparation for these diplomas only takes place in public institutions. Coexisting with establishments which depend on various Ministries are private institutions, profit-making or not, and institutions attached to, for example, professional organizations and chambers of commerce. Furthermore, study routes are also diverse: full time in school, apprenticeship (sandwich courses), continuing vocational education, and, more recently (2002), through Accreditation of Prior Experiential Learning (APEL). *Diplômes* are organized in levels. The first level *diplôme* in vocational education is the *Certificat d'Aptitude Professionnelle* (CAP), which is the normal qualification for bricklayers.

The awards (*titres*) given by the Ministry of Labour are very similar to the *diplômes*. They are also recognized nationally and valid for all time and are particularly related to continuing vocational education. A *titre*, however, does not have the dual (that is, academic and labour market) currency of a *diplôme*: a *titre* awarded by the Ministry of Labour may be of the same educational level as a vocational *diplôme* awarded by the Ministry of Education but does not, for example, automatically entitle the holder to go on to tertiary education.

Finally, a *certificat* is a term commonly used to designate other kinds of qualification (that is, not *diplômes* or *titres*) that are usually awarded by private bodies, mainly those in continuing training. Since the mid-1980s, employers' organizations (and unions) have been promoting a new kind of certificate, the CQP (*Certificat de Qualification Professionnelle*). CQPs may be gained by adults seeking career progression or to move from one occupation to another but also by young people just starting out on their careers. In some sectors, this policy is clearly a backlash against the *diplôme* and the French education system with the aim of establishing their own qualification system. In other sectors, however, the aim of the policy is much more to complement the formal system and to 'fine-tune' people for specific jobs.

The second shift concerns the growing use, as in the Netherlands, of the notion of competence, which is added to existing notions but also contributes to changing the way qualifications are constructed. The notion of competence began to grow in importance at the beginning of the 1980s and took concrete form in the reference grids for vocational qualifications; however, it is also gaining ground in academic education (Rope and Tanguy 1994). Thus in 2005 a law defined the common core of knowledge and competences that students have to acquire by the end of compulsory schooling. This common core, outlined in the Decree of 11 July 2006, which applies also to VET, includes: command of the French language; ability to use a foreign language; the principal concepts in mathematics, science and technology; command of basic information and communications technology; a humanistic culture; social and civic competences; autonomy and initiative (SCEREN/CNDP 2006). The use of the term 'competences' refers explicitly to European definitions where the term is defined as 'a combination of knowledge, ability and attitudes oriented to actions in particular situations'. Formally this definition is very close to the three categories of the European Qualifications Framework (EQF), even if the common core is in fact much larger (see for example the humanist culture, and social and civic competences).

This notion of competence is growing in importance both in academic education and in VET, forming a basis for student assessment (see below the role of the grid of competences).[1] It differs, however, considerably from the British conception, where 'competence' is generally synonymous with performance and narrowly defined in a behavioural sense. And, even if its development within VET reflects its growing use in the management policies of firms' human resource departments, nevertheless significant differences with the Anglo-Saxon world are discernible (Méhaut 2004; Bouteiller and Gilbert 2005). If competences are firm-specific and attached to individual posts and to work organization, however, they are usually explained in terms of technical competences (*savoir*), operational competences (*savoir-faire*) and behavioural competences (*savoir-être*). In this respect, a part of the French model of competence-based management differs from the Anglo-Saxon model, which focuses on the psychological analysis of behaviour and individual performance, by being more holistic and relating to notions within the VET system.

Roughly speaking, these concepts are found at the heart of the *référentiels* (frameworks) that form the basis of vocational qualifications, regardless of level.

Building qualifications: the growth of the 'competence' concept

Most of the nationally recognized qualifications (*diplômes* and *titres*) are prepared by special committees on which unions, employers, teachers/trainers, and training provider and awarding body (*organismes formateurs et certificateurs*) managers are represented. All such qualifications are automatically included in the national qualification register or *répertoire national*, a national grid created in 2002 by the National Qualification Commission (*Commission Nationale de la Certification*), which brought together the different groups involved in VET (awarding bodies, employers organizations and trades unions). It is the French equivalent of a National Qualification Framework (NQF) even if its underlying principles and the stakeholders differ significantly from those in England and from the principles underpinning the EQF.

Since the early 1990s, the methodology for the design of qualifications has undergone a change (Bouix 1997; Möbus and Verdier 1997; Robichon 2001; Maillard 2005a). The first stage in such a process is usually debate and an attempt to define the occupation(s) concerned, work activities and the labour market outlook, often based on preliminary studies undertaken by experts (including Cereq – *Centre d'Études et de Recherches sur les Qualifications*)[2]. Then two reference frameworks are devised, one based on work content and job analysis (the activity framework, or *référentiel d'activité*) and the other using this framework to produce a grid of competences that is then used to evaluate individual students (the competence or certification framework, or *référentiel de compétence/référentiel de 'certification'*). In principle, these steps are independent of the course content or curriculum, which is defined at a later stage; in fact, as teachers and specialists are also involved, it is often to some extent a compromise. The next step will be to build the *référentiel de formation* (curriculum), which is undertaken by teachers and inspectors with less involvement of unions and employers and lays down guidelines for the number of hours, disciplines and content of courses.

With some differences in practice, this methodology is used by the Ministry of Labour (to govern the *titres*) and by the Ministry of Education or other Ministries. Thus the CAP for the *maçon* (which comes under the Ministry of Education) and the certificate of the Heavy Goods Vehicle (HGV) driver (which comes under the Ministry of Labour) rest on a reference grid of competences. However, *diplômes* and *titres* differ both in their goals and their clientele. The first are more oriented towards young people in initial VET and, because of this, are integrated into the mainstream education system and rest on a larger knowledge base. *Titres* are more oriented towards adults, the unemployed (young or old), and are therefore more integrated with the employment system and have less strong underpinning knowledge.

However, most vocational qualifications within tertiary education (vocational degrees or Master qualifications) are still largely academic in content and design, not necessarily occupation-specific and usually more organized around the academic disciplines. This was also the case with the nursing qualification in this study (a non-university diploma, but nevertheless a higher education (HE) qualification coming under the Ministry of Health) which was organized principally around a curriculum, a prescribed number of hours, and teaching content. However, at the time of our research, it was in the course of being revised, following the general model, with the frameworks of activity and competences.

Using competences as a basis of student assessment corresponds to the tendency, also apparent in the UK and the Netherlands, to base the design of qualifications on outputs rather than inputs. The arguments in favour of a logic of outputs are that it allows for a greater flexibility in the updating of qualifications and brings knowledge closer to the 'needs of the labour market' and away from an accumulation of subject-based knowledge. This tendency is accentuated in France by the requirement that any qualification on the national repertory of qualifications be obtainable through APEL (accreditation of prior experiential learning or

Box 3.2 An example, the qualification file for the builder

The bricklaying qualification (CAP), revised in 2002, is organized according to the typical structure of most vocational *diplômes*. The first part describes the activity and related tasks that a bricklayer is expected to perform. There are four main responsibilities: preparation; organization and execution; implementation of new projects or renovations; equipment maintenance and communication. Each of these responsibilities (*fonctions* in French) is linked to one or more activity, broken down into detailed tasks. Each activity specifies the resources required, the level of autonomy and responsibility involved, and the expected outcome. Alongside the description of activities, there is a cluster of *compétences*, which are what is actually assessed and accredited. It is, however, unclear how much further such description of *compétences* can go. In the case of builders, while some *compétences* cross-cut all activities (such as the ability to read a plan, a competence required both in preparing work and in carrying it out as well as in communication), what are known as 'execution *compétences*' are merely a list of the different types of task involved in building. The competence 'making sense of technical documents' presupposes that the individual is able to relate information from written documents to plans and charts, and vice versa, to read documentation, and to locate a particular operation in the overall planning stage – that is, to be able to read maps, specifications and planning documentation. The criterion by which this is assessed is the accuracy of response. Linked to the competences, 'related knowledge' is organized under seven headings that cross-cut the *compétences*, including, for example, organizing building operations, technical communication and quality control. Under each heading is a schedule of 'knowledge, principles and concepts' along with the extent to which these need to be mastered. For example, under the heading 'Materials' is listed: familiarity with materials groups, such as stone, wood or plaster, with the specific materials used in building, such as concrete, or with specific features, such as lintels, beams and shafts. Expertise boundaries for these knowledges relate to the ability to identify, understand and suggest a material, use technical documentation, and cite provisions for use of the material in question. The knowledge and expertise can be seen as underlying *compétences* and the efficient execution of *fonctions*.

validation des acquis de l'expérience, VAE) and therefore independent of modes of acquisition of knowledge and competences.

The movement from inputs to outcomes, gives rise to debate and disagreements among the parties involved, concerning the relative importance assigned to *savoir*, *savoir-faire* and *savoir-être* and how each is assessed. In part the debate is a reflection on the inherent tension between the twofold goal of qualifications, as educational or as labour market currency. In addition, there is the aspect raised by Michael Young (2009) regarding the way in which knowledge is transmitted within societies and the necessarily – and thankfully in this case – conservative character of education.

Debate can focus on the degree of specialization of the *diplôme* and the scope of the occupation envisaged that it might lead to. Should the *diplôme* be narrowly aligned to a precise *métier* (leading to immediate employability) or broader (facilitating labour market mobility later on, but possibly at the cost of being immediately employable)? The logic of education would incline towards the second choice but this is sometimes rejected, notably in the case of traditional 'craft' occupations, and most often by the representatives of small firms. Beyond this, discussion has also taken place on the transversal structure of an award, that is, its applicability across industries: should it, for example, be designed for one occupation in one industry or relate to many similar occupations in a number of industries? In the case of the *maçon*, if the partners are united in recognizing differences in the organization of work and in the configuration of activities according to, for example, the size of the firm, or differences in the materials used according to the region (brick in the north, stone further south), nevertheless a broad conception of a unitary *diplôme* still prevails. In the case of information technology (IT), the *diplôme* is meant to prepare equally for working in firms specializing in IT as in banks, telephony or other sectors. Nevertheless a certain consensus can be observed, resulting in the long term in a reduction in the number of specialized *diplômes*. Thus, 20 years ago there were more than 300 CAP *diplômes*, as compared to less than 200 today. Likewise, the number of BTS (*Brevet de technicien supérieur*) qualifications, after growing strongly, has now stabilized for the past ten years at around a hundred.

Another frequently debated question concerns the relevance of the *diplôme* level. The structure of such awards reflects the fact that employment is divided both horizontally ('families' of occupations) and vertically (in the educational and employment hierarchy). Conflicts and doubts around the relevance of the basic level, namely the CAP, have been numerous and as much among public bodies as among the representatives of big business. Indeed, there was a time when its abolition and replacement by higher level diplomas were envisaged, a solution that has since been abandoned (Maillard 2005b). Business, notably in metallurgy, has played an important role in the creation of a vocational *baccalauréat* (Campinos-Dubernet 1995) and, more recently, vocational degrees in order to ensure the flow of recruitment of young people at the highest level of education, without this however necessarily translating into an improved situation in the job hierarchy or salary scale (Eckert 1999).

An initial VET system integrated into the general education system

Initial VET, that is the *formation* of young people studying for an award either within an educational framework or as part of an apprenticeship, is very much a part of the education system, both from an institutional point of view and in the way the awards are structured. From this perspective, the French system is similar to the Dutch (Chapter 5) and differs from those of England and Germany (Chapters 4 and 6). The embeddedness in the education system, in a common structure of qualifications organized in levels and allowing, in theory at least, the progression of students, partly explains the broad and integrated conception of competences.

Education (*éducation*), which has in French history been strongly marked by the Enlightenment, aims to prepare individuals to be human beings, citizens and producers – the emphasis placed on each varying with the nature of the education (general or vocational), though all three are represented. A study of the history of the VET of young people demonstrates a progressive process of integration within the educational system (and within the French Ministry of Education), as the activity was gradually transferred from other Ministries (the Ministries of Industry, Labour and Commerce) and from employers, who gave up their *écoles d'entreprise* (see Brucy 1998). This meant that initial VET (*formation professionnelle initiale*, or IVET – the term used in vocational education) was integrated into the educational system of which, indeed, it was a branch. The case of 'continuing' VET (*formation professionnelle 'continue'* or CVET) was quite different, as it related only to young people or, indeed, adults who had left formal education and fell within the remit of the Ministry of Labour, albeit with some demarcation disputes.

Most of the IVET at the upper secondary level (and partly at tertiary level, two years after the *baccalauréat*) is delivered through full-time studies in what is called a '*lycée professionnel*', the term *lycée* echoing that used for academic institutions. Studies combine classroom courses and more practical periods in workshops and also include periods within firms ('*stage en entreprise*'). The apprenticeship track exists and is expanding, with apprentices – as in the Netherlands – also preparing and taking a public diploma, sometimes in the same field as full-time study as the two tracks coexist and compete. The main differences between the two tracks are, on the one hand, that the apprentice is under a labour contract and, on the other, that s/he will alternate working periods within a firm and courses within a '*centre de formation d'apprentis*'. More recently, apprenticeship is also expanding within universities: a university student, for example preparing a Bachelor or a Master degree could be under an apprenticeship contract (Arrighi and Brochier 2005). Thus between 1995 and 2003 the number of apprentices pursuing a first-level qualification (the CAP) decreased slightly, while the number of apprentices enrolled in a vocational *baccalauréat* doubled and even tripled in the case of the two-year higher education vocational tracks. These 'new territories of apprenticeship' (Simon 2001), while not very significant in quantitative terms, have nevertheless had the effect of extending apprenticeship into occupations and sectors that until now have not been involved in this type of VET, as well as creating new apprenticeship streams (CAP/BEP (*Brevet d'Études Professionnelles*) → vocational *baccalauréat*, vocational *baccalauréat* → BTS). These new streams are more attractive to young people and they have become incorporated into training establishments' strategies. One of the four qualifications studied in this book, that of bricklayers, is thus prepared in 80% of cases through apprenticeships, either in vocational colleges (*lycées professionnels*) or – most often – in VET centres run by employers' organizations.

As in the Netherlands, and in contrast to England or Germany, vocational qualifications have, at least in theory, a dual currency (Méhaut 1997). In 'general' education, the main currency of an award is its value within the education system: courses and awards are primarily designed to ensure that the distillation tube works and students can be selected and given progressive access to education up to higher education level. Their currency on the labour market is low. With VET, in contrast, the labour market value of an award is its main value. However, to remain true to the ideals of republican education and to parity of esteem for all awards, guarantees have to be in place for students to progress within the education system as a whole. In theory there are bridges between vocational and academic education, though they remain notional and are little used. However, since VET is also organized in levels, a *diplôme* must allow access to the next level. The *maçon* CAP in this study allows access both to the labour market and to further study for a vocational *brevet*.[3] The same applies to the DUT (*diplôme universitaire de technologie*) in software engineering. This dual currency of the qualification ('internal', that is within the educational system, and 'external', that is, on the labour market) creates marked tensions between the two functions. If the occupation at which a qualification is aimed is defined too narrowly or the curriculum is too strongly vocational, the holder will not be able to progress within the education system. Conversely, a vocational qualification used to gain access to HE can lose part of its vocational content and, hence, of its value on the labour market. Thus for example the DUT in software engineering has progressively become more a foundation for a third year in higher education. Almost 80% of DUT students opt for a 'vocational bachelor' or for engineering colleges, and this then becomes the benchmark for recruitment by firms.

This dual value is a strong argument for the teachers to support 'general' elements (such as language studies or history), in the VET syllabus. Employers do not dispute this.[4] Thus for example the representatives of the employers who met in the context of the *maçon* CAP insisted on the importance of mastery of French and basic mathematics and considered that knowing a foreign language was an individual asset, even if not necessary in the exercise of the professional activity.

So IVET in France retains the triple focus (human being, citizen and producer) with a relatively 'holistic' concept of awards (*diplôme*). Courses always (albeit sometimes under pressure) contain some 'general' education, including such topics as language, history or civic education, with the aim of maintaining a balance between these three foci while at the same time allowing for further studies in the vocational field. This holistic concept is also an attempt to prepare students for life in the broadest sense; rather than preparing them for the immediate demands of the labour market at a given point. The aim is also to anticipate how employment will evolve and to give individuals a knowledge base that will enable them to benefit from mobility (Bouix 1997; Kirsch 2005). However this broad conception does not necessarily signify a strong connection between *diplômes* and the labour market.

Qualification and qualifications: what relationship with the labour market?

French usage of the word *qualification* typifies the 'labour market' facet of the relationship between *formation* and employment: *qualification* is not identical with *diplôme* and, indeed, in certain respects, overlaps with the English term 'skill' though it also carries a connotation of something that has been 'negotiated'. The *Trésor de la langue française*[5] indicates that the term first appeared in employment usage around the time of the Popular Front[6] in connection with the conclusion of collective agreements; in a 1947 entry, Villemer specifies that '*professional qualifications* are the capacities recognised in a worker by virtue of his empirical or methodological *formation*'. The concept was then widely used in industrial sociology (Naville 1956) where it referred to a 'social relationship' rather than to an objective and inherently measurable quality.

The concept then re-emerged in the 1970s in a work entitled *La qualification du travail, de quoi parle-t-on?* (CGP 1978), when discussion centred on the dual usage of the term: *qualification* for a particular job in the sense of its position in a hierarchy of employment and, hence, its position in a '*grille de classifications*' in a collective agreement, from unskilled employment to skilled; and *qualification* of the individual worker, that is, a personal attribute resulting from the complex interplay of that individual's level of *formation*, vocational experience and position. The relative nature of *qualification* as an expression of a social or employment relationship has also figured prominently in the way employment has evolved: through disputes and in bargaining, jobs formerly categorized as 'unskilled' (*non qualifiés*) became 'skilled' (*emplois qualifiés*) as, too, did those who did this work.

What is then the relationship between diplomas and *qualifications*? As we have seen, diplomas are clearly organized on a system of levels, with progression to the higher levels always possible in principle within the VET system. This school-like hierarchy more or less reflects the hierarchy of *qualifications* and found official expression at the end of the 1960s in a nomenclature which tried to rationalize the number of students leaving the *formation* system to correspond with the needs of the labour market (Tanguy 2004). Thus, for example, those leaving without a qualification were supposed to be in a corresponding position to an 'unskilled' worker (*ouvrier spécialisé* in French) in Taylorized industry. The first level of the vocational diploma, the CAP, was meant to correspond in principle to the level of the skilled industry or 'craft' worker. And this hierarchy of levels finds its theoretical counterpart in qualification grids resulting from collective agreements (Jobert 2000) and in the wider society in the social hierarchy of occupations and professions.

Thus the collective agreement in construction firms of more than ten employees refers to the level II skilled worker position, which is defined as 'carrying out of routine work within a specialism, following general instructions, without continuous supervision . . . with a certain latitude regarding choice of methods'. The agreement specifies 'the possession of basic technical knowledge . . . respect for regulations within the work environment' as well as 'flexibility . . . notably through continuing vocational education' and the fact that workers 'can be called upon for others to benefit of their experience, and to use their ability to lead'. The holder of a *diplôme* (CAP or equivalent) is expected to be classified at this level. In the same way, in the public health sector grid, nurses (who in France are classed as civil servants) are classified as category 'B', itself defined at a theoretical level equivalent to diplomas which follow two years of study after the *baccalauréat*.

This hierarchy was clearly based on the pyramid model of both the school system and major manufacturing organizations as well as on civil servant status. At the beginning of the 1970s, it also corresponded to the dominance of internal labour markets. Entry into large firms was most often into positions at the lowest level of the hierarchy; progression then followed either on the basis of length of service and/or further *formation*. However, this model has profoundly changed. Growth in the availability of qualifications at different levels allows firms to select candidates and offer positions at each level of the hierarchy. The rules of internal mobility are changing. As we saw above, they rely now more on 'competence' and less on length of service alone. Moreover, the relative abundance of qualified candidates, together with the systematic sending into retirement of older workers, has – at least in the largest firms – transformed the composition of the labour force, as has the use of continuing *formation* (shorter, more adapted to the needs of the position). In certain respects, it is nowadays possible to talk of internal markets increasingly based on occupational criteria.

However, unlike in the Netherlands and unlike, to a lesser degree, in Germany, the correspondence between the qualification and the employment category is far from automatic. It depends on labour market conditions and bargaining power. In general, when drawing up collective agreements, employers refuse to make qualifications correspond automatically to certain positions, in the name of the freedom of the employers to match the position to the individual. And the unions themselves are also very careful, as to make the correspondence automatic and a diploma compulsory would risk closing the door into skilled jobs to non–diploma holders.

To take bricklayers as an example, only a small majority of those classed as 'skilled' bricklayers hold a CAP in the sector; the remainder either have a diploma from another sector or only have relevant professional experience. This is even more the case for HGV drivers. The case of nurses differs from both these two in that the diploma is necessary in order to practise; therefore the correspondence between diploma and position is very strong. But this case highlights the complex interplay between academic and vocational hierarchies. The nursing diploma requires three years of post *baccalauréat* study. In principle, therefore, it is at the same level as a university Bachelor degree, though not recognized as such until now. Making use of the Bologna agreement, nursing unions and professional organizations of nurses have claimed and obtained recognition of their diploma as a Bachelor degree, opening up the way to study at Masters level. And one of the probable consequences of this recognition will be the reclassification of nurses as category 'A' civil servants (a higher category, opening up better perspectives for salary and career development than the present category 'B'). This subtle interplay between qualification levels, position and salary levels is likely to have major consequences in the referencing of French levels to those of the EQF (Méhaut and Winch 2009).

Conclusion: what relationship with the EQF?

In response to the diversity of the qualifications, in France, as in many countries, the idea of a national qualification register has gradually emerged, with the dual aims of bringing coherence to the wide range of awards now in existence (and avoiding duplication where possible) and of guaranteeing a measure of transparency for both individuals and companies. Attempts to achieve this were very fragmented in the past but have since 2002 been entrusted to a body, the 'national qualification commission' (*commission nationale de la certification*) which is devising the national qualification register. This commission includes representatives of the state, employers and trade unions and thus reflects the continuing existence of a form of tripartite management of the VET system.

This chapter is essentially based on research carried out in 2007 and 2008. At that time the various players knew relatively little about EQF and ECVET (European Credit System for Vocational Education and Training) and few knew where to place their *diplômes* in the eight-level grid of the largely unfamiliar EQF or indeed saw any real benefit in doing so. Employers still have doubts about how companies can make concrete use of the grid and are reluctant to accept it, fearing that it could well change the French classification system, especially since this system is a benchmark for collective bargaining. All of the evidence points to a 'soft' application of the grid in a compromise that would see the French system merely being translated into the EQF.

The whole process is (will be) under the control of the NQF authority. This is seen as a condition both for the coherence of the NQF and for the mutual trust in the EQF. NQF managers say that the 'vertical' grid (i.e. the three descriptors) is not a major problem. As we have seen, the concepts of *savoir* (knowledge), *savoir-faire* (know-how) and *savoir-être* (knowing how to conduct oneself) can quite easily be transposed into the descriptors. However, questions do arise about the relative importance of these three descriptors. If the main goal of the EQF is the relationship between qualifications within the education system, then, from a French point of view, the first dimension (knowledge) will be the more important. If the main goal is the labour market, then maybe the second and the third dimensions will be more important. So one question is the implicit hierarchy of the three descriptors and the conceptual ambiguities between these three 'vertical' descriptors and the

French concepts of *savoir, connaissance, savoir-faire* and *savoir-être*. Another question is the coherence between the levels and these three descriptors. The French holistic notion of a qualification presupposes a strong relation between the levels of mastery of *savoir, savoir-faire* and *savoir-être*. A qualification ought to be classed at the same level in the three dimensions, even if, in fact, differences exist. For example, the competence dimension (namely autonomy) is not the same for a CAP (and) skilled worker within a Taylorist industry and a CAP for a skilled, self-employed, worker within the construction industry.

More fundamentally, the classification of qualifications in eight levels, in France as in the Netherlands, carries strong social implications as a result of the dual value of qualifications and interferes with their position in the hierarchy within the education system. Since the three higher levels actually correspond to the three levels of the Bologna process, level 5 ought logically to be shorter, higher education-based *formations* (BTS or DUT), level 4 the *baccalauréats* (academic and vocational), and level 3 the CAP. Any other classification would compromise the principle of progression within the school hierarchy.

So the relationships between an NQF and the EQF is not only a technical problem but also a social one, linked to the ability of the national social stakeholders to grasp not only national disputes but also the European perspective.

Notes

1   For a critical reading, see Rope and Tanguy (1994), Crahay (2006) and, particularly concerning the concept of competence in the workplace, Dupray *et al.* (2003).
2   A national organization in the field of applied research and expertise on the relationship between education/*formation* and employment, providing expertise to public authorities as well as to the social partners.
3   This is not the case with the *titre* of the HGV driver, awarded by the Ministry of Labour, which explains why this *titre* is more like the English NVQ (National Vocational Qualification). As for the nursing diploma, it used to be classed as a final qualification which did not automatically give access to further levels of education. Nowadays, however, unlike the *titre* of HGV driver, the nursing diploma is integrated more closely with university education and recognized under the Bologna process as a Bachelor qualification, opening access to Masters level.
4   This opinion, which is found among employers in most other occupations, is partly explained by the need for academic knowledge within the occupation and partly by a concern that *diplômes* should be attractive. In France, a diploma is attractive if it has not only a strong labour market value but also a value internal to the system by leading to further study.
5   Etymological reference-work.
6   The Popular Front was the alliance of left-wing parties that governed France between 1936 and 1938.

4

THE CHANGING RELEVANCE OF THE *BERUF*

Georg Hanf

A bit of history

Since the beginnings of modern Europe, there have been two sources of social recognition: on the one hand, the titles given by the emerging education system, promoting a culture of written knowledge and legitimizing access to social positions; and, on the other, the demarcation of social membership through the older tradition of framing of labour under corporatist surveillance (Harney and Kissmann 2000). 'Corporatist surveillance' meant maintaining the heritage of the trade through the tradition of experience in workplace practice (apprenticeship, mastership) and the protection of the social status related to it. In the course of modernization, the different nation states took different routes in dealing with the principle of corporatist surveillance: dissolving (e.g. France), marginalizing (e.g. England and, to a lesser extent, the Netherlands), transforming (e.g. Germany). Depending on the route taken, different ideal types of 'qualification styles' can be identified (Deißinger 1995): science-orientated, where the state takes control; function-orientated, where the interplay of market participants prevails; and *Beruf*-orientated, where intermediary institutions (corporations) are in charge.

In Germany (and in the other German-speaking countries) work-based practical experience under corporatist surveillance continued to be the dominant type of 'skills formation'. With the integration of principles of the school system, the explication and codification of occupational knowledge, the differentiation of theory and practice, the replacement of corporatist rites through private contracts and public exams, the principle of corporatist surveillance was extended into wider areas of labour. Hereby the institutional structure for a separate vocational education and training (VET) sub-system was established, clearly demarcated from the education system – even though VET in companies was complemented with part-time vocational schools.

Demarcations exist between different constituencies with their own legislation: the privately organized VET under corporatist administration is based on the Federal (national) Vocational Training Act (*Berufsbildungsgesetz*), closely linked with national labour and trade law, whereas the *Länder* (Federal States) legislation comprises all other forms of education (including vocational schools). There are also demarcations between different forms of progression/career spaces: the education system produces a highly differentiated hierarchy of school/university qualifications defined by a hierarchy of knowledge; the VET system based on the Vocational Training Act provides its own hierarchy of Initial and Continuing VET qualifications defined by a hierarchy of occupational competence related to positions in the labour market.

The Dual System is considered key to the generally high skills level of German society and the high productivity of its economy (Finegold and Soskice 1988; Culpepper and Finegold 1999). However, it has long been debated as to whether the system can respond adequately to structural changes in the economy and in the organization of work, as well as to demographic developments, and whether the qualifications produced are able to meet emerging demands. Tensions arising from these changes have put the *Beruf* concept under pressure, seemingly pulling initial VET in two directions at once: towards more academic education (knowledge) on the one hand, and towards more training for employability (skills) on the other. Adjustments are required to meet these challenges. Recent reforms are intended to overcome certain rigidities of the *Beruf* concept without abandoning it. Certainly, the sub-system needs to be better coupled with the education system. Here the qualifications framework approach may provide options to overcome certain limitations in the national and international context.

In this chapter we will address the following questions: what is the significance of initial VET in the entire system? What is the meaning of *Beruf* as the organizing principle of German VET? What are the specific features of an *Ausbildungsberuf*, the main qualification type of the German qualifications system? How are the qualifications of the Dual System used in the labour market? What are the main challenges for the *Beruf* as the governing principle of VET from the labour market and from the educational point of view and how does the system react to these? Finally: what might be the impact of the European Qualifications Framework (EQF) on national developments?

A brief outline of the German VET system

The VET system in Germany comprises VET in companies and in full-time vocational schools at secondary and tertiary level. The focus of this chapter is initial VET under the Vocational Training Act with the *Beruf* as its organizing principle, aimed at occupational competence at intermediate (skilled worker) level. This sub-system of work-based VET in companies complemented by compulsory part-time vocational school, the Dual System of VET, is still the main route into employment for the young generation and attracts more students than can be taken on. Table 4.1 shows the German focus on intermediate qualifications (ISCED – International

Standard Classification of Education 3–4), most of which are vocational, Dual System qualifications. School leavers with a university entrance qualification normally continue to university, whereas some of those with an initial VET qualification acquire a vocational qualification at tertiary level; 8% have a qualification equivalent to ISCED 5B.

These figures have been more or less the same for quite some time, with a continuous slow shift towards the ISCED 5A level. Some 25% of young people with a general upper secondary leaving certificate go onto the vocational track, most of them into the Dual System. Looking at the actual enrolment patterns at upper secondary level of the countries included in this study, Germany stands out as the country with by far the highest figures for dual initial VET (Table 4.2).

A closer look at the trends in enrolment patterns for initial VET in Germany shows a certain stability but also quite disturbing developments. The sector comprises the Dual System, the fully qualifying vocational schools and the so-called 'transition system'. The growth of the transition system within the last 15 years is highly problematic because it includes different VET schemes and full-time courses which do not lead to recognized qualifications. Its purpose is threefold: preparation of school leavers for the Dual System, acquisition of school-leaving certificates, and bridging the time between school and an apprenticeship. Since the mid-1990s, full-time vocational schools leading to a labour market qualification have seen a slight increase in numbers and stability in their overall share, while the transition system has grown steadily. The system evolved due to an increasing absolute number of school leavers whilst the supply of dual apprenticeship training places did not

TABLE 4.1 Population aged 25 to 64 years by highest educational attainment in Germany and selected EU member states, 2008 (%)

Country	ISCED 0-2	ISCED 3-4	ISCED 5-6
EU–19 average	30	45	26
Germany	**15**	**60**	**25**
The Netherlands	27	41	32
United Kingdom	30	37	33
France	30	43	27

Source: OECD *Education at a Glance 2010*, Paris 2010 (Table A1.4).

TABLE 4.2 Upper secondary enrolment patterns (2008)

	General	Vocational	Dual/alternance
Germany	**42.5**	**57.5**	*42.8*
Netherlands	32.9	67.1	*20.2*
France	55.8	44.2	*12.4*
United Kingdom	68.6	31.4	. . .

Source: OECD *Education at a Glance 2010*, Paris 2010 (Table C1.4.).

TABLE 4.3 Distribution of new entrants into the three sectors of the initial VET system 1995, 2000, 2005 and 2008

	Total	*Dual System*	*Full-time vocational school*	*'Transition System'*
1995	1,068,470	547,062	180,271	341,137
	100%	51.2	16.9	31.9
2000	1,217,985	582,416	175,462	460,107
	100%	47.8	14.4	37.8
2005	1,219,092	517,341	215,874	485,877
	100%	42.4	17.7	39.9
2008	1,166,330	558,501	210,552	397,277
	100%	47.9	18.1	34.1

Source: Federal Statistical Office Germany and statistical offices of the Länder. Calculations and estimates on the basis of school statistics. In: Authoring Group Educational Reporting: *Education in Germany 2010*, Berlin/Bonn 2010. Table E1-1.

increase accordingly. Every year hundreds of thousands of young people enter this system. As can be seen from Table 4.3, in 2005 there were nearly as many entrants to the transition system as there were to the Dual System.

Table 4.3 shows the distribution of new entrants into the three 'sub-sectors' of the initial VET sector within the last 15 years. Entrants to the transition system are about 16 years old and stay for about 1.5 years. Most of them (between 70% and 80%) move on into the Dual System or into full-time vocational schools. Partly as a result of the growing transition system, the average entry age for an apprenticeship has risen to 19 years and above; between 14% and 18% of the age cohort remained without a vocational qualification. These developments have sparked fierce debates about the functioning of the Dual System and about alternatives to be addressed by educational reforms.

The vocational regime (*Berufliche Ordnung*)

Beruf is a signature of modern society, linking the individual with the economy, morality with function (Durkheim 1902; Weber 1980; Kurtz 2005). The term *Beruf* denominates a certain form of labour, where the individual is acting in a certain socially defined role, making a specific contribution within a differentiated world of work. *Beruf* is a pattern for the social division and integration of labour (Harney and Kissmann 2000). This applies to all the countries we are looking at in this book. What is different is how *Berufe* are shaped in Germany and, even more so, how people are qualified for a *Beruf*.

The German workforce is characterized by a large segment working at intermediate skill level with a rather high degree of autonomy (Beck *et al.* 1980). Whereas in other countries there are strong demarcations between worker and management positions, in Germany about 60% of the workforce is at intermediate level. This is, *inter alia*, due to certain markets for quality products: German industry is characterized by 'diversified quality production', requiring a certain supply of highly qualified workers (Backes-Gellner 1996; Abelshauser 2004). The Dual System of vocational education is deeply rooted in and closely linked with the system of industrial production. The competitiveness of the German economy was – and still is – based on skilled workers at intermediate level, that is, the *Facharbeiter/ Fachangestellte* who are qualified for a *Beruf*. This has been the strategic and main type of qualification for the German path to industrialization (Greinert 2004).

The *Beruf* concept is functional for various areas: for companies, it provides transparent clusters of competences, ensuring the allocation of the right people to the right work places and constituting the basis of company productivity. The *Beruf* structures the labour market mainly at the level of intermediate qualifications. At the same time, it sets demarcation lines against the unqualified worker, on the one hand, and against the academically qualified worker, on the other. *Berufe* reduce competition in the labour market. A *Beruf* protects the one who acquires it. It represents a specialization which draws a clear line against all other competitors in the labour market. At the level of society, the *Beruf* concept (re-)produces social position, providing integration and stability, as well as social mobility. VET in a *Beruf* conveys a certain status in society, forming certain strata and levelling down social differences within these. For the individual, it is the basis for a particular biography and for employment as well as a source of social acknowledgement and identity. Finally, as regards VET, the *Beruf* concept is the basis for structuring qualification processes and their institutionalization.

The *Beruf* concept is characterized not by a single function but by this very comprehensive multi-dimensional functionality. We might refer to an 'occupational regime' (*Berufliche Ordnung*), characterizing the interplay of the structural and conceptual aspects which give *Berufe* stability and meaning. A functional deficit in one direction impacts on the entire network of functions. 'Qualification', 'activity', 'function', 'job' are terms which focus on certain aspects of labour but cannot grasp the fundamental dimension of *Beruf*, giving legitimacy to social structures (Kutscha 2000; Kraus 2007).

According to Hartmann (1968), a *Beruf* is a typical combination of work activities requiring certain specialized knowledge and skills, aiming at a permanent income. A job in contrast may be just occasional, not requiring definite knowledge and skills, with varying activities. In a functional perspective, a *Beruf* is a job somebody is engaged in and where s/he delivers a certain measurable performance. In a subject-orientated perspective, on the other hand, 'I have a *Beruf*' means that 'I am in the possession of abilities acquired through a particular VET programme and orientated towards certain role expectations which can be demonstrated in action (performance)'. From job to profession there is a continuum in the dimensions of systematic knowledge and collective orientation. Historically, work is transformed into *Berufe* or further into 'professions' (professionalization), but processes of professionalization might also be reversed (Hartmann 1968: 201–2).

A *Beruf* encompasses a typical set of activities; it has a defined sphere of operation, a workplace and company and an independent set of activities, whereas jobs are defined by the workplace. To pursue a *Beruf* the individual needs to acquire a typical systematic combination of formal knowledge, skills and experience-based competence; their deployment is not geared to any single worksite. *Berufe* are strongly linked with the collective bargaining system as well as with social welfare. A *Beruf* is a currency for trading labour for money on an occupational labour market (Marsden 1990; Reuling 1998), conferring societal status and securing a self-determined life. Beyond the individual *Beruf*, there is *Beruflichkeit* as the principle underlying the re-production and innovation of 'cultivated and qualified' labour, strongly related to 'dignity' as opposed to humiliating forms of work (Kutscha 2008).

The co-ordination mechanisms in which the *Beruf* concept is embedded give it stability as an organizing principle. David Soskice introduced the distinction between 'co-ordinated' and 'non-co-ordinated' or 'liberal market' economies (Soskice 1999; Hall and Soskice 2001). According to Soskice, co-ordinated market economies, like Germany's, provide more and better in-company training. Its skills formation regime is based on a particular set of institutions that can be seen as a special mode of self-governance, operating through the country's social partners in co-operation with the state (corporatism). Co-ordination mechanisms are in place in various sub-systems and at various levels: (1) the division of labour, qualification-related employment and related pay (co-ordination of the labour market by the social partners); (2) the regulation of *Ausbildungsberufe* (co-ordination of VET standard-setting between social partners and the state/s); (3) the provision of apprenticeships (co-ordination of the labour market and VET organization/s); and (4) the relations between company-based VET and the education system.

The specific institutions and bodies involved in legislating for initial VET are the Federal Government and its Ministries, in co-operation with the social partners and the *Länder* governments. It is the complex process of consensus-building that ensures that the regulation of VET standards is accepted by all sides. At the level of provision, self-administered bodies (chambers and similar bodies) supervise the quality of training and organize the external exams independently from individual companies. Also at this level, social partners play an important role in these 'competent bodies' as stated in the Vocational Education Act (*Berufsbildungsgesetz*). Finally, social partnership takes place at company level where employee representatives engage in all matters of practical training. For individual firms, participating in the apprenticeship system means being involved in a powerful mechanism, conferring social status and recognition on individual workers and firms alike (Deißinger 2001).

The major VET qualification: the *Ausbildungsberuf*

The *Beruf* is the organizing principle for both employment and VET. VET is structured in terms of *Ausbildungsberufe* (training occupations). An *Ausbildungsberuf* is a social construct, based on a consensual agreement between social partners and the state. *Ausbildungsberufe* constitute a type of qualification, with specific combinations of competences, preparing for certain sets of activities and normally linked to a collectively agreed wage. They are laid down in *Ausbildungsordnungen* (training ordinances) which are a combination of input, process and outcome orientation.

In 2010 there were 350 *Ausbildungsberufe*, each with its own regulation. An *Ausbildungsberuf* is an ordering category that determines the clustering of work tasks and the necessary knowledge, skills and competences. An *Ausbildungsberuf* never just mirrors the reality of a particular work place at a particular time; it always goes beyond this by achieving a wider scope of action and greater sustainability. It defines a minimum standard which is open to specifications at company level. *Ausbildungsberufe* guarantee a minimum standard, a systematic and complete programme, binding for both the training company and the apprentice (Deißinger 1995: 183).

The development of new vocational training regulations and the adaptation of existing regulations follow a systematic procedure that incorporates the Federal government, *Länder* governments, employers, trade unions and the vocational training research community. As a rule, the initiative for updating the occupational profile of a training occupation or for developing an entirely new occupation comes from trade associations, employers' associations, trade unions or the Federal Institute for Vocational Education and Training (BIBB). An *Ausbildungsordnung* is always a result of negotiations between conflicting interests about a more or less favourable tailoring of competence clusters (Beck *et al.* 1980: 40).

VET regulation benchmarks include: a) title, b) duration of training, c) occupational field, d) type and structure of the profile (monolithic or differentiated), e) timetable and f) inventory of skills, knowledge and competences (*Fähigkeiten*), outlining the minimum requirements for the occupational profile. Based on these benchmarks, Federal government experts, VET practitioners from both sides of industry, develop a skeleton curriculum for the company part, while the *Länder* experts (mainly teachers) develop a draft curriculum delivered part-time in vocational schools.

Ausbildungsberufe are defined by a combination of learning outcomes related to occupational standards (*Berufsbild*) and a strong input and process orientation with clear regulation of what has to be learned/taught when, within what period of time and where, either in the workplace or at school. The qualification is awarded after a final external exam at the end of a course by the 'competent body' as defined by the Vocational Training Act. In most cases the competent body is the local Chamber. It is possible to sit exams without having completed a VET programme but this is exceptional (*Externenprüfung*).

Ausbildungsberufe are based on the Vocational Training Act (2005: 15). According to this Act, the aim of VET is *berufliche Handlungskompetenz* which comprises 'the vocational skills, knowledge and competences necessary to engage in a form of skilled occupational activity in a changing working world'.

Throughout the Act skills, knowledge, competences (*Fertigkeiten, Kenntnisse, Fähigkeiten*) are always mentioned together, never on their own. They are not defined in detail and are explicitly understood as vocational. *Kenntnisse* represent a narrow concept of knowledge, more related to factual, declarative and procedural knowledge and less to reflection and understanding (the connotation of *Wissen*). *Fertigkeiten* are functional skills, whilst *Fähigkeiten* are understood as extra-functional (methodological, social and personal). The demands of the labour market are dominant here.

The conceptualization of competence is enshrined in the framework for vocational school curricula which takes the perspective of the learner. It is also at the core of vocational pedagogy (Bader and Müller 2002). Here *Handlungskompetenz* is not restricted to the world of work but comprises the ability and readiness of the individual to act adequately, as well as in a socially and individually responsible way, not only in occupational but also in social and private situations. *Handlungskompetenz* unfolds in the dimensions of *Fach-*, *Sozial-* and *Humankompetenz* (competence in actively dealing with objects (real or symbolic), competence in dealing with oneself, competence in dealing with others). Thus, *Handlungskompetenz* is a holistic concept integrating all dimensions (KMK 2007) (see Chapter 10). Like *Fertigkeiten, Kenntnisse, Fähigkeiten* in the vocational education regulation (*Ausbildungsordung*), these competences cannot be taught or learned separately but only in an integrated way; there is no separation or categorization in the vocational education regulations and school curricula (Ertl and Sloane 2005).

In the late 1990s a new concept was developed gearing learning in vocational schools more towards the integrative approach of *Handlungskompetenz* by structuring curricula in *Lernfelder*. The term *Lernfelder* can be roughly translated as 'fields of learning'. The concept was introduced formally by a decision of the Conference of Education Ministers (Kultusministerkonferenz, KMK 1999). It applies the notions of didactic innovations, such as task-orientated and comprehensive learning programmes, to the context of vocational colleges.

The main idea of this concept is the reconstruction and/or simulation of vocational processes in the vocational colleges. Tasks and activities the trainees are typically confronted with in training companies ('working area') form the basis for the construction of 'teaching and learning arrangements' (learning situations at vocational colleges) that constitute a field of learning (Sloane 2001). Fields of learning also draw on the knowledge that is incorporated in conventional school subjects. However, traditional subjects are transformed into a cross-curricular structure in which comprehensive tasks have to be fulfilled and real-life problems resolved by the trainees. In sum, many fields of learning represent pedagogically adapted and enriched vocational processes derived from actual work contexts; this in turn implies both a 'streamlining' with the vocational training in the company and losses in terms of general education (Kremer and Sloane 2000; Ertl and Sloane 2005).

Following the discourse on education standards and learning outcomes, the process of shaping *Ausbildungsordnungen* has taken a new twist. The concept of

Kompetenz is being further developed by research and development into 'competence-based VET regulations' (*kompetenzbasierte Ausbildungsordnungen*). The aim is to create a nationally applied basis for measuring and validating vocational competences in the sense of competence diagnostics (Lorig and Schreiber 2007; BIBB 2009: 287–98). *Ausbildungsberufe* are divided into six to eight units, derived from occupation-specific, typical work processes, paying regard to the principle of complete action, that is, in each of these processes all dimensions of action (planning, executing, evaluating, adjusting) have to be represented. These units are further broken down into single competences.

The competence discourse in Germany had already begun during the great educational reform era when an integrated structure of the entire education and training system was conceptualized (Roth 1971). The then developed overarching concept of *Kompetenz* was about the rational organization of the self. According to this concept, learning always includes something that is not tangible but which, by means of planning and control, helps to develop the potential of the individual. Whereas 'qualification' is understood as the standardized expectations of society, *Kompetenz* (also in relation to a *Beruf*) is conceived as a property of the person. Can this understanding be maintained in the face of recent attempts to make this potential measurable?

Berufsausbildung (dual VET) in the education system

VET in Germany represents a structure linking education with the employment system. The structural characteristics are: the combination of the workplace and the vocational school as learning venues for practical learning and for systematic studies of vocational and general subjects, with different curricula based on different (Federal and *Länder*) legislation, conferring a double status on the learners as apprentices and as students.

Since the beginning of the nineteenth century, the divide between VET and education, especially higher education (HE), was legitimized by Wilhelm von Humboldt's theory of education. In his plan, public education is defined as the education of human beings and citizens. Vocational training for certain trades exists only subsequent to and outside the public education system (Benner 2003). As a consequence, vocational training and its qualifications developed outside the education system, underpinned by a separate body of legislation. Through the part-time vocational school with its educational mandate, which became compulsory around 1900 for all general school leavers up to the age of 18, the one world (*Bildung*) was loosely coupled with the other (*Beruf*).

Initial dual VET provides a surplus beyond that which is necessary for certain job functions; it includes systematic-theoretical knowledge and has a strong educational dimension. The concept, integrating skills formation with the formation of character and good citizens, goes back to Georg Kerschensteiner and the foundation years of the Dual System and has now been adapted to modern times (Winch 2006; Gonon 2009).

Even though training and education were linked in a 'Dual System' (the term was only coined in the 1960s), vocational qualifications from outside the school system do not – in principle – necessarily provide entitlement to access to further studies in the education system or to careers requiring particular general or academic education. Only in recent years, with an ever growing demand for more general education and a general academic drift, have the demarcation lines softened.

On the supply side, tensions have been growing over the last 15 years. Structural changes in the economy have made it more and more difficult for people to enter the dual training system because of a lack of company training places. Companies have not provided the volume that would have been necessary given the growing size of school-leaving cohorts, most of whom still see the dual VET route as the most attractive. While more and more school leavers with an *Abitur* (university entry qualification) start an apprenticeship (approximately 20% of all apprentices in 2008) those from the *Hauptschule* (basic secondary school) find it increasingly problematic to enter the initial VET system. Short-term lack of apprenticeships has a long-term effect on the life course of a cohort (Blossfeld and Stockmann 1999: 13). Those without an initial vocational qualification have little chance to get on track later and risk being excluded for life.

Within the Dual System the two components (company and part-time school) have clearly defined and different tasks. The term 'dual' refers primarily to the division of VET into two separate learning environments, each with its distinct curricula but also with different personnel (company trainers and teachers). Trainees spend about three or four days a week in companies and up to two days a week in vocational schools. Learning processes in companies focus on guided learning in the workplace or instruction in company training departments with an emphasis on the practical elements of the occupation but also including industrial, cross-sector and occupation-specific knowledge.

The function of the *Berufsschule* is to provide students with general and vocational education in order to deepen and supplement workplace learning. *Berufsschulen* equip their students with basic and specialized VET, adding to the general education they have already received. Due to the inclusion of these general subjects, individuals completing a Dual System programme can also acquire the intermediate school-leaving certificate (*Realschulabschluss*).

In defining the purpose of initial VET in the dual system, the Vocational Training Act also states that it has to lay the foundation for continuing VET. This holds true for any advanced vocational qualification (*Meister*, Higher Technician, etc.) where an initial VET qualification is required, but it applies also in a more general way. The *Ausbildungsberuf* is an essential basis for continuing VET which offers the chance to continually renew knowledge during working life by making use of the learning opportunities and learning options available for individuals and provided by employers (Harney *et al.* 1999: 287). Since the majority of German employees start their working lives with an initial vocational qualification and occupational mobility is rather low, there is relatively little participation in lifelong learning. The need for this is defined less by the individual than by changes within the *Beruf*.

For some time now, efforts have been undertaken to overcome the divide between VET and HE. To identify and agree on uniform criteria for access to higher education by vocationally qualified applicants, the Standing Conference of *Länder* Ministers of Education took a landmark decision on 5 March 2009: general university access will be opened for persons holding *Meister*, technician and equivalent qualifications; subject-restricted university entrance will be possible for vocationally qualified persons after a successful final initial VET examination and three years' work experience. HE qualifications are becoming more vocational, reflected in the growing number of dual degrees (apprenticeships at tertiary level) or with the introduction of Bachelor and Masters degrees in vocational subjects.

To adapt to changes in the economy and to provide better opportunities for more young people to acquire a qualification, the Federal Ministry of Education and Research established the think tank 'Innovation Circle on Initial Vocational Education and Training' (IKBB). Its ten Guidelines for the Modernization and Structural Improvement of Vocational Education and Training are to form the basis for VET policy in the coming years (IKBB 2007). In their analysis, the experts identified a lack of permeability in the system: between vocational preparation and regular VET, between full-time vocational schools and the Dual System, between qualifications on the same level, between initial and continuing VET, and between VET and HE. To a large extent the guidelines aim at making VET more flexible and creating pathways for lifelong learning, at the same time strengthening the *Berufsprinzip* (occupation principle). Throughout the guidelines, opportunities for credit transfer in the education system are a high priority and transfer between the various sectors of education is emphasized. This is seen as a necessity not only in order to guarantee equality of opportunity but also to meet the increasing demand for HE graduates. Most of the recommendations were already prepared by the Vocational Training Act in 2005.

The IKBB also proposed to step up the introduction of modular structures. Modules (*Ausbildungsbausteine*) are being tested as a means to help previously unsuccessful training applicants, drop-outs, young people with learning difficulties, and returning-to-learning adults make the transition by having their previously acquired skills and competences credited towards the regular training period or enabling their admission as external candidates to chamber examinations.

Modularization has long been the subject of fierce debate at national level. The *Beruf* concept is considered compatible with more flexible, modular qualification approaches as long as these lead to a recognized qualification (*Abschluss*) and to employment with progression options. The *Abschluss* concept is important to the German system of accreditation of *Berufsfähigkeit*; sections may be composed of modules but the whole qualification cannot be seen merely as a bundle of modules (Ertl 2003). Modules may, however, be used for enabling access to a regular VET programme, for transfer between qualifications, and for progression.

Concepts and programmes have been developed to promote lifelong learning across and beyond formal qualifications. The ANKOM initiative (Credit of vocational competences towards higher education study programmes) developed models for the crediting of vocational competences towards HE study programmes (http://ankom.his.de). With the DECVET initiative, a credit system for VET is being developed (http://www.decvet.net/).

Within VET, more flexible delivery structures have also been developed within recent years, and this process is set to continue. The final examination can now be taken in two parts, administered at different times; for the final examination, credit is given for the period of training already undergone pursuant to the rescinded provisions. Initial VET in another relevant occupation may be credited towards initial VET in the occupation governed by the initial VET regulations, taking into account the vocational skills, knowledge and competences acquired in the course of such previous training.

The modernization of the VET regulatory framework in terms of the number and types of occupation is supposed to make its provision more transparent, efficient and flexible. The aim is to form groups of occupations with common core skills and options for further specialization in order to give talented young apprentices an opportunity to acquire additional creditable skills and qualification modules during their course. The justification for such occupational groups is threefold: for the companies, there is more flexibility in the provision; for the apprentices, there are increased options for mobility after completion of their initial VET; for the vocational schools, occupation-related classes can be maintained in times of shrinking age cohorts.

These new developments have been greeted with some concern on the part of those guarding the *Berufskonzept*. According to the director of the section responsible for training ordinances in the Ministry of Education and Research, too much flexibility in terms of individually (person or company) designed profiles and qualifications may be counterproductive since it can restrict the mobility of the employee. On the other hand, a too-broadly conceptualized qualification may also be counterproductive, since the specific purposes of a qualification would disappear and it would lose its particular value. Both would contradict the *Berufsprinzip* (Leskien 2008: 7).

An occupational labour market – how does it work?

The German labour market is structured around occupations (*Berufe*). *Berufe* describe the national workforce potential; they are central categories for the recruitment of skilled workers; and they form a core criterion for the collective bargaining structure. The *Berufsabschluss*, the certificate of the Dual System, implies a high degree of social security for the 'owner': the qualification comes with the entitlement to a particular wage, if employed according to the qualification. It also comes with certain entitlements to social benefits related to the qualification in case of unemployment or occupational disability.

The countries included in this study differ, *inter alia*, according to the relative dominance of certain principles of labour market organization. A common distinction is that of internal labour markets (ILMs) versus occupational labour markets (OLMs) (Marsden 1990). OLMs are predominantly structured along occupational segments related to corresponding tracks of vocational training. Prospective employers receive strong signals concerning the labour market value of standardized and specific vocational qualifications. While an OLM features skills that are needed in many firms, those developed within an ILM are less transferable. An OLM relates to persons holding a particular qualification sanctioned by a diploma or by the judgement of their peer group. The two types of labour market are associated with different VET patterns. In OLMs it is likely that VET is concentrated (in the form of apprenticeship) at the beginning of working lives. The close co-ordination of supply and demand in Germany is the basis for an OLM with significant positive effects for successful entry and stable early careers (Hillmert and Jacob 2008: 50–84).

The high labour market value of qualifications from the Dual System of VET is achieved by involving employers and trade unions as central partners in the process of designing training regulations, providing and monitoring training, examinations and quality assurance. The result is a high level of transparency and confidence, shared by all parties, in the value of the qualifications – which is always higher than for qualifications acquired in full-time vocational schools.

The majority of skilled employees receive fixed rates of pay laid down in the collective agreements concluded between the social partners. In 2007, those with an initial vocational qualification earned approximately 26% more than those without such a qualification.

The labour market value of vocational qualifications is shown in the subsequent offer of employment in the company after completion of VET for between 50% and 60% of the apprentices. Youth unemployment in Germany was around 10.5% at the beginning of 2009 (when general unemployment was 7.4%), rather low compared to the figures for EU27: 18.3% and 8.2% respectively. Average unemployment within recent years was about 10% for individuals with a vocational qualification, about 25% for those with no vocational qualification, and – since 1990 – never above 5% for university graduates (Reinberg and Hummel 2007).

The value of qualifications is also manifest in their match with the occupations of employees. According to a survey of 20,000 employees (*Bundesministerium für Bildung und Forschung* 2008: 43ff), the matching of 'dual' qualifications is quite high: 84.3% with such a qualification work at skilled worker level or above; 15.7% were overqualified, working below their qualification level. An improving match of all vocational qualifications with the related occupation is shown over a longer period of time compared with HE qualifications. Within the socio-economic panel (SOEP) in 1984, 1995 and in 2004 employees were asked whether they were employed at the level of their qualification. For VET qualifications the match was 81.6%, 82.6% and 82.8%, respectively, that is slightly rising, whereas for HE qualifications the figures were 87.9%, 83.1%, and 80.2%, respectively, clearly declining, bringing the results for both sets of qualifications closer together (*Konsortium Bildungsberichterstattung* 2006: 185). The rather high match is confirmed by international studies (McGuiness 2006).

However, the future matching of qualifications and occupations is in question because of structural change in the economy and the system's inadequate response to this (Baethge *et al.* 2007: 75). The development of the Dual System and its 'product', the *Facharbeiter,* is interlinked with industrial and craft production. Today the manufacturing sector accounts for around 25% of the workforce. Whilst more than 70% are employed in service occupations, only around 60% acquire a qualification in service occupations. Although initial VET offers stayed nearly the same in the service sector between 1994 and 2008, offers in the manufacturing sector during this period shrank by nearly a quarter. This gap needs to be filled by education/training routes other than the dual system (BIBB 2009: 180).

Work-integrated VET with its highly experiential knowledge could not cope with the change towards more tasks requiring systematic knowledge (*Konsortium Bildungsberichterstattung* 2006: 80). With regard to the manufacturing sector, production work in general – but especially in new emerging sectors such as microelectronics, optic technology, biotechnology, renewable energy and nano-technology – is becoming more and more knowledge-intensive. Work in these sectors but also within more traditional fields requires more systematic and analytical competences and less practical knowledge based on experience. Facing these challenges, the question is, whether the German dual VET system and its qualifications are becoming increasingly irrelevant to related sectors, which are growing and prospering. However, empirical results at sector level and occupationally-specific macro data on the structural development of employment and apprenticeship do not support this pessimistic outlook. There is a backlog in the demand for further adjustment to the initial VET system particularly with regard to the growing area of knowledge occupations. But, with the modernization of the dual VET system since the mid-1990s, its stabilization in modern service occupations has been achieved (Uhly and Troltsch 2009).

There are, however, more tensions stemming from changes in work organization. The particular interconnectedness of vocational proficiency, social integration in the company and social status characteristic of the traditional *Beruf* concept is dissolving. The concept is losing its validity. Work organization is shifting towards process orientation. Changes related to this include the outsourcing of parts of the supply chain, cross-functional co-operation and flat hierarchies. In this context, not only is the profile of the *Facharbeiter* (skilled worker) fading, but companies are also moving away from patterns of social integration through individual skill-specific clusters of tasks and company-specific wage agreements and career paths (Baethge and Baethge-Kinsky 1998: 469).

As a consequence, the *Beruf* system has been undergoing subtle but significant changes in a 'segmentalist' direction, whereby the orientation towards common interests is contested by partial interests and more differentiated solutions are brought onto the agenda (Thelen and Busemeyer 2008). These developments need to be seen in a broader context where collectivism is losing ground. Transformational shifts in labour relations and collective bargaining have occurred over the past few years (Streeck 2009). There is a declining membership base of intermediary associations (employers' associations, trades unions). Only 60% of all employees are now working under collective agreements; ten years ago it was 70%. One-third of the workforce is under non-standard or precarious work contracts (not full-time, not permanent or working poor). This raises the pressure for continuous adaptation to ever-changing labour market needs. Changes in the economy appear to support a shift towards short-term employability, which undermines *Beruf* as an institution.

Occupational mobility in Germany is still rather low compared to other countries. For men with an initial VET in an *Ausbildungsberuf* (based on the subjective judgement: 'I am not working in the *Beruf* I was trained for'), it has risen from 18% to 26% between 1977 and 2004; interestingly this was the reverse for women, with a fall from 20% to 16% (Seibert 2007). But employment biographies are becoming more and more atypical. Managing change processes is turning out to be a permanent task in working life. These dynamics require a response, which is usually defined as developing 'employability' capacities (Kraus 2006, 2007). 'Employability' refers to the entire set of abilities and conditions allowing the individual to engage in employment and to stay in employment, whilst also reflecting on and evaluating the supply and demand for skilled work as well as continuously adapting individual potential. This includes taking responsibility for oneself and entrepreneurial thinking and acting. 'Employability' in the German context does not mean abandoning the *Berufskonzept*, but developing it further by maintaining the professional core, strengthened with extra-functional competences, and nurturing the ability to reflect as a condition for self-responsible action (*Selbstkompetenz*).

In this context, a new figure has appeared on the scene, traditionally more common to other systems: the *Arbeitskraftunternehmer* which could be translated as 'entreployee'. 'Entreployees' are expected to manage their own labour power and to bear the risk of market failure. Their heterogeneous and highly individualized working conditions contribute to very individualistic personality traits and, as a consequence, these dependent self-employed workers might be less inclined than other employees to join a trade union (Voß and Pongratz 1998: 152). With the weakening of organizational membership, the German system might be driven in the direction of market-based co-ordination (Harney and vom Hau 2010: 29).

The EQF and its – possible – impact on the German qualifications system

In the European context, VET is seen either as an issue of schools/universities or of work experience; *Berufsbildung* in the German sense is hardly present. The prospects for 'Germanizing' EU VET policy are rather limited, even though the Dual System occasionally receives some attention. On the other hand, the German government aims to gear the national system towards European standards and to qualify its citizens for increasingly international job requirements. In this context the Europeanization of the German system manifests itself as a proactive reform policy (Trampusch 2009). This concerns not only geographical mobility but also the structure, shape and provision of qualifications. European initiatives are used by the Federal government in coalition with big industry to promote greater flexibility in the Dual System and its qualifications. By contrast, the unions as well as the 'craft' (*Handwerk*) sector and the Chambers have adhered closer to the existing structures and claimed a more cautious course in the modernization of VET (Busemeyer 2009).

Germany has thoroughly engaged in the EQF/NQF (National Qualification Framework) approach since 2005. In the national working group on the German Qualifications Framework (DQR), stakeholders from all sectors have agreed on a set of basic principles.[1] The Framework should be EQF-compatible, taking full account of the specific characteristics of the German education and training system. It should include all sectors, putting competence at its heart. Competence depicts the ability and readiness to use knowledge, skills and personal, social and methodological competences in work or study situations and for occupational and personal development. The proposed framework comprises eight levels and four categories of learning outcome: professional competence, composed of knowledge and skills; and personal competence, composed of social and self-competence.

The development of an NQF in Germany might come as a surprise to other countries since the German qualifications system is rather exclusive and is characterized by standardization and stratification to a higher degree than other systems. Because of this and because of its strong input orientation, it appears to fly in the face of the qualifications framework approach. So, why an NQF for Germany?

From an international perspective, the clear outcomes and competence orientation of the EQF is first and foremost seen as an opportunity to classify German qualifications more adequately than in existing international classifications, such as ISCED-97 or in the 2005 EU directive for the recognition of qualifications based on types of certificates and time spent in education and training. According to this directive, the German *Meister* was placed at level 2 out of 5, the same level as the journeyman (in the meantime the *Meister* went up to level 3). This is why the *Handwerk* associations were at the forefront of the campaign for the EQF as a means to achieve a more appropriate 'ranking' of German VET qualifications internationally. This is also considered important for a more successful international marketing of German qualifications and programmes. From an international perspective, a Qualifications Framework is also expected to support the government's initiative for the recognition of 'foreign' qualifications, which is justified in terms of demographic change and the prospect of future skills shortages (Bundesregierung 2009).

From the national perspective, the learning outcomes approach is seen as a catalyst for strengthening the coherence of the entire system, for linking and eventually integrating the different sectors. The NQF provides an opportunity to demonstrate the comparability or even equivalence of VET qualifications with those from HE. It is expected to support the permeability of the entire system, creating learning pathways throughout and allowing access to the system for individuals without formal qualifications – as with the EQF, the German framework has 'for lifelong learning' in its title. Presenting options for progression is expected to make VET more attractive. The private schools, the providers of continuing training as well as the organizations providing training for those at risk of social exclusion (for different reasons) consider the framework as an opportunity for their provision to become part of one integrated system, offering their clients better access/progression opportunities. Employers' organizations see the option for a precise differentiation of vocational qualifications by levels and volume according to their specific needs; they also consider the use of the framework for personnel development.

On the other hand, there are serious concerns, especially in the light of the heavy conflicts emerging from the Bologna process in Germany, that the EQF and its adaptation through an NQF might undermine the value of qualifications by creating confusion, mixing different spaces of recognition and blurring the distinction between different types of knowledge. There are fears too that the learning outcomes approach could split up the *Facharbeiter* qualification into different levels and – in combination with a general credit point system – lead to the fragmentation and individualization of qualifications. And, finally, because in principle the learning outcomes approach is based on the detachment of qualifications from publicly controlled institutions, there are concerns that it might lead to a vast commercialization of education and training. In this respect, the implementation of the EQF with the establishment of an NQF is seen as an attempt to accommodate the German system to a neo-liberal regime (Drexel 2006).

Despite their different interests, unions and employers act like the 'united VET league' in the national group working on the NQF. Whereas the VET sector in general is expecting to retain or even gain territory and power within the system, the sharing of power between the different governance structures and between various competent bodies of the different sectors (Schools, VET according to Vocational Training Act and HE), which is constitutive for a qualifications framework, seems to be a real threat to the *Länder* authorities and the universities. They want to play it down to just a transparency tool.

The national qualifications framework discourse instigated by the EQF provides a platform for the discussion of many issues: appropriate recognition of the 'real' value of what somebody knows, understands and can do; progression across various sectors; and access from outside into the qualifications system. The qualifications framework approach is expected to be a panacea for all of this. But will it alleviate fears and will it deliver on expectations?

Last words

The *Beruf* concept was already considered to be questionable in 1968 in the face of modern society – but indispensable at the same time (Blankertz 1968: 23). The erosion of the concept by changes in the real world is a recurrent theme in German – mostly academic – debates. Analysing future worlds of work, one could imagine the *Beruf* might maintain a function in terms of entry to employment in certain segments without being an absolute condition, because there are other company-related means of identifying the value of labour. In other segments, with more open forms of labour where such ties do not exist, the *Beruf* with its comprehensive and at the same time open structure and its relation to professionality might gain new relevance. But, even if the *Beruf* concept is losing its relevance for companies, it remains important for young people in terms of finding their place in society and building trust in the future (Harney 1998: 3).

The 'territory' ruled by the Vocational Training Act with the *Beruf* at its core will be smaller in future. The system will not disappear, but there will be structural changes making the system more flexible and adaptable to changing demands. At the same time, the core concept, the *Berufsprinzip*, will not be replaced by other principles but rather be further developed, with a focus on self-reflexivity. In the foreseeable future, it will still be most influential for structuring German VET.

Note

1   *www.deutscherqualifikationsrahmen.de.*

5

THE MEANING OF COMPETENCE

Anneke Westerhuis

Introduction

Differences between vocational education and training (VET) systems cannot be explained only in terms of their differing position within national education systems, but also in terms of differences in educational concepts. Moreover, these concepts are affected in turn by VET's position within the system, as illustrated in the understanding of competence in Dutch VET. Although the *competence* concept was introduced in the most recent innovation round in Dutch VET, it will be argued in this chapter that its meaning is coloured by the long-standing and recurrent debate on the position of VET within the education system.

For Mulder (2007: 7) the concept of competence is 'quite confusing, and it is no surprise that therefore so many differences of opinion exist about the meaning of it . . . . But the more concrete meaning of the concept is strongly depending on the context of use'. One major context of use is VET, but it is not the only one. The competence concept is one of the basic concepts of the European Qualification Framework (EQF) and a key-stone of the European Union (EU) lifelong learning agenda, which emphasizes that competences can be developed through formal, as well as informal and non-formal learning, irrespective of the routes of acquisition (Le Deist and Winterton 2005).

In the Netherlands, the dominant context of use of the competence concept is VET. But is this also true for England, France and Germany? This chapter will explore to what extent the Dutch context of use is similar to or different from that in the other countries and how these differences affect understanding of the concept.

A brief outline of the Dutch VET system

As a result of extensive merger rounds in the period between 1980 and 1996, Dutch vocational education (from now on: VET) came under one Law (*Wet Educatie en*

Beroepsonderwijs 1996). VET is provided by some 70 educational institutes, offering courses for all sectors at four levels and two equivalent tracks (a school-based and a work-based, or dual, track). However, only 10% of VET students are found in Education Centres for the Agricultural sector and a small number of specific sector-based schools for the printing, fishing and shipping industries, as well as housepainting, which stayed out of the 1980–96 merger process with explicit backing from the social partners of the respective sectors. It is clear from Table 5.1 that the vast majority of VET students attend courses in the 40 multi-sector Regional Education Centres.

VET has now been embedded in the Dutch education system for 90 years. The first law on Vocational Education (1919) was in fact a trade-off between the National Government and local School Boards. Schools for vocational education were originally founded by local employers and philanthropists, but from then on vocational education was subject to national policy and laws, resulting in government subsidy of almost 100%.

The ambition of the Dutch system is to guide the masses of young people through publicly-financed education facilities to the labour market in the most effective and efficient way. The VET programme structure, with its four levels and two tracks, is valid for all types of providers (see Table 5.1). In other words, since 1996 a comprehensive VET system regulates entrance to almost all job positions in the Dutch labour market segment between unskilled labour and professional positions. In terms of Marsden's (1999) classification of employment systems,[1] Dutch VET corresponds to an occupational labour market (OLM), where one is admitted to skilled jobs when in possession of the relevant formal qualification.

The Dutch education system is highly selective; as early as in the final year of primary education (which takes eight years), 12-year-olds are assessed for their abilities in a semi-obligatory, national ability test and, depending on the results, advised either to enter general education tracks preparing for higher education (HE) or to enter junior general and prevocational education preparing for VET. Early detection of abilities is supposed to prevent young people from entering secondary education at a level below or above their abilities. This rather formal response to differences in abilities is also the organizational principle in VET; someone's qualification level in VET largely depends on performance in junior general and

TABLE 5.1 Number of students by type of vocational education provider

Type of school	*Number of students 1-10-2007*
Agricultural Education Centres	26,688
Regional Education Centres	466,871
Sector-based VET schools	22,730
Other	4,902
Total	**521,191**

Source: MBO Raad 2009.

TABLE 5.2 Participation in VET and higher professional education (x1000)

	1995	2005	2007	Rise 2005:2007
VET	436	483	513	+6%
HPE	271	357	374	+5%

Source: CBS 2009.

prevocational education; proceeding to a higher qualification level within VET varies from 14% at level 3 to 30% at level 1 (CBS 2009, data from 2006).

It was not until recently that VET was accepted as a route to HE (in particular: higher professional education, ranked at BA level) in its own right. With the growth in awareness that the Netherlands (and the rest of the EU) need to raise the numbers of students with a HE degree, possibilities to fast track from VET to HE have been created. These routes are only open to VET students with a diploma at level 4.

Table 5.2 shows the development of participation in VET and higher professional education. The still growing participation of students in VET has two sources. The first is the increasing number of youngsters continuing their education after junior general and pre-vocational education (as intended). A new source is working people using VET for upgrading their qualifications; in 2007–8 19% of the VET population was over 23 years old (CBS 2009). Qualifications designed for young people to enter an occupation-based labour market are also used for adult education, signifying that the Netherlands has no parallel system for lifelong learning; a great many providers are active in the Dutch lifelong learning market, which still lacks market regulations in terms of transparency, coherence and procedures for client protection/consumer complaints (Onderwijsraad 2009).

Aims and purposes of Dutch VET

The incorporation of VET into a comprehensive education system in 1919 faced all stakeholders, the government included, with the question of how it should relate to other elements of the system. Should VET address its students as workers only or also as members of a civic society? Should it be exclusively dedicated to preparation for occupations and trades or also for proceeding to HE levels? Many debates on VET have since addressed these questions. The history of the 1919 law itself is a good illustration.

With the 1919 law, the country obtained a system with a great variety of educational forms that were – however separately – regulated and subsidized by the state. This educational system was dual in character as, with this new law, the concept that the lower classes should have their own general education provision was abandoned due to its distinct lack of success. The 1919 law regulated the schools for trade and industry, founded from private initiative. However, the law clearly stated that vocational education should not be restricted to practical training, as occupational training should also contribute to personal development. The State was only willing to fund VET when it served a broader educational aim. This principle had already been asserted by the liberal Minister of Home Affairs, then responsible for education, in 1862. Workers, tradesmen and crofters were to be addressed as citizens: 'also the lowest classes belong to the citizenry and are to conduct themselves in working life in a worthy way'[2] (Goudswaard 1981: 237).

Another significant illustration of the role of VET is the debate concerning the rebuilding of the country after the Second World War. As the state had a pronounced role in economic policymaking, it saw in VET an important instrument for post-war economic reconstruction. A key question was how to attract sufficient numbers (in terms of the capacity needed for industrial expansion) of young people to attend VET schools. Very influential was the advice given by the Goote Committee not to reduce VET to practical training, suggesting that, by providing general education and focusing on preparation for the skilled trades, rather than on producing mere tradesmen, this form of education would not alienate itself from general education but would share the same culture (Commissie van Onderzoek 1948). One of the arguments was that pupils wishing to go back on their school choice would be able to transfer to a more suitable form of education with little delay; there would be no dead ends in the system.

Industry was not opposed to a more general character for VET. In 1958, the central organizations of employers and employees, meeting in the Social-Economic Council, produced a report emphasizing the need to concentrate on general technical thinking in vocational curricula (SER 1958). This report concluded that it would not be sufficient merely to deliver trained specialists in future. The new generations of skilled workers and technicians must be able, both as skilled employees and as human beings, to rise above the narrow confines of their trades. Such a mentality was also necessary for occupational mobility and social change. In the future there would be an increasing demand made not only upon the specialist knowledge of skilled workers but also upon their personal capacities. VET would need more than ever before to be concerned with general education (Westerhuis 2007).

It was not until 1981 that relations between education and industry were re-evaluated. The common sense belief was that, subsequent to the international industrial crises in the late 1970s and early 1980s and the extension of the Welfare State, the international – export-oriented – position of Dutch industry had deteriorated. To regain industrial competitiveness, new answers were needed. A high-profile Commission, chaired by the former Shell Chief Executive Officer Wagner, launched a White Paper with a great many suggestions for industrial revitalization. The report, called 'Towards a new industrial *élan*', also pleaded for a greater educational contribution to economic growth, in particular by granting the social partners the responsibility for the validation of national qualifications in VET (Heijke 2008).

An essential characteristic of Dutch VET debates, worth pinpointing here as it is relevant for understanding post-1981 developments, is that tensions between stakeholder positions are accepted as consequent on the fact that three major stakeholders (Ministry, social partners, schools) share responsibility for VET. The bottom line, shared by all, is that compromises are (for the time being) inevitable. This is why debates on Dutch VET have a pragmatic, rather than a philosophical or conceptual, nature, as apparent from, for instance Keep and Brown's conclusion that the key point in Dutch VET reforms is the 'clear and explicit attempt to plan the reforms systematically and to design a new system as a whole' (2004: 258). The observation, illustrating not only Dutch policymaking preference for addressing issues at system level but also its pragmatism, is shared by other researchers from abroad. For instance, the German researcher Reuling concludes that in the Netherlands education policy debates concentrate on the pros and cons of pragmatic solutions rather than on principles (Onderwijsraad 2000).

The introduction of the competence concept into Dutch VET

The government accepted the Wagner Commission's advice and in 1986 introduced a procedure for the development of outcomes-based qualifications for all VET courses (Ministerie van Onderwijs 1986). The production of national programmes by sector-based social partner committees was common practice in the Dual System, but not in school-based VET which was still separated in the pre-1996 era. Looking for a qualification concept valid for all VET programmes, the outcomes-based English National Vocational Qualifications (NVQs) were highly appealing to Dutch policymakers, in particular their potential for standardization which meant that from now on all VET qualifications could be expressed in a common language. The NVQ was also seen as a model for performance criteria founded in occupational practice; the point that NVQs were introduced to overcome deficiencies in skill formation in the UK, through a strategy of widening opportunities for the recognition of skills developed in non-formal and informal learning rather than curriculum reform, was surprisingly missed.

NVQs suggested a linear procedure for developing task-based VET programmes, starting with occupational analyses via standard setting and proceeding to curriculum development, which fitted perfectly with the working procedures of the new sector-based qualification bodies (Nijhof 2008).

The sector-based bodies set up to execute this procedure produced first-, second- and third-generation qualification frameworks, all heavily criticized by the VET schools, in particular those not accustomed to deduce programmes from national qualification standards produced by third bodies rather than by themselves. However, it was not only the fact that new frameworks were launched at an almost manic tempo, confronting the schools with the necessity to adopt programmes at very frequent intervals, but also the quality of the information in the documents which was criticized for not being very helpful for curriculum development (Hövels *et al.* 2006). In government circles and in standing National Advisory Bodies the qualifications also met growing criticism. Significantly, the NVQ-inspired outcomes-based attainment goals were found to be too partial in their emphasis on the technical–instrumental aspects of working life and too detailed and hence vulnerable to permanent revision as even the smallest change in occupational practice had to pass the validation procedure.[3] These criticisms revealed a real dilemma as qualifications and goals should, in the spirit of the Wagner recommendations, be valid and recognizable for people in industry, their moral owners. The dilemma is aptly verbalized in a call for advice formally put to the National Social Economic Council by the junior minister for Social Affairs in 1997 (one year after the introduction of the new law on VET!):

> How will it be possible to formulate qualifications and attainment goals in Secondary Vocational Education in such a way that they are relevant both for lifelong learning ability and for flexibility on internal and external labour markets and, at the same time, maintain their validity for firms and the practical character of VET?
>
> (SER 1997)

The Council's (in fact: the social partners') advice contains two key points. The first is a plea for a broad qualification concept in VET, encompassing vocational qualifications and general qualifications and relevant for continuing education at a higher level as well as to civil and cultural qualifications. This advice should not be read as a new aim for VET but as the social partners' confirmation of the indisputable relevance of a VET system embedded in a comprehensive education system. Secondly, vocational qualifications should not only contain occupation- or job-specific skills, but also so-called 'key skills'. The Council's definition of key skills – or 'key qualifications' as they are also called in an almost careless choice of words – is almost identical to what were only a few years later to be called 'competences':

> Key qualifications encompass knowledge, skills and attitudes belonging to the core of an occupation or a family of occupations. They will facilitate transfer to other and new positions in an occupation and innovation in an occupation, contribute to the capacity-building of people in employment and help to bridge career changes.
>
> (ibid.)

A year later the influential Education Council for the Netherlands advised a broadening of the definition of qualifications, as had been previously advocated (Onderwijsraad 1998). However, it was reluctant to use the concept of 'key qualifications' because of its ambiguity and preferred 'competence'. According to the Council, the concepts of qualifications and competence were exchangeable and had a similar meaning; the only argument for preferring *competences* to *qualifications* being their lack of ambiguity (ibid.: 9). The idea to define occupations not in terms of occupational skills but of broad sets of personal '*Handlungsfähigkeiten*'

– such as methodical, social and participative competences – was also advocated by influential researchers (e.g. Hövels *et al*. 1995).

The advice culminated in a White Paper with the significant title 'A turn to key competences', issued by the social partner-led ACOA Committee responsible for the assessment of all new qualifications (ACOA 1999). This paper met hardly any opposition and the Minister of Education concluded that: 'the implementation of the *competence* concept is the obvious way to solve the problems now experienced in VET' (in a letter to the Second Chamber of Parliament of April 2002). A new and competence-based qualification framework was needed but, in contrast to the past, included in the development process were not only the bodies producing qualifications but also the VET schools responsible for the development of competence-based curricula. Typically for the Netherlands, the Ministry allowed VET stakeholders to organize this implementation process themselves.

Looking back, what has been achieved in the 20 years following the introduction of social-partner led bodies for the validation of VET qualifications and a national qualification framework for VET? For me, it is the inclusion of social partners in the debate on the aims and position of VET on a regular basis. It was never a point of discussion that Dutch VET should prepare for rather narrowly defined occupations. And, although this period started with the introduction of an NVQ type of vocational qualification, they were thought to be expressed in a language too close to the shop floor. It took little time for the limits of this approach to be felt and all parties, social partners included, welcomed the competence concept as a better language in which to express the aims of VET, encompassing methodical, social and participative aspects of working life. Dutch VET's traditional outcomes were in fact converted into competence jargon through the identification of four types: vocational/ occupational, career, civic and learning competences.

The competence concept in Dutch VET

The first competence-based qualification framework was produced in 2004. In contrast to the previous introduction of new qualification frameworks, schools were invited to experiment with the translation of the new qualifications into new competence-based programmes. Schools with no intention of using the new qualifications for the innovation of programmes also volunteered to join the experiment (van den Berg and Doets 2005). For many schools the development of competence-based programmes was a logical step in their tradition of school-based innovation. It is quite possible that the competence concept was new for schools, but not what it stood for. Independent of the introduction of competence-based qualifications, schools had been experimenting with various forms of competence-oriented programmes for a long time (Hövels *et al*. 2006).

The bottom line of this sector-led implementation strategy was that, in the absence of a national curriculum, teachers took on themselves responsibility for developing competence-based programmes through a 'learning by doing' approach. However, due to a distinct lack of progress, complaints from VET students and a change in public opinion (preferring results instead of experiments with young people!), this implementation strategy came under fire and the Ministry of Education was pressed to take a more active role. In 2007 the strategy evolved into a policy-dominated process, focusing on the transformation of all VET programmes by 2010. Table 5.3, taken from Hövels *et al.* (2009), illustrates the progress of this process of implementation.

The change in strategy is particularly relevant from a conceptual point of view. Arguments for the introduction of the competence concept were originally founded in changes in industrial relations, production concepts and learning theories. Almost all policy advice was based on studies forecasting – if not dreaming of – new types of work, changing industrial relations and labour market developments.[4] The competence concept was welcomed as the universal and uncontroversial answer to these changes. The main problem in the initial implementation strategy was a lack of interest in the success of the new competence-based programmes in addressing these ambitions. Implementing the competence concept was an end in itself. As a frame of reference for the new strategy, nine output criteria were agreed by all stakeholders, whose choice illustrates the new focus in of the implementation strategy in addressing stakeholder value and system efficiency:

- better useful/dedicated 'professionals'
- increased motivation (to attend school) of VET students
- more students leaving VET with a diploma
- decrease of early school leaving in VET
- greater numbers of students proceed to higher forms of VET and HE
- increased professionalism of teachers and company trainee supervisors
- growing company and social partners appreciation of and involvement in VET
- more appreciation from teachers
- more appreciation from students.

Competences were welcomed, as a reaction to the narrow and activity-based NVQs and as a better concept to fulfil VET's historic mission of preparing VET students

TABLE 5.3 The development of competence-based programmes in VET

Total numbers of students by school year	*2004– 2005*	*2005– 2006*	*2006– 2007*	*2007– 2008*	*2008– 2009*
Number of experimental programmes	152	825	2,841	3,923	5,928
Number of students in experiments	9,634	43,717	122,431	203,992	365,195
Total of VET students (number or prognosis)	474,165	485,000	490,821	503,388	503,388
Students in experiments as a % of all VET students	2	9	25	41	73

Source: Hövels *et al.* 2009: 78.

for life rather than for specific job demands, anticipating the evolution of employment and giving individuals the knowledge to enable them to benefit from lifelong learning and mobility. Based upon rather strict formats and assessed by a national co-ordination unit, sector-based bodies have produced an unambiguous set of competence-based qualifications (Coördinatiepunt 2009). However, schools cannot refer to conceptual models or key characteristics of competence-based programmes. The competence concept has been introduced into VET programmes through local trial and error processes, hence the wide variety of interpretations of the concept. The introduction of the nine output criteria has stimulated the development of a variety of practices, as the materialization of competences in school curricula is explicitly shared with local stakeholders to respond to their needs and appreciations. There are now as many models for competence-based education as there are education programmes, much to the annoyance of the national employers' organizations. These organizations stress the need for programme uniformity at sector level, implicitly confirming the – in terms of Marsden's (1999) classification – OLM orientation of Dutch VET and the role of local firms in contributing to a public VET system (VNO-NCW and MKB Nederland 2008).

Dutch competence concept in a European context

In the Netherlands competence is understood as an integrative concept, aiming to cover a wide set of human abilities required to cope with complex tasks. Integrative stands for the facts that (1) competences are multi-dimensional and (2) competent performance is only possible if all dimensions are addressed according to a set of standards. As defined by Mulder (2001), for instance:

> Competence is the capability of a person (or an organisation) to reach specific achievements. Personal competences comprise integrated performance-oriented capabilities, consisting of clusters of knowledge structures, but also cognitive, interactive, affective and, if necessary, psycho-motor capabilities, as well as attitudes and values. All are required for carrying out tasks, problem solving and, more generally, effectively functioning in a certain profession, organisation, position or role.
>
> (Biemans *et al.* 2004: 530)

With this definition, a new perspective – or frame – was created for identifying the essential aspects of work to be translated into VET vocabulary. Instead of defining this essence as a narrowly defined set of skills, as is the case with English NVQs, this concept of competence refers to a broad set of human capacities appealed to in working life (Onstenk 1997; Boreham 2002).

One could even argue that definitions of the essence of work are rooted in VET concepts in the sense that these define what aspects of work are taken as input for curriculum development. This would mean that competence concepts are essentially educational concepts. However, this is not the whole truth. Mansfield and Mitchell's Job Competence Model in particular widens the perspective of the outcomes of work, to include (possibly conflicting) expectations of supervisors, clients and colleagues concerning the outcomes of activities as well as the definition of activities to include in what is termed contingency and task management (Mansfield and Mitchell 1996). In this model, work is also about dealing with changing conditions and disruptions and responding to planning problems and priority setting, thereby in its performance concept sharing with competency-based Human Resource Management (HRM) the inclusion of personal and social behaviour under various conditions (e.g. Dubois and Rothwell 2004).

In the definition in the template of competence-based VET qualifications,[5] competences are 'capacities' (that can be developed) of human beings, enabling them to act in an adequate and dedicated way with a focus on processes and results or, in other words, to select and apply appropriate procedures to attain the desired outcomes. Competences are multidimensional and refer to underlying skills, knowledge and attitudes, based on Bloom's Taxonomy of cognitive, psychomotor and affective domains (Bloom 1956).

The significance of competences is context-dependant or, as Rychen and Salganic put it: 'Competences are the ability to successfully meet complex demands in a particular context through the mobilization of psychosocial prerequisites (including both cognitive and non-cognitive aspects)' (2003: 43).

This understanding of competences differs significantly from the competence concept introduced in the 1970s in the United States of America (USA) when Competency-Based Education (CBE) was advocated as a utilitarian, behaviouristic curriculum design approach, focusing on someone's ability to perform, rather than demonstrating the possession of knowledge (Finch and Crunkilton 1999). The use of performance objectives to provide structure for lesson plans, criterion-referenced measures of task completion and reliance on incumbent worker task lists for the primary source of curriculum in CBE, derive directly from behavioural learning theory (Doolittle and Camp 1999). In the CBE approach, competences are functional, based on job requirements and trained according to the principles of behaviouristic learning theories. The focus is on performance, at the expense of complex intellectual processes, and reflection in and on action (Sultana 2008, 2009). While the CBE approach defines competence only as a performance category, the integrative approach advocated in the Netherlands assumes that a performance is only successful when conditions are met; prerequisites have to be fulfilled in terms of skill development and the acquisition of knowledge. Nijhof (2008) assumes a causal relation between performances and prerequisites: without – in particular knowledge-based – prerequisites, a performance cannot be adequate; both pre-requisites and performances should be the subject of learning. The CBE approach does not differ from the integrative approach by defining learning goals in terms of 'real life' situations taken from working life, but rather by excluding intermediate goals, relevant for the organization of learning or, in terms of Bloom's taxonomy, the identification of domains of educational activities.

It is precisely this characteristic, that prerequisites have to be derived from working life situations, that makes the integrative competence concept vulnerable. How much knowledge and what exact knowledge does one need for an adequate, if not state of the art, performance? And does it matter how competence development is organized? A recurrent critique of Dutch stakeholders, also at firm level, of the new competence-based VET programmes is, for instance, that the knowledge component suffers from too little attention (van der Meijden *et al.* 2009). And while this discussion is only about the amount of knowledge inserted in a curriculum, what about the locus of competence development and the organization of competence development? Are loci, or a variation of learning processes, also essential prerequisites?[6] The Achilles' heel of the integrative concept is its lack of clear implications for the development of educational standards and the design of learning processes. For this, the concept, with its chameleon-like nature – taking the meaning invested by its users when developing qualifications, standards and curricula – has been given the epitaph 'fuzzy concept' (Boon and van der Klink 2002).

As in the Netherlands, the introduction of the competence concept in Germany is associated with educational reform, when in the early 1970s an integrated structure of the entire education and training system was envisaged. It took about 15 years to develop a specific concept of competence for the dual VET system. Central to the German understanding of competence in VET is the idea of *Berufliche Handlungskompetenz,* competence in the workplace, whereby *Beruf* has a significant meaning. While in the Netherlands the breadth of national VET programmes is decided by social partners on rather pragmatic grounds, German dual VET programmes are defined by *Berufe,* more or less stable identities strongly linked with the collective bargaining system and with social welfare regulations. The underlying concept is the notion of 'complete action' (*vollständige Handlung*) which includes the planning, execution and evaluation of tasks. As in the Netherlands, the triptych *Fertigkeiten* (practical skills), *Kenntnisse* (non-systematic knowledge) and *Fähigkeiten* (extra-functional – methodological, social and personal – abilities) are foundation stones of the German competence concept.

In 1996 the German education system adopted an 'action competence' approach, moving from subject (inputs) to competence (outcomes) and curricula specifying learning fields rather than occupation-related knowledge and skills content (Sultana 2009). A standard typology of competences now appears at the beginning of every new vocational training curriculum, elaborating *Handlungskompetenz* in terms of subject competence (*Fachkompetenz*), personal competence (*Personalkompetenz*), social competence (*Sozialkompetenz*), procedural competence (*Methodenkompetenz*) and learning competences (*Lernkompetenz*). There is a strong common conviction that *Fertigkeiten, Kenntnisse, Fähigkeiten* can only be learned in an integrated way. So, also in Germany competence is defined as an integrative concept that includes prerequisites in terms of training provision. The German Vocational Training Act states for instance, that: initial training shall, through a systematic training programme, impart the vocational skills, knowledge and competences (vocational action competence) necessary to engage in a form of skilled occupational activity in a changing working world (Hanf 2009: 21).

In its dedication to competence development and its triple focus on addressing students as human beings, citizens and producers, the French context resembles the Dutch and the German in its application of competences within the country's school-based VET system. As in the Netherlands and Germany, competence is approached as an integrative, multidimensional concept involving the combination of *savoir* (knowledge), *savoir-faire* (know-how) and *savoir-être* (social and personal qualities and attributes) in a given work situation. It is this combination of components that defines levels of professionalism; competences are the practical expression of an individual's ability to apply *savoir*, *savoir-faire* and *savoir-être* in a practical, work-related situation (Méhaut 2009). However, unlike the Netherlands and Germany, in France the competence concept is not the exclusive domain of VET. VET qualifications are just one segment in the French qualification register, devised by the National Certification Commission, that includes diplomas issued by the Ministry of Education, *titres* issued by the Ministry of Labour's own VET organization, and *certificats* issued by private bodies (for instance the CQP: *Certificat de Qualification Professionnelle*) (see Chapter 3). The gradual emergence of the term 'certification' is significant and symbolizes its dissociation from knowledge acquisition, a principle that was formalized with the introduction of the accreditation of prior (vocational) learning.

Growing rapprochement between the various national learning arrangements in France is also evident from the use of the competence concept in VET provision, whether for young people, adults (respectively called initial VET (IVET[7])), continuous (CVET) or HRM. In the Netherlands and Germany, there is a clear distinction between these different processes of competence development, and they do not share a common definition of competence. This is not to say that it is not used in HRM, but that in these countries the definitions applied in HRM and in VET are deliberately not harmonized. What will be the effect of this growing rapprochement in the understanding of the competence concept in France? What influence will the use of the competence concept in CVET or HRM contexts, with their emphasis on competence assessment and accreditation of informally acquired competencies (*bilan de compétence*), have on the French understanding of competences?

The HRM approach, competence-based management, emphasizes concrete competences at workplace level associated with individual jobs. These are explained in France in terms equivalent to their use in IVET, distinguishing between technical (*savoir*), operational (*savoir-faire*) and behavioural competences (*savoir-être*), even though – contrary to what is intended – the *bilan de compétences* tends to focus on IVET diplomas rather than on informally acquired competencies (Mulder 2007). In this respect, the French competence-based management model is influenced by notions coined in the IVET context though there is also a shift away from the classic conception of learning (from a French perspective) as synonymous with school-based learning, with the workplace and work experience now valued as equivalent venues for competence development – both for adults (CVET) and young people (IVET). Together with this, there is also a shift away from collective rules towards personalized arrangements (for example, individual rights and duties based on individual experiences and individual career paths) and from the internal labour market (ILM) model, perhaps heralding a competence concept neutral to specific prerequisites and moving away from organized learning (Méhaut 2009).

As illustrated in Chapter 6, the integrative conception of competence has been absent from policy debate in England where the dominant definition refers to the NVQ model, as a competence-based qualifications system. From the NVQ perspective, individual competencies are identified on the basis of a detailed analysis of functional tasks and activities in the workplace, with the focus on what is required by the job, defined as a distinct range of operational tasks. Hence the conception of competence is concerned with the performance of prescribed tasks to a defined standard. This task-based system of specifying knowledge and skills for a specified list of tasks corresponds with the CBE approach, but contrasts with the integrative conception of competence as found in France, Germany and the Netherlands. A further difference is in the lack of attention given to prerequisites in the definition of competences as English competences constitute the skills deemed necessary for a particular job. Qualifications are also separated from learning processes in being assessment-led and thus not commonly linked to curricula but relying more often on the accreditation of skills commonly learnt on the job, underpinned by a belief that knowledge needed for the execution of tasks is acquired through experience in the workplace.

The differences between the Dutch, English, French and German conceptions of competence, each emanating from differences in the relations between the competence conception and VET, can be summarized as:

*   English competences refer to specific job requirements rather than – as in France, Germany and the Netherlands – to nationally agreed conceptions of occupations, whether defined for VET/IVET only (Netherlands, France) or for a wide range of public applications (Germany).
*   The integrative competence approach, associated with the development of curricula (France, Germany and the Netherlands), denotes the *potential* of the individual worker to draw on multiple resources, including knowledge, know-how and social and personal qualities to deal with complex and unpredictable tasks and situations, increasingly supported didactically through self-directed learning within authentic work situations. In contrast, when the process of competence development is dominated by an emphasis on competence assessment, as in England, the use of the competence concept is confined to an assessment context and to the development of processes for the demonstration of skills and abilities (Mulder 2007; see also Chapter 6 of this book).
*   In Germany and the Netherlands the competence concept is used exclusively in the VET context. Competences are content for the curriculum, developed through various kinds of learning and formative assessments of the prerequisites

deemed necessary for their performance. In France the concept of competence is shared by IVET and HRM and links between competences and VET are less exclusive. However, institutionalized processes for curriculum development for IVET compensate for this lack of exclusiveness and attend to VET specific interpretations of competence. In contrast, in England, competences are not associated with curriculum development at all but – predominantly – with the validation of *in situ* performance of a range of tasks.

Conclusions

Delamare Le Deist and Winterton (2005) conclude that a one-dimensional framework is giving way to a multi-dimensional framework whereby cognitive and behavioural competences are being added to the English occupational functional competence model.[8] This chapter has shown that the EQF, as an example of an integrative framework, still has a long way to go to impact on English definitions of competence as used in daily practice. Of perhaps even greater significance is the suggestion that overarching competence definitions tend to be neutral with respect to prerequisites for learning environments, organized learning and systematic attention to methodical, social and participative aspects of working life.

From the case studies of France, Germany and the Netherlands, it can be deduced that the outcomes-based approach to education, perceived as Anglo-Saxon, has had a major impact on recent innovations in VET. The competence approach is also an expression of this trend, but – particularly in Germany and the Netherlands – the competence concept has been absorbed into VET to acquire a distinct meaning, while in France it is used to cover a wide set of contexts for competence development, dropping specific prerequisites in terms of organized learning and the conditional mastering of knowledge and skills.

In the EQF implementation process, the Netherlands is a 'late adopter'; only recently was the decision taken to develop a National Qualification Framework (NQF). The Dutch NQF will be a minimalist, bridging framework,[9] not limited to eight levels beforehand as this number will be the outcome of the implementation process. This is because system discussions are extremely sensitive in the Netherlands. Many initiatives come to an untimely end with the mantra 'no system changes'. The ultimate ranking of formal qualifications to the EQF levels will be anything but an exciting process. It is understood by all stakeholders that the major challenge in developing a Dutch NQF and linking this to the EFQ is the allocation of the current levels in HE (4), VET (4), Senior General Education and Junior Vocational and General Education (6) to the eight EQF levels.

The implication is that it will be non-regulatory, only formally relating to education subsystems and lacking transparent indicators for progression routes. The single new element is the (conditional) inclusion of non-formal qualifications besides the formal qualifications of General Education, Vocational and Higher Education. These basic assumptions of the Dutch NQF envisaged illustrate the distinct position of youth education as a system for learning. This has far reaching consequences for Dutch assessment of prior (informal) learning facilities, as informal learning is assessed against VET qualifications, designed for the allocation of young people to an OLM. Consequently, assessment procedures operate as intake procedures for VET courses, by and large the exclusive domain of public education providers. The almost exclusive route for the assessment of prior (informal) learning through VET providers explains the low uptake of accredited prior learning (APL) in the Netherlands, despite the availability of well-established procedures and quality assurance systems.

The strong association of the competence concept with VET is one side of the coin; the other is the absence of stimuli for the development of an equivalent system for lifelong learning, based on a competence definition that encompasses the different positions of young people with no work experience and adults. Not surprisingly, Germany also lacks a well-organized CVET system (*Weiterbildung*), apart from the nationally regulated facilities for Master training (*Meisterausbildung*) for a number of *Berufe*. For countries with competence concepts which are embedded in the VET system, with the *raison d'être* of preparing young people for an OLM, the barrier to stretching the concept to include wider aims of occupational learning and wider sets of target groups is definitely higher than for countries familiar with the ILM concept (England and France). The fact that internal labour markets have of late considerably weakened does not seem to affect the position of VET systems directly (Marsden 2007).

The EQF defines competence as:

> the proven ability to use knowledge, skills and personal, social and/or methodological abilities, in work or study situations and in professional and personal development. In the context of the European Qualifications Framework, competence is described in terms of responsibility and autonomy.
>
> (EC 2008b: 11)

No allowance is made for learning processes and learning environments in this definition. As a consequence of the European Lifelong Learning policy, these prerequisites are carefully omitted. What will be the impact of an overarching European framework, neutral to the variety of contexts of use, for understanding the competence concept in countries where competence has a specific meaning in the context of VET? Will organized learning be devalued into an interesting, but unnecessary, competence element when competences are no longer designed as a frame of reference for curriculum development in VET? And does it matter?

For Sultana (2009: 22) organized learning is conditional for competence development:

> Holistic/integrative approaches to competence-based models, therefore, seem to have successfully absorbed insights from the behaviouristic and

functionalist approaches, and additionally integrated some of the most promising practices in education and training, such as project-based and team learning, autonomous and problem-based learning, formative assessment strategies emphasising what learners can rather than cannot do, and so on.

Organized learning, or education, is instrumental to mastering the complex nature of knowledge in the integration of knowing, doing and being, self-directedness and critical reflection. Outcomes are affected both by inputs and environments, according to Astin's Input–Environment–Outcome (I–E–O) Model (1993). Organized learning and daily life are distinct environments, having different effects on learning outcomes as the quality of the outcomes is conditioned by environmental factors, including the programme, personnel, curricula, instructor, facilities, institutional climate, courses, teaching style, friends, room-mates, extra-curricular activities and organizational affiliation.[10]

The irony of launching the EQF as a multi-dimensional integrative framework is that, while its definitions tend to refer to competence development in terms of organized learning, this intention is contradicted by the European Lifelong Learning policy emphasizing the development of competences through a variety of routes and in a variety of environments. The question is whether the creation of zones of mutual trust (ZMTs) will be sufficient to compensate for apparent differences in types of competences and *in situ* understanding of the concept. This is a question to be addressed in Chapter 9.

Notes

1 Marsden identifies internal labour markets (ILMs) and occupational labour markets (OLMs). They differ in their relations to the education system. In countries with an ILM, newcomers to the labour market start their career in low qualified jobs, learning on the job; additional courses will help them to acquire the competences needed for a career; the relation to the education system is rather loose. The United Kingdom, France and Ireland are seen as examples of ILM countries. In OLM countries (Germany, the Netherlands, Denmark), it is the role of the education system to qualify young people for the labour market (1999).

2 See also the Minister's address to the Society for Language and Literature in Ghent in 1830: 'Without good education the mass of the labourers is unable to act independently and will be reduced to unimportant numbers in the hands of the employers, living in servile dependency. Give the labourer appropriate secondary education, give them the opportunity to improve their position' (Goudswaard 1981: 237).

3 See for instance the letter from the Education Minister to the Second Chamber of Parliament dated April 2002 (reference BVE/KenO/2002/10797). Also: B. Hövels *et al.* 2006.

4 Apart from some reports in Dutch referring to international developments (Simone J. van Zolingen, *Gevraagd: sleutelkwalificaties, een studie naar sleutelkwalificaties voor het middelbaar beroepsonderwijs*, Nijmegen: KUN, 1995; SER CED-rapport, *Arbeidsmarkt, informatietechnologie en internationalisering*, SER: Den Haag, 1996), a surprisingly small number of publications referring to international developments either in VET or in the labour market can be found in these reports. The only reference publication in English is Moss Kanter's *When giants learn to dance: mastering the challenge of strategy, management and careers in the 1990s*, suggesting the fashionable character of these proposals.

5 Source: www.colo.nl/begrip.php. The elements of this definition are taken from an inductive study into the definition of competences, identifying six characteristics frequently encountered in competence definitions:

- competence is an indivisible cluster of knowledge, insights, skills and attitudes (alternatively – within an HRM or CVT framework – supplemented with the term 'qualities')
- competence is contextual
- competence is liked with tasks or activities
- competence changes over time
- the acquisition of competence assumes learning and development
- competences have a particular interrelationships (Merrienboer *et al.* 2002).

6 See for instance Birenbaum's (2003) thesis that different types of knowledge demand different types of learning environment. Or Schön's reflective practitioner concept, which argues that it is not competences and behavioural training that determine how actors behave in a particular context, but rather their prior beliefs and personal theories (cited by Sultana (2008)), a concept that has unmistakably found its way into the curricula of Dutch VET.

7 In an analysis of the French situation, the distinction between IVET and CVET is relevant, though use of the term IVET is synonymous to VET in all other sections of this chapter.

8 See also Sultana (2009): 'While there is no single, authoritative definition of the word competence, there seems to be an increasing consensus that the term should not be used in a narrowly technicist manner to refer to just skills, precisely because of the implications this has for education and training' (20).

9 A bridging framework as opposed to an integrative framework. Traditional descriptors for the various subsystems to be covered in the Dutch NQF will not be replaced by EQF descriptors. Although it will be necessary to develop a common language to describe all qualifications, this language will be used for reference purposes only.

10 See also the massive body of research on the effect of instruction time and teachers' roles on learning outcomes (for instance: David Reynolds, Peter Cuttance (eds), *School Effectiveness: research, policy and practice*, London: Cassell, 1992; Creemers, Bert P.M.; Reezigt, Gerry J., School-Level Conditions Affecting the Effectiveness of Instruction. In: *School Effectiveness and School Improvement*, v7 n3 pg.197–228 September 1996; Creemers, B.P.M., & Kyriakides, L., *The Dynamics of Educational Effectiveness. A contribution to policy, practice and theory in contemporary schools*, Abingdon: Routledge, 2008).

6

SKILL – A CONCEPT MANUFACTURED IN ENGLAND?

Christopher Winch

Introduction: main characteristics of the English VET system

In this chapter the notion of skills underlying the vocational education and training (VET) system in England is described in detail, both conceptually and in terms of the way it is embedded in the labour market and the qualification system. The implications for the nature and role of VET and the qualification system in England are drawn out and, at the same time, the ways and the extent to which this is distinct from the systems in other European countries, particularly France, Germany and the Netherlands – especially in terms of their understanding of 'skill'. This chapter is therefore challenging to an English-speaking audience which usually takes for granted the conceptual basis of the system and the domination of 'skills' in the policy agenda – from Sector Skills Councils (SSCs) to the Leitch Review (2006) on *World Class Skills*.

Although England funds much of its VET centrally, it does not have a unified vocational education system and neither is there a unified system of vocational qualifications. The years since 1979 have been marked by a shift towards an employer-led system in which the state constantly intervenes in order to ensure that the supply of ability is adequate for the needs of employers (Hall and Soskice 2001; Keep 2007). At the same time, it is increasingly recognized that employer demand is for the application of knowledge, as opposed to narrow, task-based practical abilities (HMSO/UKCES 2009: 114ff.). The governance of the English system, although strongly dependent on the state, is designed so that employers have maximum purchase on the orientation of the vocational education, both at macro and micro levels. The paradox, well described by Keep (2007), is that England operates a state-dominated VET system whose aim is to facilitate employer needs, when employers are often reluctant to articulate these, not least because their needs are, in many cases, extremely limited.

The English system, unlike in some other European countries, is not centrally organized; nor are the different vocational routes integrated, despite the strength of the English state (Hall and Soskice 2001: ch. 7). Most VET is delivered through the further education (FE) colleges which cater for young people from the age of 14 upwards. More advanced forms of VET are delivered through the various parts of the higher education (HE) system, while a small portion is work-based through some form of apprenticeship. The FE colleges are responsible for full- and part-time trainee programmes which lead to various qualifications and are, as with work-based learning provision, largely concerned with providing skills for use within the workplace. The relative remoteness of the colleges from the workplace, however, can lead to difficulties for FE graduates to access the labour market in some sectors. FE colleges also provide day and block release on apprenticeship programmes, although here they are in competition with private training providers.

Oriented towards perceived employer needs, English VET includes different forms of vocational education and certification, ranging from knowledge-based degrees in technology, such as Bachelor and Foundation degrees at European Qualification Framework (EQF) levels 5 and 6, to input-based vocational qualifications that combine theory and practice at levels 3 and 4, to behaviourally-oriented certification of highly specific workplace skills, the National Vocational Qualification or NVQ, particularly at levels 2 and 3, but also at level 1. Intermediate between these are various qualifications that also presuppose the application of knowledge to a range of tasks. Such qualifications, usually to be found at level 3 in the British QCF (Qualification and Credit Framework), presuppose that a certain amount of technical or theoretical knowledge is applied to workplace activities. This is not usually the case with qualifications below level 3 apart from such qualifications as the Technical Certificates at level 2. Such level 3 qualifications include the BTEC (Business and Technology Education Council) and City and Guilds awards, certificates and diplomas, awarded by independent and often for-profit accreditation bodies, as well as the new government-supported Diplomas, which are concerned with the largely academic study of particular sectors. These qualifications tend to be based in the FE colleges, while NVQs, usually incorporated as the major component of an Apprenticeship qualification, dominate the work-based route. The new national qualifications framework, the QCF, whose structure is congruent with the EQF, is designed to recognize previously non-recognized qualifications within a credit framework. However, work-based vocational education in England is a minor route in comparison with college-based VET. It should be emphasized that English VET is variable in quality, both across sectors and across types of qualification, with examples of both good and bad provision.

Figures shown in Table 6.1 do not include informal, unaccredited episodes of work-based learning. Most 16–19-year-olds in work-based learning are on the government-subsidised Apprenticeship scheme. It can be seen from Figure 6.1 that their overall numbers have been declining since 2004, in particular both the relative and absolute importance of the level 3 route (Advanced Apprenticeship). As Table 6.1 suggests, however, work-based provision at the initial VET stage is a relatively

TABLE 6.1 Numbers of 16–19-year-olds in work-based learning and FE, 2007/8

Programme	Female	Male	Total
Further education	358,200	348,200	706,400
Work-based learning	52,700	89,700	142,400
Adult safeguarded learning	2,300	1,200	3,500
Grand total	413,200	439,200	852,300

Source: Data Service (2010).

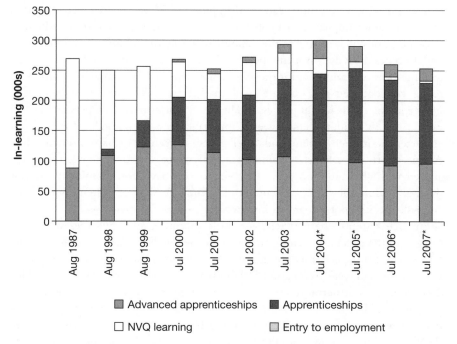

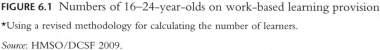

FIGURE 6.1 Numbers of 16–24-year-olds on work-based learning provision

*Using a revised methodology for calculating the number of learners.

Source: HMSO/DCSF 2009.

small proportion of total numbers – less than 20%. Of the 16–19 age cohort, around 4% is in work-based learning, making it a minor route even for those opting for vocational programmes; approximately 80% is in full-time education of which around 20% is in VET 9.4% is not in employment, education or training; and the balance is in employment but not in any form of education or training.

The story told in Figure 6.1 has four key elements:

1. An absolute decline, since 2004, of numbers in work-based learning.
2. The gradual, but absolute, decline, since 2000, in the numbers on level 3 Apprenticeship programmes.

3. The relative and absolute growth of numbers on level 2 Apprenticeships since 1998.
4. The apparent virtual disappearance of NVQ learning, living on in another guise due to its absorption within the Apprenticeship programmes.

Professional education, which is occupationally-oriented and explicitly geared to the aim of producing individuals who can apply theoretical knowledge to complex forms of practice in operational conditions, is kept distinct from the broader stream of VET and is almost exclusively located in HE at Bachelor degree level and beyond.

Nevertheless, a common feature of English VET can be discerned, that it is organized either implicitly or explicitly around the concept of *skill*. The English conception of skill is related to the political economy of skill formation in England which relies heavily on firm-specific skills, not requiring high educational qualifications or attainment for their formation. Production strategies in turn tend to be concentrated towards the mass market and rely quite heavily on the fragmentation of the labour process and high levels of managerial supervision, often carried out by graduate employees. Compliance is a key, sought-after personal characteristic in such systems and 'intelligence' is deemed to be of limited value. As one informant, a logistics training company manager put it, people who have arrived with absolutely no education whatsoever 'have been absolutely brilliant trainees because they are obedient and determined'. Skills are often highly firm- and task-specific, not integrated into broader forms of know-how.

In such systems, there is relatively little incentive for employees who have achieved little success at school to invest in their skill formation because of the limited and firm-specific nature of skills required, the relatively few opportunities within firms and weak occupational labour markets outside them (Hall and Soskice 2001: ch. 4). Furthermore, there is some evidence that, even on accredited programmes, the quality of training is assessed less on substantive benefit to trainees than on procedural compliance (Lewis and Ryan 2009). Political economy and the role of social class in limiting access to the labour market are two, but not the only, explanatory factors for understanding the English conception of skill as narrow, task-based ability. The small number in work-based learning programmes is a testament to structural difficulties in developing such provision, as well as to the related problem of the relatively low importance attached by firms to substantive skill formation in the workplace, despite the use of 'skills rhetoric' by virtually all parties concerned with VET (see Brockmann *et al.* 2010a for details on the low availability of Apprenticeships).

The concept of skill

Yet it is not so easy to say what a skill is as it is to say that a certain activity requires skills. *Skill* is a concept that differs in important ways from the French *aptitude*, the German *Fähigkeit* and the Dutch *competentie* which do not just refer to task-performance but to integrated and independent project management as well. It is, therefore misleading to translate any 'know-how' term in Dutch, French and German as 'skill' and vice versa, except in specific instances. However, the narrowness of the term 'skill' has also meant that it has become stretched within the VET system and the labour market to mean various different things, including personal attributes and aspects of project management, with the result that its use can produce a certain amount of confusion. This chapter will try to unravel some of that confusion.

The most ready-to-hand term for practical ability in English is 'skill'. So common is its use in both economic and non-economic contexts that it has become almost synonymous with 'practical ability' or 'know-how' even though it means less than either of these terms. However, it has specific connotations and is not always easy to translate into other languages. Even though the word 'skill' has crept into some other European languages, 'soft skills' being, for example, a term often employed in German, one cannot assume that its usage is congruent with that in English.

Central usages of the term 'skill'

The 'paradigm case' (Hanfling 2000) of a skill is a specific ability of an individual, typically involving manual and/or co-ordinative features, which is geared to a *task* – or, more precisely, a task type – itself quite a narrow action category, involving the application of a technique. The skill of sawing wood would consist, among other things, in the handling and gripping of the saw, being able to move it with the appropriate pressure across the wood, being able to keep sawing according to a guide mark and so on. The skill of sawing wood is closely linked to the concept of a task, namely that of sawing a particular piece of wood for a particular purpose. Someone who possesses a skill can then apply it to tasks of that type. Although the concept of skill is perhaps used most naturally in connection with manual tasks, it is also used in connection with, for example, mental arithmetic ('the skill of multiplication') and with some kinds of social interaction ('the skill of welcoming a customer'). Thus although the range of abilities that can be described by the word 'skill' seems to have grown, the term is still linked to the performance of tasks, where tasks are typically a narrow range of operations usually linked to a larger action category such as a project ('redecorating the house') or a job ('fitting kitchens').

Although the term 'skill' is now often used beyond the paradigm case, so that it is customary to speak of 'communication skills', 'self-management skills' and so on, the term is still used primarily in relation to tasks. Even if communication skills can be deployed on a large variety of tasks, they are said to be transferable from one kind of task to another. One finds, in the documentation associated with occupations accessed through HE, more emphasis on skills in these broader senses of the term, even with the attributes expected of a successful PhD candidate. However, the inadequacy of such language and of the term 'competence' for describing professional ability is recognized in some professional documentation (e.g. TDA 2007).

German, by contrast, uses the term '*Fähigkeiten*' for those abilities which are more to do with the way that one conducts oneself in the context of a range of activities than with the way in which one acts on the materials with which one is working. In German, *Fähigkeiten* contrast with *Fertigkeiten*, which correspond more closely with the English manual or co-ordinative skills. A *berufliche Fähigkeit*, on the other hand is an occupational capacity which integrates all the knowledge, practical wisdom and understanding necessary to practise an occupation (Hanf 2009). *Skill*, then, is mainly a type of practical ability or know-how, associated with a narrow range of activities. However, in professional situations, the term has undergone a sort of 'conceptual inflation', whereby attributes that used not to count as 'skills' have become so. To quote an administrator in the Health Sector:

> Nursing requires a mixture of technical and more generic, transferable skills. These would include social skills: respect, understanding of cultures, treating patients with dignity, discretion.

In this example we can see how the concept of skill is expanded to move beyond the kind of manipulative and co-ordinative abilities mentioned above (technical skills) to include *virtues* 'treating patients with dignity and discretion' and even a kind of *wisdom* 'understanding of cultures'. Although the vocabulary exists in English to describe these various attributes, the reductive use of the term 'skill' tends to hide the variety of abilities and forms of understanding that are valued in the workplace. Other languages in the study make use of broader categories of know-how. Thus French distinguishes between '*savoir-faire*' (know-how), '*aptitude*' (broadly based know-how) and '*habileté*' (narrowly based know-how). We have already noted the presence of broad action categories in German, which also has the term '*Fertigkeit*' to refer to a narrow skill or knack. For more on this, see the analytical dictionary in this volume. This reductive tendency in discussion on skills can also be seen in the *Leitch Review of Skills*, a highly influential report for the government published in late 2006:

> Skills are capabilities or expertise in a particular occupation or activity. Basic skills such as literacy and numeracy and generic skills such as teamworking and communication are applicable in most jobs. Specific skills tend to be less transferable between jobs. Most occupations use a mix of different types of skills.

(Leitch 2006: 11)

While expanding the concept of skill beyond the narrowly task-oriented, this definition nevertheless fixes specific skills within a task framework. Whether teamworking and communication can be counted as skills, as opposed to broader abilities and character attributes, is debateable, but that they can be considered as examples of skills seems to be taken for granted in the contemporary official discourse on the subject.

Skill and competence

The term 'skill' is also associated in contemporary English with the term 'competence'. But the relationships between the two are not always clear. To say that someone is competent is sometimes to suggest that they are able to exercise a skill to a certain level of minimum performance. To quote one of the informants in our study working in the health sector:

> Competence is being able to do something according to a safe, pre-agreed standard; skill means you might be able to do it, but it doesn't mean whether it's good, bad or indifferent.

But the term 'competence' is also used to designate an action category beyond that of a skill, where the activity is complex and draws upon a range of skills. As another informant, also in the health sector, describes it:

> Competences are probably more in the domain of technical skills, e.g. carrying out a procedure, for which you might need a range of skills, which would be a subset of the competences.

This suggests that *competence* is less a concept used to integrate know-how into a broader action category than one that acts as a sort of collective noun for a bundle of related skills. In everyday usage, in the most simple form, the term 'skill' is related to task performance. However, in work situations, it has undergone 'conceptual inflation' and now includes not only non-manual task-related abilities but also character attributes, virtues and wisdom necessary to be able to know how to carry out a task in real workplace conditions. The term 'competence' is used sometimes synonymously with 'skill', but more often to signify either a threshold level of performance of a skill in workplace conditions or a bundle of skills which may be applied to a complex type of task. Skills are subject to evaluation and the application of evaluative vocabulary. To work skilfully is not necessarily to be highly skilled, a concept which is related more to education and qualifications.

The labour market

Occupational category, occupation, trade

The concept of a skill does not apply to an occupational category. You cannot enquire of the skill of a carpenter as such, only of what skills s/he possesses. One can, of course, obtain an answer to this question in terms of the various skills that it is necessary for a carpenter to possess. What is lost in such a description, however, is a sense of the integrated nature of the carpenter's work which could include planning, control, teamwork and evaluation in the context of independently organized project management, as in the sense of the German *berufliche Fähigkeit*. However, the fragmentation of the labour process (as the creation of a service or product from conception to evaluation of the completed article or service), makes this broader conception of occupational capacity less salient in the English context.

A *trade* is composed of tasks which each require their own skills. Traditionally trades have been organized around the production or carrying out of a particular type of good or service. In England since the industrial revolution, the wider social organization of trades has been weak relative to the situation in some other European countries, with a large measure of informality associated with training, employment practices and boundaries between one trade and another (for an example, see Sturt 1976 on the Wheelwright). When reference to workplace ability is almost exclusively centred around skill, it becomes difficult to allow for the concept of occupational integration, as skill is a fragmenting rather than an integrating concept. 'Skill' is suited to conceptualizing the way in which the labour process (for instance, from conception to evaluation) is segmented into particular episodes of work, into tasks, although at the limit this fragmenting removes any aspect of personal ability (and hence skill) from an operation (Smith 1776; Braverman 1974). This situation, however, reflects the reality of the English labour market in which occupational boundaries are weak and relatively ill-defined.

The informal nature of trade organization and the lack of a social partnership structure to sustain it mean that trades are susceptible of reorganization according to either the perceived needs of employers in a sector or, alternatively, the perceptions of employer need identified by the state (Keep 2007). In such cases, trades become quite distinct from the traditional English notion and what is called an 'occupational profile' becomes, in reality, a group of skills brought together for the perceived needs of employers at a particular time. What remains of the English trade is often described in contemporary official documents as an 'occupation', although the use of this term differs greatly from, for example, the German *Beruf*. Occupations in this restricted English sense can be set out in terms of occupational standards and a series of skills associated with them, which relate to tasks that are then bundled together. An occupational profile is created that suits the need of an employer or group of employers, rather than being the result of the comprehensive mapping of a sector. However, such relatively *ad hoc* groupings of skills often resemble job specifications more than occupations in the European sense. Furthermore, since skills are relatively discrete (like the task types with which they are aligned), it is easy to deploy the concept of skill in relation to a flexible conceptualization of 'occupation' which can shift from one permutation of skills to another.

Such *ad hoc* arrangements have taken root in those areas of economic activity once covered by trades, organized on traditional lines or controlled through craft trade unions, and are legitimated by a qualification system designed to make these constantly-shifting, job-type specifications easier to accredit. It is important to note that bundles of skills (usually called 'competences') are descriptions of groups of task-related activities and that the criterion for their possession by an individual is that a certain behavioural description is satisfied. They contrast strongly with the professions, regulated by charter, which have a defined knowledge base, controlled entry, and well-understood and longstanding qualifications based in higher education, together with relatively independent disciplinary and accountability arrangements (Clarke and Herrmann 2004a).

The concept of a skill, although it is still significant in these professional occupations, has a less prominent role. For example, the specification of the work of teachers in England is set out in terms of *Standards and Competences* (TDA 2009), in which *standards* include values and dispositions and a *competence* is a grouping together of a range of skills. The competence specifications are broad and allow for judgement and discretion in their exercise. They cannot easily be reduced to a narrow set of behavioural criteria. Thus, although the terms 'skill' and 'competence' are used in the professional context, the use of 'competence', in particular, has undergone a subtle shift in comparison with its use in trades and other non-professional activities.

The prominence of the term 'skill' in labour market discourse in England thus reflects trends in the English labour market that have been growing steadily more important over the last 30 years. At the same time, the use of the term reflects a strong cultural disposition to think of *knowing how* in terms of visible performance rather than less easily observable underpinning knowledge. This can be seen for example in Chapter 2 of Ryle's seminal *The Concept of Mind* (Ryle 1949), in which expert know-how is illustrated as the seamless performance of arrays of different kinds of task or routine. This cultural predisposition to want concrete evidence of the possession of know-how through the witnessing of a performance ('the proof of the pudding is in the eating') has come to dominate the qualification system that has the greatest degree of influence in the English VET system, the NVQ. As Gilbert Jessup, one of the designers of NVQs, expressed it:

> Skills can only be demonstrated through their application in performance (doing something) while knowledge can be elicited through the more abstract means of conversation, questioning or talking.
>
> (Jessup 1991: 121)

The NVQ, initiated in 1986, is a good example of the way in which the English state interacts with employers and the labour market. Originally devised by ministers, civil servants and occupational psychologists as a way of making the accreditation of skills transparent to employers, their use by employers has been uneven (Raggatt and Williams 1999). Yet they are considered by successive governments to be central to the construction of vocational qualifications such as Apprenticeships (see Brockmann *et al.* 2010a).

It is, however, no part of the concept of a skill that possession implies accreditation. Adam Smith, for example, drew attention to the multifarious skills of the agricultural labourer, while pointing out that these were scarcely recognized except by those who could directly appreciate their value:

> Not only the art of the farmer, the general direction of the operations of husbandry, but many inferior branches of country labour, require much more

skill and experience than the greater part of mechanic trades. The man who works upon brass and iron, works with instruments and upon materials of which the temper is always the same, or very nearly the same. But the man who ploughs the ground with a team of horses or oxen, works with instruments of which the health, strength, and temper are very different upon different occasions. The condition of the materials which he works upon too is as variable as that of the instruments which he works with, and both require to be managed with much judgment and discretion. The common ploughman, though generally regarded as the pattern of stupidity and ignorance, is seldom defective in his judgment and discretion.

(Smith 1776, Bk1, Section 10: 79)

In the informal labour market that has operated and still operates in much of the English economy, the availability of qualifications for skills has been to a large degree very patchy. One of the problems here is that the skills employed are not officially recognized and tend not to be classified as belonging to a recognized category of skilled labour, particularly if union organization is weak. This lack of recognition occurs even though the know–how required to carry out the relevant tasks may involve a high degree of manipulative and co-ordinative ability that is difficult to acquire. The task concerned may also necessitate very low degrees of tolerance or margin of error, a high degree of contextual knowledge and be difficult to accomplish successfully in complex operational conditions. Skills are very often developed informally in operational conditions and are firm-specific and unrecognized outside the context in which they are developed.

Skills and qualifications

Although 'skill' is not the same as 'qualification', there has nevertheless been a drift in England, at least within official discourse, towards identifying skill with qualification. This trend has been encouraged by the development of forms of accreditation, most notably the NVQ, based on certificatory validation of existing skills. In addition to NVQ qualifications are the BTEC awards, offered by various exam boards, the City and Guilds progression awards and the more recent Diplomas, also offered by exam boards and City and Guilds. All these qualifications can to a greater or lesser extent constitute all or part of the underpinning knowledge for NVQs within the context of an Apprenticeship programme. However, the relationship between underpinning knowledge and practice of the relevant skills is by no means clear, since in most cases it is possible to acquire the NVQ before the certificate guaranteeing that one has acquired the underpinning knowledge necessary to practise these skills. Even in vocationally-oriented HE in England, the application of knowledge to practice, although central, is often obscured by the use of terminology such as 'learning outcome' and 'skill' to describe successful completion of degrees and other programmes. It is a continuing weakness of British VET that the relationship between theoretical knowledge and practical ability is not made clear and is, in many cases, not clearly understood (Winch 2009).

The role of qualifications like the NVQ in the accreditation of skill is also unclear. On the one hand, a skill is thought to be self-disclosing; one can lay claim to possession not through a display of propositional knowledge, but through actions that embody the skill. To quote Gilbert Ryle:

> You can't define a good chef as one who cites Mrs Beeton's recipes, for these recipes describe how good chefs cook, and anyhow the excellence of a chef is not in his citing but in his cooking.
>
> (Ryle 1946: 222)

The attribution to someone of the ability to cook – and hence of the skills of measuring, cutting, heating and so on – is justified by their performance of such actions in appropriate circumstances. The original intention of an NVQ was to assess *competence* in an occupational category (as defined by an accrediting body) as successful performance in workplace conditions of the range of tasks set out in the specification for that certificate and, hence, as possession of the range of appropriate skills. Such competence would thus consist in the ability to *display* certain skills in occupational conditions. On the face of it, therefore, an individual's possession of propositional knowledge is irrelevant to whether or not he or she possesses a skill. However, where a skill is to be exercised in a wide variety of situations, each of which has specific contextual requirements, it is not sufficient to draw attention to one instance of the exercise of that skill. Some NVQs require a statement of the range of circumstances in which the competence can be exercised and also quite commonly – as with some Apprenticeships, especially at level 3 – a Technical Certificate (Raggatt and Williams 1999). However, such requirements are neither universal nor even particularly stable in the case of the Apprenticeship and reflect the continuing ambivalence towards the role of knowledge in practical ability that exists in thinking within and about the English trades.

Thus, it is common to find that employers, are at times, focused strictly on the skills needed to perform particular tasks and, at others, concerned about the out-of datedness of particular skills or fretting about operatives' lack of knowledge of the industry in which they work. There is no settled view within the English trades in general, and not even within many specific trades, as to what the appropriate level of knowledge and practical ability should be. The engineering and IT sectors are notable for their relatively high demand for level 3 qualifications, but level 2 is preponderant in most other sectors. It is arguable that the continuing focus on skills, to the detriment of thinking about competences in a broad and integrated way, has impeded the development of a sufficiently broad conceptual map of practical ability that would enable employers to gain a clearer and more detailed picture of what is needed.

The 'world class skills' agenda

This problem is perhaps most vividly illustrated in the Leitch Review (2006) which has been extremely influential in determining the direction of funding of VET in

England and has set the target of 90% of adults with level 2 qualifications by 2020. These qualifications are precisely those for which underpinning knowledge has relatively little importance. Significantly, Leitch takes the view that 'skill' should be equated in practical terms with 'qualification': 'The most common measures of skills are qualifications' (2006: 11). However, the award of a qualification for existing workplace ability does not create a new skill but merely assigns a name to the skill an individual already possesses. To believe otherwise is to come perilously close to the magical belief that incantation of the word 'skill' over a qualification will bring a new individual skill to life, where none had previously existed. Nevertheless, the flagship 'Train to Gain' programme, heavily promoted by Leitch and strongly pursued by the previous UK government, is to a considerable degree based on accrediting already-existing workplace skills.

The context of the Leitch Review and of a large number of other government publications over the last 20 years or so in England has been the assumption that the country has an inadequate supply of the skills required by the 'knowledge economy'. Until recently, it was assumed that 'high skills' were in demand from employers, although it is now realized that this may not be the case. The 2009 report of the UK Commission for Employment and Skills (a body set up as a result of a recommendation in the Leitch Review) appears to recognize what many VET commentators in the UK have long been saying, namely that:

> The argument is that the UK, or particular sectors or geographical areas, may be 'trapped' in a low skills equilibrium or following a low skills trajectory, which presents a relatively low level of demand for skills by some UK employers.
>
> (HMSO/UKCES 2009: 124)

What is implied is not only that there is a low demand for skills (since all employers demand some degree of skill), but that the skills demanded are not 'high' enough. But what does it mean to say that some skills are higher than others?

High skills and qualifications

In contemporary times, application of the adjective 'high' to 'skill' is increasingly bound up with the association of a formal qualification with a range of tasks, a trade, an occupation or a profession (Brown *et al.* 2001). This can reach the point at which the skill is virtually identified with the possession of a qualification. Thus, the Leitch Review suggests that a workforce in which everyone is required to have a qualification will be one in which everyone is 'skilled', in the sense of having know-how which is not only valuable but has been acquired through time and effort. But the amount of 'judgement and discretion' that the performance of a task requires can only be settled by a qualification awarded as a result of a programme of study and practice, one that prescribes that a certain standard of performance be reached – following the acquisition of both propositional and practical knowledge within a curriculum. It cannot be settled through awarding a qualification for an already existing skill, if the exercise of that skill requires little judgement or discretion.

The relationship between the concept of skill, as a kind of know-how or practical knowledge related to the performance of tasks, and the concept of a qualification is a complex one. A qualification, in the sense in which the term is used in England, is a certificate, which serves to guarantee that the bearer has acquired certain skills, knowledge or understanding. It is easy to see how the guarantee that someone has a skill could come to be equated with the possession of the skill itself, since one might argue that, if the guarantee is missing, then so is the skill. Such a situation could only come about where possession of the relevant qualification is *criterial* for possession of the relevant skill, where there is no guarantee of the skill without the possession of the qualification, as for example, where there is a strict and universal licence to practise underpinned by a qualification which is a necessary condition for labour market entry. But, apart from limited areas, such as the traditional professions, nurses and gas fitters, that is not the case in England and it is not possible to equate skills with qualifications.

Notwithstanding, it is increasingly common to identify the possession of 'high skills' with the holding of a qualification, particularly a qualification that presupposes that exercise of the relevant know-how requires possession of a body of propositional knowledge. Such propositional knowledge will almost invariably be acquired through an educational process, and so the achievement of a 'high skill' tends to be thought of as contingent on following a course of education in which the acquisition of relevant propositional knowledge plays a significant role. This way of thinking about high skills is evident within the EQF as well as in, for example, the English QCF, in the sense that possession of a high degree of skill is assumed to mean that one has acquired and is able to apply underpinning systematic knowledge to tasks performed in the workplace. This, in turn, implies that one has a degree of discretion and, hence, of independence in one's workplace operations, as the question of *when* to perform an act depends on prior judgement of the appropriate course of action. It depends not just on experience and purely *in situ* considerations, but on systematic knowledge of the properties of the materials, situations or individuals with which one is working. Qualifications have a particular role to play in the realization of this conception of being highly skilled, since the key feature of possessing such a high skill is the ability to bring one's systematic knowledge to bear on making judgements and carrying out actions in operational workplace conditions.

On this view, it is neither enough to possess systematic knowledge without operational experience and ability nor sufficient by itself to have operational experience and ability in order to possess the skill. The two must be fused together in acts of professional judgement and action (Eraut 1994), suggesting that a possessor of such skills should be able to:

1. form an assessment of the nature of a problem, based on both systematic and local knowledge;

2.   plan a course of action to deal with the problem;
3.   control and, if necessary, adjust the execution of that plan; and
4.   evaluate the success of the course of action adopted.

In this sense, the highly skilled person is different from the highly skilled craftsman who predominantly relies on experience and local and particular knowledge to make tacit judgements embodied largely in action.

Craft and skill

An excellent description of the craft worker in England at the turn of the nineteenth into the twentieth century is to be found in George Sturt's *The Wheelwright's Shop* (Sturt 1926). Sturt's account of craft knowledge suggests that it is based on tradition and practice transmitted through apprenticeship and is practised within the context of a trade, such as that of the wheelwright. Qualifications were of no importance for entry into a traditional trade such as this. The skill possessed would be characterized by Oakeshott (1962) as *practical knowledge* because procedures, which are usually implicit, will be devised by the operative based on relevant systematic knowledge, local knowledge and tacit knowledge of his/her own capabilities. Such a worker is also different from the possessor of 'technical knowledge' in Oakeshott's sense, as this involves the following of rules (conceived of as recipes) to attain an end. In fact, it may be doubted whether possession of technical knowledge in its pure form could count as skill at all.

> The technique (or part of it) of driving a motor car on English roads is to be found in the Highway Code, the technique of cookery is to be found in the cookery book, and the technique of discovery in natural science or in history is in their rules of research, of observation and verification.
>
> (1962: 7–8)

Possession of an account of a technique is insufficient to count as possession of a practical ability. For example, understanding of the technique of discovery in natural science cannot be acquired simply through acquaintance with rules. Skill and technique should be distinguished from each other, even though the term 'skill' is sometimes used in place of 'technique' as in 'the skill of ice-skating is difficult to acquire'.

It may be argued, and implicitly is by, for example, Ryle (1949), that the systematic knowledge required for possession of a practical ability can be acquired through experience:

> A man knowing little or nothing of medical science could not be a good surgeon, but excellence in surgery is not the same thing as knowledge of medical science; nor is it a simple product of it. The surgeon must indeed have learned from instruction, or by his own induction and observations, a

great number of truths; but he must also have learned by practice a great number of aptitudes.

(1949: 49)

The crucial claim in this short paragraph is the phrase 'or by his own induction and observations'. If this is admitted, one could also acknowledge that the 'high skill' route can be followed through a process of learning on the job through experience. But, in fact, surgeons are not allowed to practise on the basis of their own inductions and observations and there is a very good reason why this is so. The contingent set of experiences that novice surgeons might have would most likely be insufficient for developing the knowledge to deal with the range of medical problems that the mature surgeon would be likely to encounter. The epistemological point of explicit instruction in the systematic knowledge underpinning surgery is to endow embryonic surgeons with the ability to make judgements in situations where they have never had the chance to make their own 'inductions and observations', by ensuring that all relevant knowledge is adequately covered.

While we might find the kind of apprenticeship to surgery that a 'sawbones' such as Roderick Random experienced on a British naval vessel in the eighteenth century amusing to read about in Tobias Smollett's (1748) satirical novel of that name, few of us would be amused at the prospect of having to submit to Roderick Random's professional judgement. We would prefer to submit to the surgeon who has appropriate qualifications from a respectable medical school, which are a guarantee, not just of the manipulative abilities necessary to perform surgery, but of the knowledge needed to fix on and elaborate an appropriate plan of action to ensure our good health. The main reason why the craft conception of skill is not appropriate to many professions and technical occupations is that the latter rely on systematic as well as local knowledge and the range and complexity of their operations make it difficult for sufficient knowledge of variations in conditions and cases to be acquired during the early years of practice.

Such complex professional abilities do not lend themselves easily to description as 'skills', even though components of such abilities may well do so. The vocabulary of 'skill' does not sit well with types of agency which involve planning, controlling, co-ordinating, integrating and evaluating over a wide range of connected operations. The 'High Skills' advocated by those who wish England to develop economically along the lines of Germany or Japan (e.g. Brown *et al.* 2001) are something more than skills traditionally conceived, and it could be argued that a shift in vocabulary is needed to take account of these differences in order to avoid misunderstanding.

Skill and technique

We need, finally, to consider another aspect of the English use of the term 'skill' and, more generally, the English vocabulary of practical knowledge, which causes confusion: between 'skill' as a property of an individual agent and 'skill' as the set of procedures necessary to accomplish a task. To appreciate this, it is appropriate to look once again at Adam Smith. In Book I, Chapter 10 of *The Wealth of Nations* Smith argues that the procedures necessary to carry out even complex trades can be given by instruction:

> But when both [watches and watchmaking machinery] have been fairly invented, and are well understood, to explain to any young man, in the completest manner, how to apply the instruments, and how to construct the machines, cannot well require the lessons of more than a few weeks; perhaps those of a few days might be sufficient.
>
> (Smith 1776, ch 10: 71)

Smith goes on to say that in the 'common mechanic trades' a few days 'might certainly be sufficient'. It is, of course, true that one could explain procedures to someone and that person might well understand what those procedures involved, but this would hardly be sufficient to constitute the skill as an attribute of that individual. Smith seems to labour under a real confusion on this subject, since he immediately goes on to say:

> The dexterity of hand, indeed even in common trades, cannot be acquired without much practice and experience.
>
> (ibid.)

He does not apparently notice that his first assertion, that one can 'explain' a procedure in a way that allows a young man to carry it out, is inconsistent with his view that the skill (as attribute of the individual) requires 'much practice and experience'. It is the confusion of 'skill' as technique, or the way in which a task is performed, and 'skill' as an element of personal practical knowledge. Whilst one can understand, in some sense, what a technique involves through having it explained, that is not the same as acquiring the use of that technique as a skill of one's own, let alone being able to practise a trade in real-life, operational conditions.

Such a view can also be found behind the assertion, often made, that the practice of a skill does not engage the character of the individual practising it. A recent example can be found in Hyland (2008: 133):

> The point is that knowledge and moral values/dispositions are connected to ideas of personhood in ways in which skills (and competences) are not.

This is true of skill as technique, but it is not true of skill as personal attribute. A skill can be exercised in various ways, including with care, consideration for others, with a love of excellence and so on, and the way in which one exercises a skill in this sense is partly constitutive of one's character. Learning a skill, when it is done properly and within a carefully constructed and comprehensive form of VET, can be an important part of one's personal development.

It is a paradox of English society, and consequently of English VET, that those who take a narrowly instrumental view of the skills that they believe are required from their workforce (exemplified in the Smith quotation above), share the same dismissive view of skill acquisition as those who think that it should have no part in an educational experience. Common usage does not imply that skills as personal attributes have no bearing on one's character and do not require a significant degree of judgement and discretion. Yet depersonalization of skill has been a persistent theme of the official discourse on skill, at least since the time of Adam Smith through to the Leitch Review (2006), seeking to reconstitute it as 'explanation' (Smith) or 'descriptor' (NVQ specifications) and 'qualifications' (Leitch). Trading on an ambiguity between, on the one hand, 'skill' as practical ability related to task and, on the other, 'skill' as technique or as an account of how something is done, the quality of VET in England continues to suffer.

Conclusion: skills and qualifications

The English concept of skill, as it is used in the labour market, expresses the view that to possess a skill is to have mastered a technique for carrying out a type of task within a work situation, traditionally within the context of a trade but nowadays in more technically-oriented occupations as well. The reason for this work-based requirement is that it is possible to master a technique without knowing how to use it effectively, because one is unable to function within the complexities and pressures of a work situation. Accreditation through the conferment of a formal qualification is neither necessary nor sufficient for possession of a skill and large parts of the economy still rely on the informal assessment of whether someone is able to carry out workplace tasks. Likewise, possession of a qualification indicating that someone has a skill is often not recognized by employers as sufficient for workplace know-how because they are unclear as to whether or not the skill can actually be employed in work situations.

The NVQ was seen, at least partly, as a solution to this problem through the device of only crediting someone with a skill if they could apply it in workplace conditions. However, since the NVQ was seen as a self-contained qualification, the question of what knowledge, attitude or character traits lay behind the exercise of the skill was left to one side. This decision had the unfortunate consequence of reinforcing an English conception of *competence*, as performance of tasks to a threshold level of quality, *irrespective of the conditions that underlay that performance*, as a restricted conception of know-how within the workplace. This feature of know-how, expressed in the terminology of 'skill' and 'competence' in the sense outlined above, is what most separates the English conception of workplace know-how from that of France, Germany and the Netherlands. This point needs to be borne in mind when considering how the middle column of the EQF, which in English refers to 'Skills', in French '*Aptitudes*', in German '*Fertigkeiten*' and in Dutch '*Vaardigheden*' is interpreted.

7

TRADE? JOB? OR OCCUPATION? THE DEVELOPMENT OF OCCUPATIONAL LABOUR MARKETS FOR BRICKLAYING AND LORRY DRIVING

Linda Clarke

Introduction

This chapter sets out to discover how far occupational qualifications can be regarded as transnational or as confined to their national borders, referring to the examples of bricklaying and lorry driving. This is no easy task; each country – England, France, Germany and the Netherlands – deploys different terms for 'occupation' and defines these in different ways, as evident in the German case of *Beruf* or the French *métier*. In the English language bricklaying is usually referred to as a 'trade', whilst 'occupation' is a much more general and all-encompassing term for employment 'in which one is engaged' (Oxford Dictionary 1980). Here we will seek to develop a transnational understanding and definition of an 'occupation' associated with qualifications and distinguished from a 'trade' and a 'job', also applied as abstractions or simplifications from particular wage and employment relations. A 'trade' involves an act of exchange and is thus defined and measured by its output, being historically acquired through work-based apprenticeship rather than via a process of vocational education and training (VET). In contrast, an occupation is recognized through VET qualifications – albeit acquired in part through a process of work-based learning – and represents a definite division of labour in society. Both 'occupations' and 'trades' in this sense are distinguished from 'jobs', which are bound to a single workplace.

In a historical sense, throughout Europe bricklaying can be regarded as moving from being a trade to a qualified occupation whilst lorry driving has never had the status of the traditional trade but rather tended to be regarded as a job (Clarke 2005). As the labour processes involved in both bricklaying and lorry driving have changed significantly, demanding ever more abstract, technical and social competences, so qualifications have developed as a means to recognize these and at the same time to facilitate greater mobility for both bricklayers and lorry drivers and increasing transparency of their competences. This is still an uneven process: in many countries bricklaying retains the hallmarks of a traditional trade, based on learning on-the-job, and lorry driving of a job; in others, trade characteristics have weakened or even disappeared; whilst in yet others can be found side by side both bricklaying tradesmen, often self-employed, and qualified bricklayers operating in what can be regarded as occupational labour markets. Similarly, lorry driving, whilst still predominantly a job is to a greater or lesser extent in a historical process of becoming an occupation, recognized by qualifications.

Trades, occupations and jobs

As the practitioner of a *trade* the bricklayer can be seen to possess the physical and mental dexterity needed to perform employer-defined tasks – in particular laying bricks – in the work process, on the basis of skills acquired through a traditional apprenticeship. The traditional apprentice was bound to a single employer so that skills acquired tended to be firm-specific and training depended to a large extent on the individual employer and on on-the-job learning – identified by Marsden (1999) as a 'production approach'. A key characteristic of a trade in this sense is that recognition and reward relate not to the capabilities or qualifications of a person but to performance of a particular range of tasks in the workplace. It is thus linked to a specific output – that is with 'work' as the output of labour or with what Richard Biernacki (1995) terms 'embodied labour', whereby the employment relation is seen as the appropriation of labour concretized in products. Bricklaying in England still exhibits many of the characteristics of a *trade*, bound to a particular material though – unlike in the past when trade demarcation disputes were a key characteristic of trade union activity – its scope today is defined by employers with little involvement of trade unions (Lee 1979; Brockmann *et al.* 2010a). In this respect, even the trade status of the English bricklayer can be seen to have significantly weakened and more closely resemble a job, going together with a failure to redefine its scope which has, consequently, become increasingly narrow.

In contrast to a trade, an *occupation* is here defined as a formally recognized social category, with a regulative structure concerning VET, qualifications, promotion and the range of knowledge, both practical and theoretical, that is required to undertake the activities that fall within it. Bricklaying as an *occupation* is thereby recognized through its qualifications, agreed on by the social partners of the employment relationship (employers and trade unions) and educationalists as part of a regulated framework, covering a broad and complex range of construction activities and tasks, with defined performance standards and knowledge base, and acquired through a recognized system of VET with a curriculum which also includes social and civic elements. In this way an *occupation* represents a division of labour within a sector of society and, because it refers to labour potential (which Biernacki (1995) terms 'labour power', whereby the employment relation is seen to comprise the purchase of labour effort) over a working life, is founded on abilities which are holistic and multi-dimensional rather than being confined to often narrow *trade* skills. It is linked to developing the capacity of the individual, rather than just to producing a given output, and is, as a result, potentially more able to develop with changes in the labour process (Brockmann *et al.* 2008b).

The bricklaying *Beruf* in Germany represents an example of an *occupation* in this sense. The VET (*Berufsbildung*) system is geared to the development of the individual to this particular occupational status, defined through the curricula and related to the attainment of standards at different levels, as agreed and defined in the collective agreement between employers and trade unions. As apparent from Chapter 4, a *Beruf* represents a systematized combination of formal knowledge, skills, competence and experience which, in contrast with a *job*, is not geared to any single workplace and is bound up with a particular system of wage relations (Hanf 2009). The labour process involved, social partnership and the VET system combine to produce a coherent conception of an occupation, with a recognized place and status within the social and economic structure of the society. A *Beruf* is connected with the development of the individual's occupational, personal and social competences and with the idea of project conception and execution central to Kerschensteiner's notion of *produktiver Arbeit* (Gonon 2009). In the workplace, too, occupational identity is seen to go together with *Handlungskompetenz*, which implies the ability to deal with complex and unpredictable situations (Rauner 2004; Erpenbeck 2005).

One of the problems with discussions of the relationship between trade, occupation, job, education, training and labour is the fluid nature of the termi-nology employed. *Job*, for instance, refers to a particular individual employment contract to work for a firm, for instance as a facing bricklayer, drainlayer, trades foreman or gangleader. To say that so and so's *job* is a trade foreman is to specify a range of *tasks* to perform as part of their employment contract for a particular firm. Someone with the job of a trade foreman may also belong to the *occupation* or *trade* of bricklayer or stonemason. The term *task*, in turn, refers to specific activities that someone may undertake, such as supervising, laying facing bricks and blocks, mixing mortar, erecting walls, corners and arches, snagging work or securing a load on a lorry. A bricklayer, therefore, could be employed in a series of different jobs, each of which would involve an array of tasks (Winch and Clarke 2003).

These distinctions imply three levels of ability or competence, based on some permutation of dexterity, practical knowledge, theoretical knowledge and social skills: first, to carry out a particular task in the workplace; second, to do a particular job – whether specified by the employer or through a contract – within a firm or production process; and, finally, to fulfil (perhaps only potentially) the activities associated with or negotiated for an occupation, thus relating directly to the division of labour in society. There are therefore different levels of complexity associated with ability in each sense. Although in the task sense it may involve theoretical as well as practical knowledge, in the job sense it requires a specification of the broader context into which individual tasks are integrated, together with an awareness of how the job is related to other jobs. Ability developed in an occupational sense, on the other hand, is of a more long-term nature, equipping individuals over a working life to work in a particular occupation and sector.

To fulfil the requirements of an *occupation* involves an awareness of its aims, values and social significance and of related occupations within that sector, as well as knowledge of the range of activities involved, the different ways in which these may be organized in different firms and how the occupation may alter as a result of social, economic and technological developments. In other words, competence in an occupational sense entails significant transferability between different jobs, associated with what Marsden has termed – perhaps misleadingly – a 'training approach' and with occupational labour markets (Marsden 1999). These latter are defined as institutionally regulated, involving skills recognized by certified qualifications and usually collectively and industrially organized (Eyraud *et al.* 1990).

Similarities and differences exist within and between occupations in different European countries, in terms of the activities, knowledge and competences encompassed and associated qualifications, industrial relations systems and labour markets. The conception of an occupation – as found in, for example, Germany or the Netherlands – depends on its comprehensive mapping onto an industrial sector via a social partnership-underpinned VET system. This means not only that the content and hence boundaries of each occupation are constantly renegotiated with changes in the labour process and in sectoral divisions but that the development of a qualification structure encompasses all related activities. Occupations that cross sectors are also defined by their qualification structure, suggesting that any move towards an occupational labour market needs to be in the context of occupational qualifications. In line with Marsden's 'training approach', occupations in this sense are founded on a more regulated and formal approach to the labour market, implying particular means of entry and going together with investment in training through collective industry-related associations of employers and employees together with the state (Marsden 1999: 33–39). They are attached to a labour market which might be described as 'qualification-based', in the sense that entry is dependent to a large extent on training and qualifications and employment more regulated.

The question this raises is whether the development of the European Qualifications Framework (EQF) needs to accompany the development of occupational labour markets if it is to facilitate mobility, recruitment and career development. The labour mobility of both bricklayers and lorry drivers is high compared to many other occupations and many find employment even in countries other than those in which they were originally educated and trained. At the same time, with the increasingly 'skilled' nature of the labour involved and with rapid changes in the nature and number of firms across Europe, qualifications provide a more important means of recognizing a person's level of competence, skill and knowledge than reliance only on a person's experience and personal references as proof of their abilities. Bricklaying, as an occupational category typical for the construction sector and lorry driving for the logistics sector, are as exposed as any to these changes and thus provide good examples to explore the difficulties and possibilities of recognizing across Europe the qualifications of what are sometimes – increasingly inappropriately – termed the 'manual' occupations.

Occupational disparities in bricklaying

Systems of governance

The trade-based character of the English system is nowhere more apparent than in the governance structure for bricklaying, with employer trade associations playing a critical role in defining qualifications grounded in the labour market rather than in the educational system. National Vocational Qualifications (NVQs) for bricklaying focus on existing practices within individual companies and are defined partly through a process of employer and trade association lobbying. Trade associations, which for bricklaying include the Association of Brickwork Contractors, are not industry-wide organizations but seek to defend the specific trade interests of their members. They can even be seen to have gained in importance as the organizations of trade unions and employers have become ever more fragmented and less representative. The representation of the estimated 186,000 private contracting companies in the sector, over 93% with fewer than 13 employees, was, for instance, until recently divided between the Construction Confederation, the UK Contractors Group (UKCG) and the Federation of Master Builders – all including firms which, whilst very often not directly employing bricklayers, will take these on as subcontractors (BERR 2008). At the same time, the different construction trade unions – in particular for bricklaying the Union of Construction and Allied Technical Trades (UCATT) – continue to co-exist but play an increasingly marginal role in defining qualifications.

One reason for the increasing reliance on trade associations in the English case is the particular role of the state in VET and qualifications. England is characterized by the lack of direct Ministerial responsibility and instead the use of quangos, or 'arms-length' government organizations, including the Sector Skills Councils (SSCs) covering all sectors including construction (Clarke and Herrmann 2004a). Unusually for England, but in line with many of the other countries (including Germany and the Netherlands), funding for ConstructionSkills, the SSC responsible for construction VET and qualifications, is through a levy-grant system, plus state support. ConstructionSkills, largely an employer-led body with only limited trade union involvement, plays a major role in regulating and laying down the type of bricklaying qualification in England and maintaining National Occupational Standards.

Unlike the continental countries, the collective agreement in Britain, the Working Rule Agreement for the Construction Industry, signed between employers and trade unions, plays little or no role in the governance of qualifications. Nor are the different skill qualification levels recognized through the collective agreement, which has moved from the sharp distinction traditionally drawn between Craft Operative and Labourers rates to develop intermediate Skill Rates 1–4 (NJCBI 1991; CIJC 2003). Given this lack of relation between qualification levels and wage rates, it is difficult for an occupational labour market to exist for bricklayers in England, though the legal requirement for site workers to obtain a Construction Skills Certification

Scheme (CSCS) card, intended to accredit existing skills on the basis of NVQs, has introduced some measure of recognition of qualifications.

In continental countries, in contrast, the role of trade associations is taken by industry-wide employers' organizations, which also have a role in the social dialogue between trade unions and employers. Each *Beruf* in Germany is thus, for instance, situated within a sectoral framework and subject to close monitoring and modification through tripartite (employers, trade unions and educationalists) sectoral committees under the auspices of the BIBB (*Bundesinstitut für Berufsbilding*) (Stender 2006). The occupation is closely bound up with the qualification, in the sense that it is necessary to obtain in order to become recognized, for instance, as a skilled bricklayer (*Spezialfacharbeiter*). Industry-wide collective agreements, drawn up between the one trade union and one employer association that cover the whole construction sector, are also critical to the governance of bricklaying qualifications in Germany. Here, the labourer/craft division has long ceased to exist as the collective agreement for the sector was graded into six wage groups linked directly to qualifications and as labourers also aspire to be skilled workers. Many activities previously classed as 'labouring' were mechanized or subsumed within one or other of the 14 specialized construction *Berufe* (Streeck and Hilbert 1991). In France, there is an 'implicit' reference to qualifications as collective agreements define the basic wage but the actual pay may depend on the bargaining power of the individual employee. And, in the Netherlands, though the collective agreement does contain a wage structure for young people who have come through the work-based VET track, holders of qualifications are not automatically entitled to a particular wage grade as other aspects – such as work experience and age – are also taken into consideration.

Unlike the English case too, the German, Dutch and French VET and qualification systems are all tightly regulated by government, which in the Netherlands and Germany sets minimum standards, validates and lays down rules and procedures, whilst the social partners are responsible for negotiating the precise content of the qualification. The German situation is further complicated by the division between *Handwerk* and *Industrie*, with *Handwerk* organizations, associated with small firms, still important to bricklaying, particularly through the local employer bodies or *Innungen*, where those who have qualified as *Meister* (master) play a key role. However, in the wide range of activities covered in the recognized qualification and in the relatively high level of general and vocational education required for this, bricklaying in Germany is an occupation rather than a trade. The legal framework is based on the principle of consensus, and social partners as well as educationalists have an important consultative and advisory function through a variety of bodies, such as the vocational training committee of the *Handwerk* and industry chambers which oversee the implementation of VET in companies.

As evident in Chapter 3, France is distinct for the role played by the state in the jurisdiction and supervision of the qualification, though the social partners also play a prominent role in negotiating framework agreements on developing skills, in apprenticeship policy and in running many of the training centres. In France, whilst the qualification is regulated by the Ministry of Education, it is developed and monitored by a consultative committee (CPC) consisting of social partners and experts, drawing up the 'activity' and 'competence' frameworks. In subsequent steps, a framework for assessment is developed by educationalists, while the training institutions develop the detailed curriculum. VET itself is jointly regulated by the social partners, with trade unions divided into five confederations and employers between large and small firms and between those in building, civil engineering and family-based concerns. There is strong consensus between stakeholders in terms of the comprehensive and broad nature of the qualification to prepare people for different types of firm and to ensure lifelong occupational mobility (Méhaut 2009).

In the Netherlands, all qualifications aim to ensure occupational and social mobility and are produced in consultation with the social partners and representatives from VET schools and according to a tightly regulated government framework (Westerhuis 2009). The bricklaying qualification content is based on core tasks identified by the sectoral representatives (non-governmental organizations) and individual schools are responsible for developing the curricula. The distinctness of the Dutch system is perhaps, as discussed in Chapter 5, that the social partners and the government define qualifications and VET in terms of competence and that the qualification, whilst requiring a similar level of competence, encompasses a broader range of activities than in the English case – being seen as a compromise between the needs of all-round construction firms and the specialized bricklaying firms. Unlike in England too, there is a strong link between VET qualification levels and occupational hierarchies in the labour market, with the result that there is a clear occupational labour market for bricklaying.

Thus, in terms of the governance of qualifications, the English system is characterized by the importance attached to trade associations, the weakness of government regulation, and the lack of a comprehensive industry framework of social partnership and of a link between qualification and wage levels laid down in collective agreements. In contrast, in France, Germany and the Netherlands, it is precisely the regulation of qualifications within an industry framework, underpinned by collective agreements that apply throughout the sector and implemented through social partnership at all levels, that gives bricklaying its distinct qualities, occupational identity and status.

VET and qualifications for bricklaying

A second key difference between England and the continental countries lies in the nature of the bricklaying qualification and the VET system through which it can be gained. In Germany, France and the Netherlands, VET is provided through comprehensive programmes that are part of the national education system and thus constitute the continuation of 'education' (commonly based on a curriculum, with a broad content) rather than 'training' as more narrowly focused on the labour market and the job. VET, including for bricklaying, is thereby aimed at developing the individual for the occupation and employment as well as for life as a citizen in wider society. Thus theory encompasses broad knowledge of the construction industry and occupational and firm-specific knowledge and includes underpinning subjects such as mathematics and physics. France and Germany also aim to provide the basis for further education, including progression to higher education, although in practice opportunities may be constrained.

In the case of the German Dual System for bricklaying, VET takes place in three locations: the college (*Berufsschule*); the training centre or workshop outside the firm and under regional employer associations and chambers of commerce; and the workplace (Streeck and Hilbert 1991). Competences relate to sets of activities in the workplace and are based on the integration of knowledge, practical know-how and more generic (personal and social) competences. Knowledge comprises general education (German, economics and social studies), industrial knowledge (labour law, health and safety, environmental protection), occupational knowledge (technical knowledge for the occupation, occupation-related maths and drawing), and firm-specific knowledge (Hanf 2009). The system is concerned not only with developing competences and a broad knowledge and skills base related to a range of activities within the construction labour process but also with developing socially responsible individuals, able to reflect on their own actions and to actively co-create their social environments, both in the workplace and in society as a whole (Halfpap 2000).

The construction industry succeeds in developing such occupational capacity through its stepped system of training, known as the *Stufenausbildung für Bauberufe*, which is staged over three years, with the first year providing a common basic training covering all construction training areas, the second divided into building, finishing and civil engineering, and the third involving specialization into one or other of the 16 *Berufe*, including bricklaying. The German *Facharbeiter* (skilled workers) qualification is more advanced than both the English Apprenticeship (NVQ level 2) and many of the Advanced Apprenticeship (level 3) programmes in terms of know-how, theoretical knowledge and personal attributes. However, the number of bricklayer apprentices in Germany has been dropping dramatically, from 31,024 in 1999 to 11,176 in 2007, prompting improvements in apprentice wage levels in an effort to attract more young people into the industry (Hanf 2009).

In the Netherlands, though VET qualifications can be obtained through school-based or dual tracks (work-based with a college element), bricklaying is largely dual-based, either with a specific employer or within a workshop organized by a group of firms, and the duration for the more common level 2 qualification is – as in England – two years. Qualifications are awarded on the basis of successful performance of activities or tasks and competences and are, as in Germany, based on the integration of knowledge, know-how and social and personal dimensions and relate to comprehensive occupational profiles with a broad scope of activities (Westerhuis 2009). Indeed in the Netherlands the qualification file (on which the curriculum is based) includes theoretical underpinning knowledge, notably mathematics, as well as 'occupational' and 'civic' competences, with the latter consisting of lifelong learning, career and citizenship competence and including 'liberal' subjects of general education, such as Dutch, English and mathematics, political participation and personal health. Occupational knowledge relates to core tasks seen to define the occupation and which, for a level 2 bricklayer, include bricklaying and gluing.

Similarly, in France, the most common route, the Certificate of Professional Ability (CAP), is integrated within the education system, regulated by the Ministry of Education, and takes two to three years to complete. For bricklaying, however, apprenticeship is dominant (80% of trainees) and the relevant qualification is that of '*maçon*' or mason rather than 'bricklayer', reflecting the different nature of the occupation. The qualification is defined in terms of four main functions (preparation/organization, implementation and execution, maintenance of equipment, and communication) which relate to: preparation of the work; organization of the workplace; installation of a structure; dealing with site waste; scaffolding; shell construction in blocks and bricks; masonry; reinforcements; formwork; concrete; components; rendering and waterproofing; piping and conduits; keeping equipment in good condition; exchanging information. These then relate to three competences that provide the basis for the curriculum – information and communication, organization and decision-making, and execution – and in turn break down into detailed competences and specific expertise and knowledge deemed necessary for underpinning the performance of the tasks. As in Germany and the Netherlands, VET in France is aimed at the person as a whole, preparing individuals as human beings, citizens and producers. Thus, CAP includes substantial elements of theoretical knowledge (mathematics and physics) and of general education (French and a foreign language, sports, history, geography and citizenship) with civic and social competencies explicitly part of the curriculum.

In contrast, the bricklaying qualification in England attached to the apprenticeship framework, consisting of the work-based NVQ and the Construction Diploma (the theoretical element as well as key skills which tend to be largely remedial), is considerably more restricted compared with that on the continent. Construction VET courses are characterized by a strong demarcation between different construction trades with no common basis and NVQs themselves are not linked to a curriculum but derive from an analysis of job functions and rely on assessment of performance in the workplace (Brockmann *et al.* 2009c). Competences refer to a narrow set of activities, defined in terms of detailed tasks and representing an accumulation of individual skills, whilst underpinning knowledge is limited compared with Germany (Steedman 1992). The NVQ 2 in bricklaying is largely concentrated on erecting and setting out masonry structures, though it also includes general workplace safety, conforming to efficient workplace practices, and moving and handling resources. A typical course of bricklaying in a further education (FE) college covers: building solid and cavity walls, piers, chimneys, flues and arches; drainage systems; basic scaffolding; setting out a rectangular building; health and safety on site; and a key skills element (English, Maths, ICT) (Lambeth College 2006). There is a paucity of the general and civic education elements provided in many continental countries, though the Standards do make reference to knowledge of the role of the occupation and the industry (CITB 2006).

The long-term tendency has been one of decline in the number and proportion of construction apprentices, that is those with an employer, who in 2008 represented only 9,877 of the 35,217 trainee starters on construction 'craft' training courses, mainly (70%) at level 2 (Construction Skills 2008). Of all starters 55% or 19,370 were studying for a Construction Award (now Diploma) and 8,949 were bricklaying students, implying that many, even the majority, are not apprentices but college-based. Indeed, there are increasing numbers seeking to become apprentices who are unable to do so due to diminishing training places with employers (Blackman 2007). Many trainees as a result follow full-time college-based courses to achieve Diplomas but then experience difficulty obtaining sufficient work experience to succeed in subsequently finding employment within the occupation, and hence in achieving an NVQ.

In summary, in the continental countries VET constitutes the continuation of general education through the occupation, with trainees following a regulated programme of VET linked to a curriculum. Programmes aim to develop the person as an active citizen in wider society as well as for the occupation and cover a broad knowledge and skill base which enables learners to work in a variety of functions and areas of construction. While the VET systems in England, France and the Netherlands have been reformed to become competence based, so as to more closely reflect the needs of the labour market, the notion of competence in the two latter countries encompasses a broader range of activities and is multi-dimensional, representing the integration of theoretical knowledge, practical know-how and social and personal competences. Bricklayers have an understanding of the labour process as a whole and their position within it and are able to exercise professional judgement and to work independently and in co-operation with others. The majority of bricklaying trainees in France, Germany and the Netherlands are – despite the embedding of VET in the education system – on the dual-based track, either with a single or group of employers, whilst in England they are on the school-based track, despite the labour market-based nature of the NVQ.

Currency of bricklaying qualification in the labour market

Given the broad occupational capacity embodied in the bricklaying qualifications of France, Germany and the Netherlands, it is no surprise that the resulting scope of activities of bricklayers is far broader and the level of autonomy higher than in England. The bricklaying qualification enables the holder to carry out complex tasks in relation to the wider work processes whilst in England it conforms to the 'skills-based model' described in Chapter 6, being based on narrow specialization and on the accreditation of existing skills rather than on occupational capacity as the outcome of a regulated programme of VET.

The English bricklaying qualification reflects the reality of the labour market where adherence to the traditional trades has meant a reduced scope of activity and ever larger areas lying outside these that resist classification in terms of VET and the recognition of qualifications, including partitioning, formwork, ground-works and concreting. Indeed, with this narrowing down of skills, the status of the English bricklaying trade has weakened and the labour market has come to conform more closely to the 'secondary labour markets' of Piore and Sabel (1984), which depend on external recruitment markets and arise when skills are depleted and institutional regulation and VET are weak. These differ from occupational markets in the lack of empowerment of employees and of stability of employment, the exercise of managerial prerogative, lack of training and low qualification levels.

In conformity with this picture, the bricklayer in England generally has a 'self-employed' status and is employed by bricklaying subcontractors, taking on contracts for bricklaying work on different sites and from different main contractors and resourcing each contract anew so that levels of labour turnover are high (Brockmann et al. 2009c; EFBWW 2010). Such employers are more interested in skills for the immediate job in hand which, together with the deregulation of the labour market, has meant a fragmentation of the labour process into discrete work processes in which the intellectual functions of labour (planning, co-ordinating, controlling, evaluating) have often been sharply separated from the executive (manual) function. Bricklaying is thereby generally restricted to erecting and setting out masonry structures while activities such as setting out, reading drawings, ordering and selecting materials, and the planning, monitoring and delivering of the work may be carried out by managers, site engineers or supervisors. As a result, it represents a diminishing area of activity, with bricklayers numbering 97,030 out of a total construction workforce of about 1.9 million (BERR 2008). The restricted nature of the bricklaying trade is particularly the case in the housebuilding sector, where the bricklayer is largely confined to laying bricks and blocks; on commercial projects, they may be required to carry out a wider range of tasks, including working with stone and concrete, erecting arches and using sophisticated bonds. Because of the job-specific nature of qualifications, there are also few opportunities for career progression and a reduced permeability to move from the trade level to site management and beyond, as graduates are increasingly recruited into such roles.

As a trade, bricklayers are rewarded for their outputs, rather than for their personal competences or occupational qualifications per se. Wages thereby generally refer to a specific performance, so that – even when on day rates – they are generally paid according to the price agreed for the job-in-hand, implying variable rates, rather than to the rates laid down in the collective agreement. They are also – as with a traditional tradesman – still invariably expected to provide their own tools. In this situation, the currency of bricklaying qualifications remains low as entry to the labour market is not dependent on the completion of a regulated VET programme. What is valued on the labour market above qualifications are skills and experience, certified by the CSCS card commonly obtained through on-site assessment of skills performance and completion of a health and safety test. Many have as a result picked up skills informally and are confined largely to laying bricks and blocks; many too are migrants, who are employed on a large scale, given often acute labour shortages (Chan *et al.* 2010). The weakness of occupational labour markets in Britain is of course not just peculiar to bricklaying and represents a characteristic of the labour market, associated by Marsden (2007) with the weakness of the VET system on which they are founded.

The actual scope of activity in the workplace strongly depends on the firm and the labour market and, as a result, bricklaying associated with the trade labour market in England contrasts with bricklaying in the more recognizably 'occupational' construction labour markets of continental countries such as Germany and the Netherlands (Clarke and Wall 2000; Clarke and Herrmann 2004b). Occupational labour markets rely on recognized qualifications, acquired through the VET system, for transferability between firms and jobs. So in Germany and the Netherlands the currency of qualifications is high as these are critical for labour market entry, a guarantee that the person has completed a comprehensive and nationally recognized VET programme, and a means to progress to higher qualification levels. In the Netherlands, for instance, where the bricklaying qualification is part of an integrated education system, there are clear progression routes to level 3 and beyond. However, despite this, the Dutch bricklayer pales in significance against the far more prominent carpenter and is less important even than the English, with bricklayers representing only 3% of the workforce and bricklaying trainees rapidly decreasing in number (Clarke and Wall 1996). Thus, unlike Germany, where the bricklayer is the dominant construction occupation, in the Netherlands it is the carpenter. Compared to the wide scope of activity of the carpenter, the scope of activity encompassed in the Dutch bricklaying qualification is relatively narrow, largely restricted to brickwork, and of a lower level – typically the equivalent of the English NVQ level 2. Whilst VET provides the overwhelmingly dominant route into the labour market, 36% of bricklayers, or 21% of those less than 30 years old, are not qualified (Brockmann *et al.* 2009d).

In Germany, in contrast, bricklayers represent 15% of the construction workforce and their social identity is especially strong, claiming, as a *Beruf*, respected social recognition (Brockmann *et al.* 2010b). Responsibilities of bricklayers embrace a broad range of activities in relation to the wider labour and work processes such as carpentry and civil engineering. They are able to work autonomously and in co-operation with others, set up construction sites, and process contracts from initial planning to handing over the completed work, may undertake building work in a variety of contexts (newly built, restoration, industrial) and work with a variety of materials (including bricks, stone and concrete). As a result, they represent the main occupation within the construction sector, one which is pivotal to further progression to site foreperson and beyond (Clarke and Wall 1996). However, the proportion of bricklayers with the qualification *Maurer*, whilst very high, has also been decreasing (from 85% in 1999 to 82% in 2005). Indeed everywhere the average age of bricklayers has been increasing and there is a high labour turnover amongst younger workers.

In France too the *maçon* is by far the most important construction occupation, representing 39% of the construction workforce of 1.4 million. However, here, significant numbers of bricklayers are not qualified (Brockmann *et al.* 2010b), so that, whilst qualifications have a strong currency for labour market entry, there is only a loose relationship between the qualification and the occupation of *maçon*. Indeed, bricklayers are employed and can progress on the basis of their qualifications or their work experience. The breadth of the occupation *maçon* is particularly pronounced, with bricklaying itself as only one component of a much broader occupational scope. The *maçon* has no clear occupational boundaries and is, in collaboration with other occupations, expected to build a house from the foundations to the roof, including preparing, monitoring and delivering the work and embracing activities such as stone masonry, plastering, finishing, concreting, steel fitting, formwork and mounting door and window frames. Whilst the 'craft' tradition remains strong, it is gradually giving way to an industrial and occupational concept, marked by the abolition of the difference between the *maçon* and the *maçon* specialized in concrete.

A key difficulty in comparing bricklaying qualifications and in implementing the EQF thus arises from the variation in the scope of activities bricklayers carry out in the workplace. Each country varies too in the extent to which recognized qualifications are a prerequisite for labour market entry and provide a degree of occupational mobility and capacity sufficient to allow bricklayers to work across a wide range of functions, across firms and sub-sectors of construction and even across countries. In the English 'skills-based model', based on specialization, rather than occupational capacity, the emphasis is on the accreditation of individual sets of specialized skills (Clarke and Winch 2006). In contrast, in countries such as France and Germany and, to a lesser extent, the Netherlands, whilst there is generally a higher degree of specialization in large enterprises than in smaller firms, the vast majority of bricklayers are employed by small and medium enterprises (SMEs) who require polyvalence, commonly encompassing activities of related occupations such as plastering or even carpentry. They have a high level of autonomy and an understanding of the entire work process, the wider industry, and their position within it. The occupational capacity of bricklayers, based on a multi-dimensional concept of competence, integrates manual and intellectual tasks and requires them to draw on and integrate a range of resources of different types of knowledge, practical know-how, and social and personal competences to deal with complex situations in the workplace. Thus, there is concern with the ability to plan, carry out and evaluate the work, based on professional judgement and responsible decision-making in co-operation with other occupations in the construction process. Bricklayers are expected to use a variety of materials (bricks, concrete, reinforced concrete and prefabricated elements) and tools and to work within a broad range of construction areas: new build, urban regeneration, restoration, and repair and maintenance.

To conclude, in attempting to align bricklaying qualifications across Europe the first difference to be considered is the level of qualification, with the typically NVQ level 2 qualification in England and an equivalent level in the Netherlands being more restricted in scope and lacking the underpinning knowledge found in the equivalent of level 3 or above of the German qualification. In these countries, too, compared to France and Germany, bricklayers represent a smaller and steadily decreasing proportion of the construction workforce. The second difference between the four countries is in the scope and depth, in part relating to the different nature of bricklaying and the labour market in which the bricklayer operates, as well as the system of regulation governing both the VET system and recognition of the qualification. At one extreme, bricklaying remains a trade, with bricklayers rewarded for their particular output and largely restricted to laying bricks with little concern for their potential and social and personal development over a working life. At the other, bricklaying is an occupation, with bricklayers valued for their often broad and social qualities as well as potential ability, both assumed to be embodied in the qualification which acts as a key means of entry into the labour market. This latter type of bricklayer therefore depends on an occupational labour market, which contrasts with the secondary labour market on which the more narrowly trained bricklayer depends.

Lorry driving: a regulated occupation?

Lorry driving provides an interesting contrast to bricklaying, never having had the traditional status of a trade, unless we consider the carter, and struggling to become an occupation in its own right with a recognized scheme of training. In France, Germany and England, only a small proportion of drivers hold a specific LGV driving qualification above the driving licence (25%, 10% and less than 10%, respectively). The driving licence is compulsory and subject to European legislation since 2009, when the Directive on the Certificate of Professional Competence (CPC) came into effect, extending current requirements for the initial qualification by requiring a minimum of 35 hours additional training every five years. Already some years ago, France added a compulsory module (FIMO) to the licence which incorporates most of the CPC elements.

The scope of activities of the lorry driver in England and France is very restricted, largely confined to driving, and there are few opportunities for career progression. Qualifications are correspondingly job-specific, of a narrow nature, and add no automatic labour market value. Just as with bricklaying, lorry driving in England conforms to a skill-based model, underpinned by a sharp demarcation of functions and division of labour between different tasks such as driving and planning. The NVQ L2 Driving Goods Vehicles – as the lowest qualification above the licence – has been developed to improve the profile of the industry but is not linked to a training programme or curriculum and, being restricted to driving and operating the vehicle, is held by few drivers. Competences relate directly to narrowly defined tasks and performance standards, rather than to individual development, and are derived from an analysis of job functions. The focus is on the skills required for a particular task or job, rather than on social, personal or civic aspects, so that general and civic education is deemed largely unnecessary.

The VET system in England is regulated largely by the relevant Sector Skills Council, Skills for Logistics, and is designed to be employer-led, though there is no collective interest representation of either employers or trade unions. The Council simply consults with a limited group of larger employers and some training providers and the involvement of trade unions is minimal. The English NVQ for lorry driving does not usually involve training although courses are provided, without, however, involving underpinning knowledge or general education. As a result, lorry driving represents an extreme case of an occupation in which the expectations of some employers and VET organizations are low. Indeed, the manager of a Heavy Goods Vehicle training company considered that the main aim of training in this area was to induce obedience and rule-following rather than judgement and discretion and that significant prior educational achievement did not constitute any advantage for gaining competence, thereby reflecting the English view that competence is about performing narrowly prescribed tasks. However, this view was not universally expressed by our informants, one Business Manager for an international haulage firm considering that the ability to diagnose problems was a valuable attribute for a driver and contributed to the efficiency of the firm.

The main French lorry driving qualification of *titre* is rather different not only from the English one but from the CAP qualifications of the mainstream VET system in being regulated by the Ministry of Labour and not by the Ministry of Education, though it is similarly developed and monitored by a consultative committee consisting of social partners and experts. One reason for the predominance of the *titre* is the regulated age restriction for lorry driving, from either 18 or 21 years old depending on the type of lorry, which is incompatible with the classic entry age of 16 for the CAP. The *titre* aims to prepare trainees (unemployed adults and/or employees) for a specific job and, as such, does not contain elements of general education though a national framework for assessment is developed by educationalists, with the training institutions developing the detailed curriculum (Méhaut 2009). The *titre* is less comprehensive than the less often acquired CAP lorry driving qualification and constitutes something of a hybrid model, linked to a curriculum but consisting largely of practical training of skills with a training provider (500 hours in the case of the public one), complemented by courses on legislation, health and safety, basic vehicle maintenance and the use of ICT. Other forms of knowledge, such as mathematics, as well as social and personal competencies, which may be regarded as desirable or even required by employers, are not covered in the curriculum. The competence framework with performance indicators on which it is founded is derived from a framework of activities, based on an analysis of tasks. Competences refer to these tasks and to the 'general and technical skills and expertise' and 'related knowledge' which form the basis of the curriculum.

In terms of the currency of the qualification in the labour market, the German qualification – unlike in England and France – is linked to a higher wage grade, whilst in the Netherlands it is an important condition for labour market entry. As with bricklaying, both systems are tightly regulated by government and conform to the model of social partnership. The only lorry driving qualifications available are those through the traditional, comprehensive VET routes, with trainees following a regulated programme which includes a broad knowledge and skills base. The resulting scope of activities of drivers in these two countries is far broader than in England and France, with a high level of autonomy and responsibility including: planning and co-ordinating transport, negotiating with customers and with other actors in the work process (e.g. transport office), administration and vehicle maintenance.

The German lorry driving qualification of the Dual System is distinct from that of the other countries in that, as with bricklaying, it is not developed according to a task analysis but aims to develop 'competence of action-taking' (*Handlungskompetenz*), conceived in terms of different dimensions of occupational, social and personal competence. Individual competencies, or the learning outcomes specified in the training profile, serve as indicators of whether the aims of the VET programme have been achieved. So the lorry driving qualification involves 840 hours of general education – including German, mathematics and economics – and classroom-based occupational education structured to reflect situations in the workplace and organized around 'learning fields' (*Lernfelder*), which also include a foreign language. The knowledge base is extensive and includes theoretical occupational and industrial knowledge (e.g. knowledge of the labour process, planning and logistics, labour and industrial relations regulations).

In the Netherlands, the lorry driving qualification is also part of an integrated education system, with clear progression routes to level 3 (planner) and 4 (manager – storage and transport), and produced in consultation with the social partners and representatives from VET schools according to the government-validated framework. Like other qualifications, the drivers' qualification is broadly conceived, covering a set of activities aimed to ensure occupational and social mobility, with its content based on four core tasks identified by the sectoral representatives and sub-divided into work processes, which are in turn broken down into 'components of competences' with associated performance criteria. Whilst VET qualifications can be obtained through the school-based or dual tracks, LGV driving is largely dual-based, over two years, with the qualification file on which the curriculum is based containing elements deemed necessary to ensure competence in a broad sense and including 'occupational' and 'civic' competences, such as Dutch, English, mathematics, another foreign language (French or German) as well as social abilities. The occupational knowledge base relates largely to non-systematic, factual and practical knowledge, including, as in the German case, legislation, administration and vehicle maintenance.

Thus, LGV driving qualifications differ between countries in important respects, though these differences are similar to those found for bricklaying. Crucially the

Dutch, English and French frameworks are 'competence-based', derived from an analysis of tasks in the workplace, related to the underpinning knowledge and skills deemed necessary for their performance, and awarded on the basis of performance assessment. The main difference is that, in the Dutch and German cases, competence is holistically defined, serves as the basis for curriculum development and embraces the notion of development of the individual, building on the multiple resources drawn on when confronted with any particular task. In the Netherlands, the qualification has a twofold value, for labour market entry as well as for further study. And in Germany it covers both freight and passenger transport and offers opportunities for progression through the vocational route. In England and France, in contrast, whilst measures have been introduced to raise the profile of the occupation so as to attract new entrants, qualifications are not linked to the wider education system but prepare specifically for labour market entry for the job of lorry driver, with the French qualification also including the driving licence. In England, a qualifications structure has been introduced to improve the status of drivers but has not been widely taken up as employers see little value in training beyond legislative requirements. Only in the Netherlands is the qualification a prerequisite for labour market entry.

Conclusions

As we have seen in the case of bricklaying, an occupation in the sense in which the term can be applied in Northern Europe is an established category of labour, involving a defined range of activity demarcated by the social partners within a sector. It represents a definite division of labour, mapped onto the sectoral or industrial structure of the national economy and formed through the VET system. At the same time, the conception of labour embodied in an occupation retains some sense of the unity between the intellectual and manual aspects of labour, however attenuated that may sometimes be. Entry into such occupations is predominantly on the basis of qualifications obtained through the VET system and in turn recognized through collective bargaining agreements. Bricklaying in France, Germany and the Netherlands represents – to a greater or lesser extent – an occupation in this sense, with qualifications grounded in the education system through the curriculum whilst at the same time referring to activities in the labour market. In the case of England, the bridge between the VET system and the labour market is less apparent, as the qualification reflects labour market realities, whereby bricklaying continues to exhibit trade characteristics more than social and educational principles. However, here too the situation is changing as VET, even by default, becomes more grounded in the education system, so challenging the trade status of the bricklayer. Is the implication that the labour force is becoming more dependent on occupational qualifications obtained through a state and social-partner regulated VET system for entry into the labour market?

In the case of lorry driving, we can also begin to see an emerging occupational labour market, particularly with respect to the Dutch and German systems which are – unlike the English and French – embedded in the VET system. The important difference between bricklaying and lorry driving is, however, that on health and safety grounds the latter is governed by European legislation requiring minimum levels of training in order to acquire a licence to practise. Though there are also critical health and safety considerations in the case of bricklaying, such a licence is not required. The question raised, therefore, is how far the EQF alone will succeed in establishing a system of equivalence between qualifications like those for bricklaying or whether regulation is not also necessary to improve and ensure adequate levels of VET.

8

HIGHER EDUCATION QUALIFICATIONS: CONVERGENCE AND DIVERGENCE IN SOFTWARE ENGINEERING AND NURSING

Michaela Brockmann

Introduction

This chapter examines qualifications and vocational education and training (VET) for nursing and software engineering in the four countries – England, France, Germany and the Netherlands. VET systems are never static but in constant flux in the context of socio-economic change. The chapter will seek to identify the main drivers of change, including those pertaining to the labour market, the (vocational) education system and also society at large, and explore the ways in which countries have responded by adjusting and reforming their VET systems and particular qualifications. In doing so, it will identify tendencies of convergence and divergence in relation to qualifications in software engineering and nursing. Thus, part of our investigation will examine the prospects for zones of mutual trust (ZMTs) (Coles and Oates 2004) as a precondition for the feasibility of the European Qualifications Framework (EQF) (see Chapter 9).

In both nursing and software engineering we found evidence of an ongoing tension between, on the one hand, demands for broad educational profiles and, on the other labour market pressures for workplace-specific skills. This appears to mirror Rauner's (2006, 2007) distinction between VET models that focus on education of the person for an occupation ('*berufliche Bildung*') on the one hand, and those aimed at the 'employability' of individuals, on the other. In the first model (exemplified by the 'Dual System of apprenticeship'), VET is integrated into a comprehensive education system and designed to develop the ability to act autonomously and competently within an occupational field. Qualifications are obtained through the successful completion of courses developed through negotiation with the social partners, integrating theoretical knowledge and workplace learning. In the second model, prevalent in Anglo-Saxon countries and presuming a high level of general knowledge, a 'market of qualifications' enables individuals to enhance their employability through continuing vocational education or certification of sets of competencies acquired either through work experience or modularized courses.

In a recent publication, Kraus *et al.* (2008) suggest that the notion of employability epitomizes the close interrelationship between the labour market and education and the ways in which economic developments have required changes in education and training. Notably, and echoing Rauner's (2006, 2007) conceptualization, employability is premised on the need for lifelong learning and emphasizes individual responsibility for updating skills and competences. It has been high on the political agenda at both national and European Union (EU) level and has been actively promoted by the EU as part of the Copenhagen Process:

> The European Council set the strategic objective for the European Union to become the world's most dynamic knowledge-based economy. The development of high quality vocational education and training is a crucial and integral part of this strategy, notably in terms of promoting social inclusion, cohesion, mobility, employability and competitiveness.
>
> (EC 2002: 1)

Our investigation found that calls for greater workplace orientation are common in relation to both nursing and software engineering VET. However, while software engineering is characterized by an increasing emphasis on 'flexibility' and on lifelong learning as an individual's responsibility, reflecting the notion of employability, comprehensive VET for nursing is safeguarded by national and EU regulation.

At first glance, there seemed to be considerable convergence in relation to the nursing qualifications in the four countries. Indeed, it is arguable that a ZMT has been established through EU regulation on the basis of an 'input'-based system, that is, one related to curricula, complemented by common structural changes to the sector and the occupation. However, there are considerable variations between the national qualifications, reflecting the different national contexts. Our investigation suggested further convergence in relation to software engineering. We found, for instance, an increasing focus on high-level transferable skills and competence and on workplace learning, indicating what appeared to be an emergent ZMT underpinned by common global developments in the sector. However, for any comparative analysis of qualifications, it is important to contextualize the changes that have taken place in order to fully understand the meaning and significance of particular approaches.

Nursing: convergence through regulation?

Nursing VET has seen significant developments over the last two decades, resulting in changes in the status and role of nurses and contributing to a degree of convergence of nursing qualifications and occupational profiles across the EU.

Socio-economic factors, including an ageing population and restructuring of health services, have led to changes in the role of nursing in terms of both the scope of activities and levels of responsibility. These changes, combined with calls from nursing bodies for nurses to have professional status in their own right, have resulted in a preference for broad educational profiles for nurses and the integration of nursing VET into higher education (HE) (Spitzer and Perrenoud 2006). Employers, trade unions, regulatory bodies and practitioners alike supported a broader profile so as to enable nurses to adapt to continuing changes in the nursing role in response to societal change and to encourage lifelong learning (ibid.). However, not unlike the situation in relation to software engineering, the increasing professionalization of nursing has led to concerns regarding the integration of theory and practice as nurses are perceived to lack practical skills, provoking in turn moves towards competence-based profiles linked to particular skills requirements. With the exception of Germany, where there have been no moves so far towards outcomes-based qualifications, these developments are apparent in all our countries, albeit to a varying extent.

A distinct driver of change is governmental regulation, which seeks to uphold certain standards related to the breadth of knowledge and skills. Thus, in contrast to software engineering, which is characterized by increased flexibility, nursing qualifications are subject to legislation safeguarding the boundaries of the occupation. As a regulated profession, the qualification, obtained in a highly formalized VET system, is a pre-condition for registration. Indeed, VET is subject to strict regulation both through national bodies and EU legislation. At national level, all countries conform to some extent to the social partnership model, with inputs from employers, unions and educationalists. The European Directive 2005/36/EC for Health and Social Care Professions regulates the number of hours to be devoted to theory and practice, as well as the broad content of the curriculum in terms of scientific knowledge, clinical experience and ethical conduct. The intention of the Directive is to enhance EU-wide mobility of qualified professionals through the mutual recognition of qualifications 'with a minimum of red tape but with due safeguards for public health and safety and consumer protection' (Department of Health 2007: 3). By effectively regulating the broad input of VET programmes, the Directive creates an important basis for mutual trust. In addition, the integration of nursing VET into HE is bound by the regulations of the EU Bologna Process, designed to harmonize European HE, further consolidating moves towards a 'unified European platform of more solid pre-registration programs' (Spitzer and Perrenoud 2006: 150).

The professionalization of nursing VET in the four countries

In all four countries, VET in nursing is school-based with clinical placements. In Germany, the nursing qualification is obtained after three years through programmes in vocational schools. In England, it is awarded after obtaining the Diploma through a three-year course located within the HE system, and the trend is towards degree-level education. In France, a three-year VET programme is provided in nursing training institutes but moves are underway to provide part of the VET in universities. In the Netherlands nursing qualifications are obtained predominantly through the four-year VET programme, although there is a HE route.

As the International Council of Nurses has observed, the development of 'advanced nursing practice', defined as 'registered nurses who have acquired the expert knowledge base, complex decision-making skills, and clinical competencies for expanded practice', has been a global phenomenon (Sheer and Wong 2008: 204). It has emanated from a combination of factors, including the restructuring of health services to cope with increased demands, skill shortages in nursing, and attempts by practitioners and educationalists to establish nursing as a profession in its own right, independent of medical doctors (Kirpal 2003, 2004). However, beyond a common standard achieved through EU regulation, there are important differences in nursing practice and VET between countries within Europe.

While degree-level education pathways have been created in all four countries, the increase in degree-level nurses has been much more significant in England and France. In these countries, this development has coincided with the creation of nurse specialists and consultants. There is a high overlap with roles from related professions, notably medical doctors, as new responsibilities increasingly include medical tasks (such as inserting a needle into a vein). The process has involved a controversial shift towards increasing the theoretical scientific input at the expense of practical (caring) tasks. The new role has been reinforced in England and France by the delegation of routine caring tasks to care assistants. The specialist positions of nurses in these countries have given nurses their own area of expertise, their own caseload and high levels of autonomy (Yam 2004).

In all countries the role of nurses in the workplace has changed from a traditional caring one towards the performance of more 'technical' tasks. However, the extent to which they have been required to take up tasks previously carried out by doctors varies significantly across the countries. Thus, in Germany and to a lesser extent in the Netherlands, nurses have not been able to encroach on areas associated with the medical profession, perhaps reflecting the degree to which it is protected in these countries. In the Netherlands, nurses with HE level qualifications have taken on more specialized tasks in line with technical innovation, for example in intensive care. In Germany, there is a strong division between the caring and medical professions. In addition, the lack of support for advanced nursing practice has been attributed to a higher ratio of General Practitioners (GPs) to nurses (thereby reducing the need for nurses to perform GP tasks), underlining the significance of labour market pressures in shaping occupational profiles (Sheer and Wong 2008). Equally important is the traditionally low status of nursing VET in full-time schools in Germany, compared to both the German Dual System of apprenticeship and nursing education in other European countries. Nevertheless even in Germany, changes have taken place in nursing roles, reflecting increased concern with financial constraints as they are entrusted with a growing administrative workload and responsibility for documentation and budgeting in a tightly monitored health system.

Integration of theory and practice

Nursing serves as an example of the potential conflict between broad academic education and workplace-relevant skills, epitomizing the trend towards workplace-oriented learning evident in many European countries since the 1980s.

It is striking that in the two countries that have gone furthest down the route of degree-level education, England and France, the move towards a broad academic knowledge and skills base in nursing has led to concerns about a lack of integration of theory and practice. While, as in software engineering, employers in all our countries valued academic 'generic' skills such as problem solving, there was severe criticism, particularly from employers and regulatory bodies, of the lack of practice-relevant skills. In all four countries, the changes have led to role conflicts and debates concerning the neglect of 'the art of caring' or, in other words, nurses' responsibility for holistic patient care. In order to enhance the workplace relevance of qualifications, many countries have introduced competence-based approaches, identifying specific clinical competences which then serve as the basis for both VET programmes and job profiles (Spitzer and Perrenoud 2006). France and the Netherlands have established competence-based qualifications systems and the nursing qualifications have been mapped onto these. As Spitzer and Perrenoud (2006) argue, this has produced a shift away from the broad academic profile originally envisaged. However, as has been shown in Chapter 5, the notion of competence is interpreted very differently in different national contexts.

In the particular approaches taken by the different countries, we can detect a degree of path dependency (see, for example, Pierson 2004) in terms of adherence to established education and labour market systems. Competences in France and the Netherlands still relate to comprehensive qualifications and rely on the integration of theoretical knowledge, practical know-how and personal and social competences. England, on the other hand, where the tension between broad academic education and employer-specific skills is greatest, has opted for a more skills-based approach. The exception is Germany, where nursing is not based on the principle of *Handlungskompetenz* or competency of action-taking, which underpins the *Berufe* of the Dual System (see Chapter 4).

In England, the trend towards professionalization has long been evident, involving a break with the apprenticeship model and – through NHS (National Health Service) Project 2000 – the introduction of supernumerary status (Bradshaw 2001). Today, there is a strong move towards an all-graduate profession. All major stakeholders, including the body representing nurses and employers, the Royal College of Nursing (RCN), and the regulatory body, the Nursing and Midwifery Council (NMC), support a broad scientific knowledge base, including medical and social science which is seen to underpin nursing practice (although the extent to which social sciences in particular are desirable is highly controversial). To some extent, our informants subscribed to a multi-dimensional notion of competence based on theoretical knowledge, practical know-how and social competences, particularly observation and interpersonal skills. However, the notion of competence is not an integral part of VET, which lacks, for instance, civic competences. Indeed, recent developments are indicative of the English task-based approach to competence. Echoing earlier studies (e.g. Spitzer and Perrenoud 2006), a conflict is evident between, on the one hand, the current 'input' model and, on the other, initiatives – favoured by the NMC and by NHS employers – to structure learning according to 'essential skills clusters' relating to particular tasks in the workplace. Continuing VET has, in contrast, been dominated by the outcomes-based model, with for example, a framework which facilitates progression in terms of skills and knowledge defined by the employer (Department of Health 2004). Similarly, the National Workforce Competences developed by Skills for Health (2007: 1) 'describe what needs to happen in the workplace – not what people are like'.

In France and the Netherlands, a multi-dimensional model of competence is integral to nursing VET and an outcomes-based approach, with competences relating to workplace situations, is not seen as contradicting the development of the person. In France, the three-year programme currently provided in special training institutes (IFSI) comprises broad scientific and industrial knowledge as well as social and personal competences. On the one hand, there are plans to deliver part of the course at university level, acknowledging the need for an enhanced status and academic knowledge base for nurses in view of the changing nursing role. On the other, the nursing qualification is to be integrated into the competence-based qualification framework. In France, there are clear tensions between the academic and vocational models of education, with different stakeholders favouring different approaches. However, the need for a high level of education may be reconciled with an outcomes-based approach, centred on a multi-dimensional notion of competence.

In the Netherlands, nursing education is well established at the vocational or further education (FE) level and students follow a four-year course. While this may reflect the lack of a perceived need for advanced nursing practice, the qualification is embedded in a qualification framework for health which includes HE and there are clear progression routes. At FE level, there has long been a concern with the integration of theory and practice. The Dutch VET system is centred on the notion of competence (see Chapter 5) and is explicit about the desired attributes and attitudes of nurses to deal with potential conflicts arising, such as finding a balance between involvement and detachment. In view of socio-economic change and a new ethos of patient-centred care, there has been a concern with situated learning and promoting student construction of knowledge; of the four countries, Dutch VET has gone furthest down the route of self-directed learning, albeit with varying success.

Nursing VET in Germany has probably the lowest status compared to the other countries, as well as, and particularly, to its renowned Dual System of apprentice-ship. It is provided through three-year courses in full-time vocational schools and permeability with HE is severely restricted. As yet, occupational profiles for nurses have not been defined in terms of competences, as it remains an input-based system; neither is *Handlungskompetenz* an organizing principle.

Notwithstanding the broader academic knowledge in England and France, the occupational profiles of nurses and staff development in all the four countries are governed largely by the requirements of employers in terms of skill needs. In the context of restructuring and efficiency gains sought through, for example, the merging of wards, there are greater demands for flexibility, with nurses required to work across tasks and in different departments, according to staffing demands (Kirpal 2003/2004). An example of this is the French *Service de Compensation et de Suppléance*, constituting a pool of nurses who are allocated to different hospital departments according to demand.

The trend towards professionalization has sparked debates about whether nursing will in fact become too elitist, at odds with contemporary initiatives based on equal partnership between professionals and lay people (Gerrish *et al.* 2003). However, to the extent that the body of knowledge associated with nursing, as well as the nursing role in the workplace, is controlled by health care managers rather than by the nurses themselves, the occupation can be more accurately described as a semi-profession (Etzioni 1969).

In summary, beyond certain standards of knowledge and practical know-how legislated by the EU, we can discern considerable variation in VET provision for nursing in the four countries. Different countries experience different pressures and deal with these within their particular societal, VET and labour market contexts, for instance the greater perceived need for an expanded nursing role in England, France and to a lesser extent in the Netherlands. Therefore, in these countries nursing education is integrated with higher education to a greater extent than in Germany. The German qualification has yet to undergo major reform. VET provision in France and the Netherlands displays greatest similarity in terms of the competence development of the person. Both countries have strong VET traditions and, in resorting to a competence-based approach, have safeguarded the multi-dimensional conception of competence. In England and France, while there are clear tensions between the academic and outcomes-based model, the stronger academic basis of nursing education implies that the respective qualifications have to be aligned with a higher EQF level than that associated with requalification of German and the majority of Dutch nurses.

Software engineering

Information technology (IT) is at the core of what has been coined 'the knowledge society', which, at a basic level, refers to the production, organization and exchange of knowledge rather than products (Temple 2004). However, the term has not been without controversy and commentators have pointed to a polarization of skills within the sector, with a segment of low-skilled work marked by a high level of routinization (Warhurst *et al.* 2006). IT is a relatively new sector, without a long-standing tradition of VET, and marked by accelerated change in technologies and product development at a global level, accompanied by innovative work organization. Software engineering, as a critical occupation within the IT sector, can be characterized by the notion of 'employability' and the need for lifelong learning, so integral to software engineers' work (Nerland 2008).

Labour market pressures have resulted in different requirements for VET qualifications, with clear shifts in content at national levels, mirroring changes in the skill requirements of software engineers. While there are differences, there are also common trends in VET across the four countries, evident in the increased emphasis on:

- competence-based qualifications, oriented towards situations in the workplace;
- social competences; and
- work-based learning, as part of both initial VET (for example, through apprenticeships) and continuing VET and lifelong learning.

There is a great variety of IT-related qualifications as the industry is marked by a diversification of roles, making for important differences *within* as well as *across* the four countries and for wariness in attempts at generalization. While reference will be made to the most dominant routes in each country, we will draw specifically on the four case study qualifications selected for our research which represented typical or common routes into the labour market. These were: the HE routes in England (BA – Bachelor of Arts, three years) and France (DUT – *Diplôme Universitaire de Technologie*, two years), the vocational route in the Netherlands (four years at vocational school), and the continuing vocational education route in Germany (Software Developer, no prescribed duration but typically one year).

Notwithstanding the differences in VET, a common trend towards greater workplace orientation is apparent in all four countries, as reflected in, for example, a greater concern with workplace performance and the use of apprenticeships. In addition, there has been a shift away from a reliance on knowledge-based initial VET to work-based continuing VET. Initial and continuing work-based VET rely increasingly on self-directed project-based or on-the-job learning, with knowledge acquired only to the extent that it is perceived as necessary to perform tasks. In the context of a fast-changing industry, the ability to perform tasks is increasingly valued over formal qualifications.

Converging labour markets

Prompted by extreme skill shortages in the IT sector, a great deal of work has already been undertaken at EU level to develop a European meta-framework for IT so as to facilitate the identification of skills needs, workforce development and mobility of labour (e.g. CEN 2006). Interestingly, this initiative has so far faltered on the differences in national VET systems and no agreement has been reached. However, in the absence of a formal framework, the sector is marked by high levels of national and cross-national workforce mobility, centred on 'competence', skill performance and work experience, and the proliferation of multi-national companies (Brown *et al.* 2008).

In IT, rapid technological advancement has gone together with sweeping labour market changes on a global scale, contributing to what Steedman *et al.* (2003: 60), in their Anglo-German comparison of IT firms, have described as 'technological convergence', including similar forms of work organization, hard- and software systems. The authors identify two main drivers for convergence: the near monopolistic position of hardware and software manufacturers and the competitive pressure for continuous innovation. These have led to similar skill demands, for example in relation to programming languages, such as Java, UNIX and C/C++.

Echoing previous research (e.g. Brown *et al.* 2008), our study found that, overall, the role and scope of activities of software engineers in the four countries has broadened over the past decade. There have been a number of changes, notably the integration of IT into businesses, leading to a diversification of the sector, and in work organization, characterized by flattened hierarchies. Concerned with developing bespoke customer solutions, the role has changed from specialist straightforward programming to software design, with a pivotal involvement in customer negotiation and 'end-to-end' management (see also Marks and Scholarios 2008). Social and personal competences – including communications, team-working, problem solving, but also the ability for self-directed learning and a personal interest in technology – are highly valued and may take priority over formal qualifications based on comprehensive and nationally recognized VET programmes (ibid.). There is movement away from technical specialism to generic skills and an understanding of relevant business needs. Thus, the trend towards convergence in relation to IT skills coincides with considerable diversification of roles as IT professionals are required to have industry-relevant competences, such as knowledge of accountancy or banking.

These developments are underpinned by the changing nature of IT knowledge, much of which has been processed (and is readily available in the form of codes), the emphasis now being on its application, oriented towards finding solutions for customers. There is evidence of a shift in software engineering away from the creative activity of software development based on theoretical knowledge and towards the application of codified knowledge to practical problems (Nerland 2008). This shift is attributed to rapid technological advancement and changing work organization. Exploring the knowledge culture of software engineers, Nerland refers to the high level of codification of knowledge and standardization of practices in the IT sector. She describes the global 'epistemic infrastructure' (ibid.: 49) or the global distribution – notably through the internet – of knowledge structures, new products and updates by companies such as Sun Microsystems. In addition, software engineers participate in on-line communities, often specializing in particular products, with individual members depositing particular solutions, thus contributing to a collective knowledge database. Nerland (2008) observes a move towards technical problem-solving and the use of applied knowledge:

> This is to a large extent what their work is about: Knowing the technological standards that are in play, knowing how they may work or not work

together, and knowing how to perform different tasks within the different technological regimes.

(Nerland 2008: 59)

The decline in the need for the highly technical end of software engineering was confirmed by Marks and Scholarios (2008) in their study of IT companies in Scotland. While there was still a need for creative development work, overall the skills profile had changed to include both technical skills, focusing on the application of codified knowledge, and, importantly, social competences. What was important was the constant updating of skills in line with employer needs, and that these skills could be taught on the job (ibid.).

Importantly, and emphasizing the salience of individual 'employability', research emphasizes software engineers' individual responsibility for their own professional development (Kirpal 2004; Marks and Scholarios 2008; Nerland 2008). As a result of changes on a global scale, notably shortened cycles of innovation and production in the organization of IT work and in the types and structures of knowledge, work-based learning has assumed a heightened significance with a concurrent decline in the importance of formal initial VET qualifications.

VET provision

In all four countries labour market pressures have had implications for the provision of initial and continuing VET. There has been a heavy reliance on graduates for software engineering roles as employers value academic theoretical knowledge and high-level generic skills, such as problem-solving (Steedman *et al.* 2003; Brockmann *et al.* 2009a; Hanf 2009; Méhaut 2009; Westerhuis 2009). In France, of all DUT graduates only 10% enter the labour market while the vast majority obtain the Bachelor degree, a qualification increasingly in demand by the industry. In Germany, HE IT courses are provided by traditional universities (after a minimum of five years) and by more applied universities (after four years).

In all countries, there has been growing criticism, voiced by employers, that HE IT qualifications do not meet the changing demands in the workplace in terms of both technical skills (with technical knowledge seen as outdated by the time people graduate) and social competences such as communication and team-working skills. In particular, employers have complained that graduates lack an understanding of the business environment (Steedman *et al.* 2003; Kirpal 2004).

In response to such employer criticism as well as to labour market pressures, all four countries have adjusted or reformed their VET systems. However, despite common labour market developments, there continue to be important differences in VET programmes, reflecting particular traditions and socio-economic contexts. Thus, for example, initial VET in the three continental countries is centred on broadly conceived occupational profiles and a broad base of theoretical knowledge developed through initial VET programmes. These concentrate on a knowledge base of underlying principles and comprise general education as well as social and personal competences, thus reflecting the continental model of education. Degree courses in France, Germany and the Netherlands prepare students for a wide range of roles and do not allow for any form of specialization. For example, the DUT focuses heavily on theoretical knowledge, such as computer science and mathematics, but also covers non-technical subjects such as economics, management, labour law, English and generic competences. Eighty per cent of the curriculum is compulsory. Importantly, theoretical knowledge is deemed fundamental in order to transcend contexts and develop new knowledge and skills. In France and Germany, a degree in computer sciences or a cognate discipline continues to be critical for labour market entry, providing the basis for broad occupational profiles and knowledge production and thus acting as a driver for innovation in high-end roles of software development and strategic management. However, the heavy reliance on degrees led to severe labour shortages in the 1990s in Germany and an inability to respond to the surge in intermediate-level positions (Steedman *et al.* 2003). In the Netherlands, as HE became seen as over-qualifying young people for many positions, a new IT qualification was developed at VET level, which has now become the main route into the labour market. Importantly, this has retained a broad occupational profile.

By contrast, in England, there has traditionally been a much greater reliance on work-based learning with a particular employer *after* graduating. Qualifications in IT are commonly generic with specialization at company level. While the HE degree is an important entry qualification, it serves predominantly as an indicator of academic ability. Echoing previous research (Steedman *et al.* 2003), we found that English IT companies recruit graduates from a diverse range of disciplines, albeit that computer science graduates provide the core. One effect of this strategy is that new recruits are expected to undergo graduate training of up to two years within the firm, where the emphasis is on developing particular skills, largely meeting employer skills needs. This is in contrast with Germany where graduates are expected to take up fully functional positions after only a brief initial training period.

Also, perhaps more than in any of the other countries, HE in England has responded to calls for greater workplace orientation, developing close links with employers in a very competitive market in order for courses to reflect the demands of the industry. Within computer science degrees there has been a shift from subject-based theoretical knowledge to business-relevant skills acquired in project work. As suggested by our English informants, there is less emphasis on theoretical knowledge and more on practical know-how and the application of non-systematic knowledge, such as programming languages. Multi-dimensional competences are, as in the other three countries, deemed highly important because of the changing role of software engineers, including increased customer negotiation. However, in England, such competences are developed in the workplace rather than in the classroom-based VET of FE or HE.

To some extent, our findings reflect the traditional concern in the English system with the workplace and the task at hand. Formal qualifications for the large IT and Communications (ICT) company in our study played a secondary role to work experience (both formal and informal) and to the social and personal qualities people bring to the job, including above all a 'passion' for IT as well as 'soft' skills related to team working, problem solving and leadership. The company also played down the importance of broad theoretical knowledge and favoured people with a 'strong academic background' who they could develop through their graduate development training 'to be the leaders of the future'. Echoing existing studies (Marks and Scholarios 2008), the importance of practical know-how, particularly programming languages, was stressed, exemplifying the new knowledge infrastructure based on a global community of software engineers:

> The necessary knowledge is about knowing which modules are needed to build the particular customer requirement. Many applications are available in the public domain and can be reused . . . [it's about] borrowing, stealing, creating bits of coding.
>
> (*assignment manager*)

Our findings also confirm earlier research with regards to the recruitment practices of British firms which, given the large pool of candidates from diverse backgrounds, have to rely on elaborate selection processes in order to identify people with the desired competencies (Steedman *et al.* 2003).

To some extent, all four countries have, in response to labour market pressures, reformed or adapted their VET systems towards greater workplace orientation. One common response has been, on the one hand, to enhance the role of apprenticeship, and, on the other, to improve permeability between VET and HE, thus enabling the integration of workplace skills and academic 'generic' competences. There is greater use of IT apprenticeships in all countries, both at tertiary level (France, Germany and, to a lesser extent, the Netherlands) and below (England and Germany). As illustrated by Steedman *et al.* (2003), this has occurred within Germany's Dual System in response to a highly rigid and unresponsive HE system which, because of the long study period required, contributed to severe skill shortages in the 1990s. Open to non-graduates, the four new Dual System qualifications have provided a much needed intermediate workforce for middle-level positions and, importantly, greater flexibility in terms of occupational profiles, thus proving the 'innovative potential' of the Dual System (ibid.: 12). Assessment is, for example, based on company-specific projects, much of the content of which may be oriented towards employer needs (for the training occupation of 'mathematical-technical software developer', see BIBB 2007). In England, despite the introduction of a Higher Apprenticeship framework in IT in 2006, apprenticeship has remained a minor route, attributable to the prevalence of work-based training of graduates from a wide range of disciplines but also to a lack of information on the part of employers (Steedman *et al.* 2003). The IT apprenticeship frameworks system itself is highly responsive to employer needs with 'areas of occupational competence' being almost entirely modular, allowing for specialization at company level (E-Skills 2005).

In England, Germany and the Netherlands measures have been put in place to facilitate progression between VET and HE qualifications. For example, in England a new route has been introduced facilitating progression from (Higher) Apprenticeship to Foundation Degrees. In all countries, the introduction of IT apprenticeships reflects a concern with integrating academic knowledge and competences with workplace experience, which is of heightened importance given the requirements of new customer-facing roles including an understanding of the whole process of system design. A differentiation in qualifications can be discerned between the non-graduate level of intermediate positions in IT user service and maintenance and the graduate level of the high end of software development and design.

The value of multi-dimensional competence

Multi-dimensional competence, best encapsulated in the German term *Handlungskompetenz* (literally meaning competence of action-taking, reflecting a concern with performance in the workplace: being able to deal with complex situations by drawing on a range of resources or abilities) was deemed highly important in all countries. It is particularly imperative in software engineering, where responsibilities centre on developing individual IT designs according to customer demands and in a rapidly changing environment. Thus, the ability to work across functions and to understand the labour process of system design was valued by employers in all countries. However, while there are similarities in the understanding of the concept of competence in the workplace, it has different meanings in relation to the VET systems.

The development of competence-based qualification systems has been a prominent means of enhancing the workplace orientation of VET. IT VET qualifications in England and the Netherlands are, for example, based on competences, derived from an analysis of tasks in the workplace, with assessment based on their performance. However, underlying these qualifications are very different conceptions of competence. In the Netherlands, the IT VET programme aims to develop multi-dimensional competence and comprises occupational as well as social and civic competences; importantly, competences combine to form a comprehensive occupational profile. By contrast, the English IT apprenticeship framework lacks a holistic notion of competence and is characterized by a modular structure which facilitates narrow specialization; in the HE context, competence is not an official concept. Interestingly, employers in England stress the importance of multi-dimensional competence, and this dominates staff recruitment and development.

In the three continental countries, the HE route and, albeit to a lesser extent, the vocational route, encompass a broad theoretical base and aim to facilitate the integration of theoretical knowledge, practical know-how and social and personal competences. Knowledge is seen as crucial both for underpinning skills and to facilitate the learning process and self-directed learning. A broad knowledge and skills base thus prepares for a wide range of roles in fast changing environments. Multi-dimensional competence is developed within comprehensive initial VET programmes through a combination of classroom and workplace elements.

In Germany, the so-called 'specialist' qualification of 'Software Developer' constitutes a radical departure from the traditional occupational model of the *Beruf*, relying on an assessment of competences developed through a company-based project, not linked to a curriculum but requiring students instead to self-direct their learning according to what they perceive as necessary to solve the set tasks. Thus, the content of programmes is shaped by the requirements of the company and the learning needs of the individual. As a continuing VET qualification, it contains no general or civic education but rather epitomizes the notion of *Handlungskompetenz* as developed through confrontation with the task (Rauner 2004).

In response to the proliferation of new skills and tasks in the sector, England and Germany have developed IT-specific skills frameworks both to recognize existing skills and to develop new ones. Steedman *et al.*'s (2003) comparison of the German (AITTS) and English (SFIA) IT frameworks shows how these reflect the different VET traditions: while the German framework is built on comprehensive occupational profiles, the English one differentiates discrete skills only in terms of the level of responsibility. This distinction could be indicative of a strong path dependency (compare Chapters 3 and 4); however, the picture may be more nuanced. German continuing VET qualifications, dependent on individual employers, may result in highly variable knowledge and skills bases and have been criticized for being potentially narrow and lacking in transferability and permeability (Grollmann *et al.* 2007).

Overall, while much of IT skills training in England is left to individual employers, there is a higher level of standardization of qualifications in the three continental countries, with young people obtaining comprehensive qualifications through regulated VET programmes. However, in all countries we can observe an increased emphasis on work-based learning both in initial and in continuing VET. Where VET is largely located with an individual employer, there is always a risk that narrower skills profiles based on fragmented knowledge and occupational profiles may vary despite standardization.

Possibly more than in any other sector, because of rapid technological development, employers everywhere have placed increasing emphasis on continuing VET of graduates in the workplace. This is generally directed at meeting short-term skill needs and commonly involves product-related knowledge acquired in short courses (rather than more comprehensive education, such as Master-level degrees). These so-called 'vendor qualifications' carry strong labour market currency. Beyond initial VET, the focus is on skill portfolios and the constant updating of immediate individual skills rather than on long-term development based on a broad underpinning of theoretical knowledge (Kirpal 2004).

Developments towards work-based learning reflect a concern with a better integration of theory and practice, given the changed roles of software engineers, the declining need for the highly technical end of software engineering, and the corresponding need for an intermediate workforce. In all countries, beyond initial VET it has become the responsibility of individual employees to acquire the necessary skills in the context of a rapidly changing technology, in line with the notion of individual employability (Rauner 2006, 2007; Kraus *et al.* 2008).

The outcomes-based nature of continuing VET in IT generally and in software engineering in particular and the increasing focus on workplace learning, vendor qualifications and the acquisition of immediate skills, together with the high value placed on social and personal competencies, form the platform upon which workforce mobility (national and cross-national) between often large multi-national enterprises takes place.

Conclusions

As this chapter has demonstrated, qualifications in software engineering and nursing have undergone reform in response to changing labour market requirements and skills profiles, socio-economic changes, advances in technology and – in the case of nursing – the regulatory framework. While there are some commonalities in the development of qualifications across the four countries, nursing and software engineering are subject to a quite separate dynamic, based on tensions between the conflicting demands for broad academic profiles and employer-specific skills and played out differently depending (to a considerable extent) on the specific national context.

With regards to software engineering, there is in all countries a certain degree of convergence to be observed in the greater emphasis on flexible occupational profiles, on individual acquisition of competences and on work-based learning. Labour market pressures are of a global nature and have resulted in similar work organizations, a global knowledge infrastructure, similar IT roles and skills profiles, and specific competences (such as programming languages) with international labour market currency. On the other hand, there are differences in the provision of initial and continuing VET that are rooted in each country's VET tradition.

In relation to nursing, EU legislation has contributed to some convergence, resulting in broad occupational profiles based on comprehensive VET provision and echoing Rauner's (2006, 2007) occupation model. Beyond this, there is considerable variation in the content and structure of nursing qualifications, implying EQF classification at different levels. Changes in the requirements and occupational profiles of nurses are not uniform across the four countries and reflect differential pressures. Nursing qualifications have been reformed in response to the particular national contexts in which nurses operate and in accordance with existing VET systems.

The following conclusions can be drawn concerning the convergence and divergence of nursing and software engineering qualifications and the prospects for future implementation of the EQF based on the development of ZMTs. Trust based on EU regulation, as in the case of nursing, depends on the imperative of patient safety, which in turn ensures that the initial nursing qualification in each country serves as a guarantee of safe practice in a wide range of caring and medical activities. Thus, one mode of trust generation proceeds from regulation governing initial qualifications and a licence to practise.

A further mode of generation of mutual trust that we have identified occurs through labour market convergence, as in the case of software engineering. In this case, multinational enterprises have developed internal labour markets and work within a wide sector which uses many standard industrial applications, competence in whose use is often underpinned by highly regarded vendor qualifications. An internal labour market structure is complemented by elements of an occupational labour market across the countries (Eyraud *et al.* 1990). A HE qualification is not necessarily regarded as an occupational qualification, let alone a licence to practise, but it does impose a degree of common educational experience across the sector. Continuing VET, although highly specific and often project-based, depends on the application of transferable skills on the basis of previously developed underlying competences. This forms another, albeit more nebulous, basis for the development of mutual trust.

9

ESTABLISHING EQUIVALENCE THROUGH ZONES OF MUTUAL TRUST

Linda Clarke and Anneke Westerhuis

Introduction

An employer wishing to determine the level of ability and knowledge of a prospective employee from another country, or an employee wishing to gauge the level of his or her qualification in a country to which he or she has moved, should be able to use the European Qualifications Framework (EQF) for such purposes. The extent to which the framework can be relied on as a valid instrument for expressing the standing of qualifications remains, however, open, particularly as it is based not on direct regulation but on 'soft law' in the form of the Open Method of Co-ordination (OMC), involving joint identification and definition of objectives to be achieved, establishing measuring instruments and benchmarking (EC 2009).

As shown in the different chapters in this book, implementation of the EQF is likely to involve very significant conceptual and practical difficulties at both sectoral and occupational levels. Above all, in order for the framework to work within labour markets mutual trust must exist between employers and employees in the different countries. This trust may involve simply validating the level-allocation of qualifications or, given a certain level, be built around identifying and agreeing on what differences exist between particular qualifications and determining how or if equivalence can be established. The latter consideration would, therefore, need to build upon a variety of factors such as, for example: the possession of similar VET systems; EU regulation of the occupation or industry concerned, as in the case of nursing or even lorry driving; or extensive and established cross-national operations, as we have observed in Chapter 8 with respect to software engineering. However constructed, what is envisaged is the development of cross-national, cross-sectoral and cross-occupational zones of mutual trust (ZMTs), establishing arrangements for recognizing equivalences in qualifications in terms of mutual knowledge and methods of working (Coles and Oates 2004). A ZMT is defined as:

An agreement between individuals, enterprises and other organisations concerning the delivery, recognition and evaluation of vocational learning outcomes (knowledge, skills and competences). They offer practical help with decisions about the value of qualifications and certification, further learning and recruitment into employment. They may be dynamic in nature and may become more or less formal in scope and form according to the mutual confidence and needs of the stakeholders involved.

(Coles and Oates 2005: 8)

The key question this raises is whether trust alone is sufficient to establish some form of equivalence between qualifications. Trust in a mutual sense involves each party relying on the other to do something, agreed on implicitly or explicitly, without the need for external scrutiny. Unlike direct regulation, it implies no legal obligation. Is such 'trust' sufficient in relation to qualifications? This is likely to depend on how we understand qualifications, what they stand for and what their currency is in the labour market. How too can ZMTs be established? What will they solve? Are there alternative ways to establish cross-national equivalence? These are the questions, arising from previous chapters, which are addressed in this chapter.

What do qualifications stand for?

One of the first problems to be confronted in establishing equivalence between qualifications, one with which we have wrestled throughout the book, is what is a qualification? However we translate terms and understand them differently in each country and however differently an occupation itself is defined and bounded, an occupational qualification still signifies that the owner has the knowledge, skills and competences recognized by the education system and associated with a particular labour market occupation. It represents a construct straddling and at the same time acting as a bridge between the system of education and the labour market. Nevertheless it may refer more strongly to one than the other.

What is evident in previous chapters from the qualification systems of England, France, Germany and the Netherlands, and above all from our four occupations – nursing, bricklaying, software engineering and lorry driving – is the very different nature of qualifications, whether they are grounded in the education system or in the labour market. This fundamentally affects the knowledge element underpinning the qualification. Qualifications in France, Germany and the Netherlands almost invariably come under the Ministry of Education; only in the case of the French lorry driver is there also a qualification under the Ministry of Labour. In England, in contrast, qualifications, particularly National Vocational Qualifications (NVQs), are rather under the purview of the Department of Business, Innovation and Skills than the direct responsibility of the Ministry of Education and are based on what is perceived as employer demand, or, in other words on the imperatives of the labour market.

The difference between a qualification grounded in the labour market and one grounded in the education system is evident from the different understanding of 'learning outcomes' in each case. The EQF is described as a 'learning outcomes' framework but the scope for misunderstanding and confusion about this fundamental concept is considerable (EC 2006a). It may be described as: output of a learning process (the 'official' EQF definition); educational standard (waymark of progression through a curriculum); and as lesson objective (the way it is often used within educational institutions). The term is perhaps most often used in the sense of a 'standard', that is a set of criteria marking progress through a curriculum and serving as the basis for the design of assessment instruments (Brockmann *et al.* 2008a; Allais *et al.* 2009). These instruments may, in turn, determine the degree to which a candidate following the curriculum has or has not met the standard (Coles 2007).

Learning outcomes in this sense relate in some way or another to a curriculum, and hence to the education system. So in Germany, for example, their key reference point is the development of the individual in a particular *Beruf*, as defined through the curricula. Even in France, learning outcomes may be thus defined in terms of curricula, though they also act as performance descriptors. The real contrast arises in the English case – above all with NVQs – where the key reference point for learning outcomes is performance criteria in the workplace related to a particular task or function, irrespective of whether or not the individual has followed a course of education or training. It follows that such tasks must be narrowly specified in order that they can be identified for assessment purposes so that the approach cannot be based on standards as this would involve sampling across a range of knowledge, skill and understanding (Coles 2007: 13). In other words, in England learning outcomes in a NVQ sense refer directly to the labour market whilst in Germany learning outcomes refer to the national, tripartite-agreed *Beruf* concept, built on the attainment of standards at different levels in the *Berufsbildung* or vocational education system.

In the EQF design it is assumed that performance output in the workplace can be directly associated with learning outcomes as standards through its incorporation of accredited learning which may have taken place outside an educational setting. This is one reason why the EQF – together with modularization, accreditation of prior experiential learning (APEL) and the promotion of 'learning how to learn' – has been seen as part of a long-term movement towards the empowerment of labour market institutions at the expense of educational ones (Young 2009).

What is the validity of the process?

The EQF is just a 'translation device' whose aim is to enable comparison to be made of the level of any particular type of qualification, in terms of general indicators and not specific content, in one country with one of the same apparent type available in another country. As such it is, like a qualification, also a construct, involving a political procedure for any effective implementation, though unlike a qualification it is constructed only around levels and not also around specific contents. Its success, as with a qualification, will inevitably depend, first, on a process of negotiation, involving different partners to different degrees in the different countries and, second, on whether a comparison of levels alone is sufficient to generate trust without taking into account also the content of qualifications.

The EQF is a 'meta' framework in the sense that it should allow different National Qualification Frameworks (NQFs) to be compared, presupposing thereby either looseness in the use of language or the use of transnational categories, and for different qualifications to be assimilated. Strictly speaking, what are to be compared through the EQF are the levels of different qualification systems, not the qualifications that individuals possess. In justifying the setting up of the framework, the Joint Interim report of the Commission and Council of 2004 states that: 'The European labour market cannot function without a European framework to stand as a reference for the recognition of qualifications' (EC 2005a: 1). The effectiveness of this depends on the degree to which the nature and currency of the qualifications differ and, in particular, on whether they are within or outside the general system of vocational education. It depends too on how far the frameworks developed are inclusive or exclusive. Exclusive frameworks are those where qualifications have to meet strict criteria to be registered; these inevitably achieve high validity or trust because the qualifications all meet these criteria. Inclusive frameworks, on the other hand, are those where qualifications do not have to meet strict criteria to be registered and which aim to cover as wide a field as possible; these run the danger of low validity or trust by incorporating also low quality or poor qualifications.

In order for the EQF to work, it is necessary for countries, industries or occupations wishing to engage with it to trust the integrity of the way in which their qualifications are referenced with the EQF. The process of referencing national qualifications with each other will, therefore, need to be carried out in such a way that trust within the labour market is promoted. It does not follow that employers or trade unions will automatically have confidence in the referencing that a country gives for qualifications within the EQF, particularly if they suspect that the exercise was influenced by political or special interest considerations.

'Referencing' national qualifications or NQFs with the EQF is taking place throughout the EU and is crucial in order that there is at least a nominal equivalence between the status (level) of a national qualification and an EQF level. It should then be possible to determine equivalence by aligning any qualification in any country with a potential equivalent in any other country party to the EQF. However, the lack of a standard procedure for referencing or of a clear status – with sanctions – for the outcome of the international peer review of national referencing exercises heralds the danger that the process will not be trusted, particularly as there is a potential conflict of interest between impartial referencing at the EU level and the political and economic imperatives of individual countries. For example, the referencing exercise of the English NQF (known as QCF or Qualifications and Credit Framework) to the EQF, which took place through the agency of a consultant in 2009, contrasts strongly with the very thorough process being carried out in France, and Germany, involving also the parallel construction of NQFs, where national and regional stakeholder involvement is central and the main aim is to ensure transparency and quality assurance (Bjørnåvold and Pevec Grm 2010).

What is the labour market currency of occupational qualifications?

As any occupational qualification depends for its validity on the involvement and agreement of all stakeholders, it follows that the less the agreement and involvement of all those concerned, the weaker its currency in the labour market is likely to be. This too has important implications for the EQF and for the establishment of ZMTs as the weaker the currency of the qualification in the labour market, the less effective is the framework also likely to be and the greater the difficulty in mutually trusting and recognizing qualifications. For instance in England, as we saw in Chapter 7 concerning bricklaying, the process of recognition of occupational qualifications is based largely on consultation by government agencies with employers and minimal input from other stakeholders, such as trade unions or the further education (FE) sector. It represents a top-down approach designed to be employer-led and to favour market-based solutions. This implies no meaningful partnership with those whose commitment is essential to establish ZMTs and is again at odds with France, Germany and the Netherlands, where governance is based on social partnership between the employers and the trade unions and encompasses the distinctive interests of young people and those working in the occupation (Brockmann *et al.* 2010a). Social partnership is generally favourable to the development of consensus, through attention to the sometimes conflicting interests of the different partners and to the fostering of stable and long-term arrangements for VET.

Throughout this book, the English case is shown to be distinct, posing a problem for the comparability and transferability of qualifications. The fluidity, fragmentation and confusion of the governance structure for VET in England is symptomatic of what might be regarded as a weak system, given the ease and speed with which changes in policy are introduced (Keep 2007). This instability is compounded by the lack of direct Ministerial responsibility and the weak and fragmented nature of the social partners. Government policy seeks to create a 'demand-led' system, which responds to employers' short-term labour market needs rather than to the long-term educational needs of young people or to the long-term needs of the economy. The danger with such a system, based on and bounded by a 'skills'-based approach (see Chapter 6), is that it may simply perpetuate a low-skilled labour-intensive economy, as employers continue to build on traditional skills, 'the skills of yesterday', thus restricting the capacity for the development of new areas (Clarke and Winch 2004: 515). Ironically too, as we saw in the case of bricklaying, the lack of regulation and of social partnership arrangements in the governance of VET leads to a lack of labour market currency and credibility of particular – though by no means all – qualifications.

Such differences in the currency of qualifications across Europe are associated with distinct notions of occupation which in turn reflect differences in the labour market and systems of governance (Brown *et al.* 2001). The difficulty in the English case is that, unlike the other countries considered, the scope and content of many occupations – with important exceptions such as, for example, nursing – tend to be defined on the basis of custom and practice, particularly when they are of a lower level as in the case of bricklaying. This is not the case in France, Germany and the Netherlands where validation involves lengthy negotiation and discussion on a social partnership basis and at sectoral level, with all the parties involved, including trade unions, employers and educationalists, with the result that qualifications represent a compromise which is mutually accepted as relevant. Thus in the continental case the qualifications attached to occupations such as bricklaying are valued by all for the often broad and social competences which they embody and act as a key means of entry into the labour market, creating occupational labour markets (Marsden 2007). Indeed, the general tendency even in England is the development of qualification-based labour markets, involving defined entry routes, though these may or may not be predicated, as in the Dutch construction sector, on a qualification which is in turn related to collectively agreed wage grades.

In many respects the EQF can be seen as a response to the further development of qualification-based labour markets. At the same time it represents the results of decades of effort to establish transparency and recognition of VET qualifications and competences as a necessary concomitant to the free movement of labour across Europe. The relative lack of regulation of VET at European level until now is also increasingly challenged given, on the one hand, the priority given to training and associated health and safety issues in the social dialogue established at European level between employers and trade unions and, on the other, the threats to national VET systems posed by migration. For instance, a number of sectors in England suffering from the relatively low levels of VET and qualifications have benefited from an influx of migrants trained and educated – at considerable cost and effort – in other European countries (Chan *et al.* 2010; Ruhs and Anderson 2010).

The labour market currency – and hence ease in establishing equivalence – across Europe of qualifications achieved at HE levels is perhaps greater than those achieved at vocational education level and associated with the traditional 'manual' occupations, even despite considerable labour market mobility (see Chapter 8). This is apparent with nursing, whilst the currency of software engineering qualifications, which tend to be achieved after HE and thus form part of continuing VET, depends on the multi-dimensional and knowledge-dependent character of the competences they encompass as well as on common (global) developments.

The EQF, together with ECVET (European Credit System in VET) and EQAVET[1] (European Quality Assurance in VET), are as a European Union (EU) policy trio premised on qualifications that are expected to be part of an education system and hence the product of particular learning processes. In this respect, the currency of qualifications depends on the quality of learning provided through different VET systems. Indeed, if VET systems are grouped in terms of structural typology, then distinct families of trust are evident (Green *et al.* 1999). The basis on which VET is constructed and its underlying assumptions in systems such as the German are indicative of the importance attached to vocational education and the commitment to a broad education, as well as the role, value and status accorded to labour, and the place of occupations in establishing social identity. Likewise, countries such as France and the Netherlands adopt an 'educational' model in their VET systems, where considerable emphasis is laid on broader educational elements such as civic education and underpinning knowledge (e.g. mathematics). As Rauner (2004, 2007) suggests, families of occupational qualifications may be grouped around what he terms the 'vocational education' model of these three countries, where VET programmes, regulated by the social partners and integrated into the education system, lead to recognized qualifications and competence in a defined occupational field. Each is likely to find it easier to understand the other than the English 'training' model, where the emphasis is usually on the skills required for specific workplace activities rather than on regulated VET programmes and recognized occupational profiles (Brockmann *et al.* 2008b).

Besides the credibility of the governance system and the quality of the VET system, a third and associated factor affecting the currency of qualifications in the labour market is their level. EQF consists of eight levels, ranging from primary/low level secondary school completion (level 1) to doctoral (level 8), with each level having a descriptor in each of the three vertical categories: knowledge, skills and competence (Brockmann *et al.* 2008b). But difficulties are likely to arise in implementing the framework in relation to vocational qualifications at skilled operative level – that is between levels 2 and 4 – due to the different level typically associated with particular occupations in different countries. For instance, NVQ level 2 is the typical qualification of an English bricklayer and is largely confined to the development of bundles of task-specific skills, with the minimal educational input necessary for long-term individual development. The qualification in the Netherlands is at roughly the same level. In Germany, in contrast, the qualification is at least the equivalent of NVQ level 3 and concerns vocational, general and personal development (Brockmann *et al.* 2010b). A further controversial difficulty relating to levels is the question of learning outcomes. If these are detached from curricula, achievement at a certain level is implicitly presupposed and, at the same time, previous achievements below the level currently assessed are regarded as irrelevant.

A final and critical factor affecting the currency of a qualification relates to its content and scope, or what might be termed 'occupational capacity'. The breadth or scope of activities of the occupational qualification is a dimension not addressed directly by the EQF but one of key importance to the development of mutual trust and to implementation. In many continental countries, including Germany and the Netherlands, nationally recognized qualifications are incorporated within a wider sectoral and occupational framework, based on broad occupational competence and awarded on completion of comprehensive VET programmes. Their strong labour market currency is attributable to the occupational capacity they represent, enabling transferability between firms and jobs with diverse requirements in terms of activities (Marsden 2007).

Differences in the scope and occupational profiles of bricklayers, for instance, are reflected in the structure and content of VET programmes and qualifications, such as the very comprehensive VET programmes in Germany which represent the continuation of general education and aim to develop the person as an active citizen in wider society as well as for the occupation. They cover a broad knowledge and skill base which enables learners to work in a variety of functions and areas. The notion of competence as the integration of theoretical knowledge, practical know-how and social and personal competences is central to VET. The scope of what might be termed the continental 'occupational' model contrasts with that in England where traditional occupations such as bricklaying continue to bear the hallmarks of 'trades' (see Chapter 7), focused on the performance of output, confined to a restricted range of tasks, and with an increasingly narrow scope of operations. VET in turn is restricted to the particular activities associated with that occupation, without covering other related occupations or providing an industrial overview and with restricted transferability and permeability (Brockmann *et al.* 2009c).

This means that occupations themselves differ in their nature according to country, raising the key question of how far occupational qualifications reflect and perhaps even shape the reality of occupations in the labour market. If a qualification seeks only to mimic a traditional, restricted and shrinking area of labour market activity, then it will inevitably have low labour market currency and become quickly out of tune with changes in the labour market. It is the educational element, in particular the integration of the theoretical knowledge component with practice, which gives a qualification its longer-term value and which can in turn facilitate rather than impede the development of the labour process (Clarke and Winch 2004). Occupations whose scope is broadly defined require substantial underpinning knowledge for the performance of the range of activities encompassed and more complex personal characteristics and abilities than simple, visually observable skills. They imply qualifications whose learning outcomes represent standards rather than narrowly conceived performance descriptors. The EQF too, as an umbrella for all 'learning outcomes' at all levels, necessarily consists of broad descriptors of knowledge, skill and competence at each level.

Where and how can ZMTs be established?

General tendencies throughout the European labour market, in particular the growing significance attached to VET and the greater reliance on qualification-based labour markets, give added impetus to establishing the equivalence of vocational qualifications through ZMTs, with or without the mechanism of the EQF. Indeed, as long as the EQF does not distinguish between the different qualities of occupational qualifications, implementing the framework will be fraught with problems. As discussed in previous sections, these differences revolve above all around whether qualifications are grounded in the VET system or are purely labour market based and around their currency in the labour market, including the quality of the respective VET system, the level typically associated with the occupation concerned, and the occupational capacity or scope. A further important consideration relates to changes taking place within many occupational qualifications, which have in turn important implications for which qualifications are aligned with which. And finally, there is the question of learning outcomes, whether these are just performance descriptors or represent standards in a broader sense.

In addition to these considerations is that of the degree of trust, low or high, which is needed to set up a ZMT. As defined by Lane and Bachmann (2002), trust in economic, social and organizational theory has three elements: a degree of interdependence, that is social relationships, between trustor and trustee; a way to cope with the inevitable risk and uncertainty in exchange/social relationships; and a belief or expectation that vulnerability resulting from the acceptance of risk will not be taken advantage of by the other party. In mutual trust arrangements, this will be a two-way process. If the initial level of trust in social relationships is relatively high, only broad agreement might be sufficient. If, on the other hand, agreement has to be established through negotiation at the level of detail, this might indicate a low level of trust between parties. In other words, the establishment of a ZMT needs careful 'process-design', as it might have a positive as well as a negative effect on the level of trust in social relationships.

Another problem to be confronted is the different layers of policymaking at European level. EQF classifies all qualifications in terms of Knowledge, Skills (or, more broadly, know-how) and Autonomy/Responsibility. The EQF can provide only a broad template, necessitating considerable occupational and sectoral adaptation in order to make sense of particular qualifications and to provide a way of comparing them across countries. Sectors across Europe that share common ways of working and are accustomed to the mutual recognition of qualifications across borders are likely to be the first to establish such zones, however gradually. It will be more difficult to establish ZMTs across sectors that have not had experience of the cross-recognition of qualifications and between countries that have dissimilar VET systems. Some sectors, for example construction, have already agreed sectoral qualification frameworks (SQFs) through the social dialogue committees of the respective European social partners at sector level, consisting of employer and trade union representatives from different countries (Syben 2009).

Within a SQF might be situated an occupational qualification framework (OQF), which would need to take up the issue of the scope of the qualification and develop minimum specifications. As apparent from Chapter 8, increasing convergence can be identified in higher level qualifications such as for nursing and to some extent software engineering, both of which share common trends, such as the broadening of roles, the higher status, and increasing prevalence of a multi-dimensional model of competence. In contrast, the traditional manual occupations discussed in Chapter 7, such as bricklaying, display greater divergence, including in terms of the respective VET system. How far agreement can be reached at occupational level remains therefore to be seen, though the European Commission (EC) has supported a number of projects to identify problems likely to be confronted, including one related to bricklaying qualifications (Brockmann *et al.* 2010b). Similar occupational qualifications, such as for nursing, may be found across national VET systems that are, in other respects, quite divergent and vice versa. This suggests that cognate occupations and occupational families, such as in the health sector, may establish mutual trust across national boundaries. Here though there already exist statutory comparators based on EU regulation of occupations such as nursing, which arguably make the EQF redundant, at least at the level of the basic 'licence to practise'. Another potential occupational family could be software engineering, where similar initial VET routes in each country, cross-national employers and globally recognized vendor qualifications might serve as binding agents. Indeed, a meta-framework has already been achieved in ICT, using outcomes as the basis for comparability (CEN 2006).

A gradual and incremental process of mutual trust may also arise between countries, based on families of cognate VET systems. Research has already indicated similarities between particular countries in terms of the role that VET plays and the philosophical and ethical underpinnings of different systems (e.g. Green 1990; Ashton and Green 1996; Green *et al.* 1999; Clarke and Winch 2007). Regions within the EU are more likely to evolve systems across those economic sectors with the most pressing need for mutual recognition, such as co-operation across the Scandinavian systems or between Dual System-based countries within certain sectors. However, the complexities revealed by previous such attempts, in particular with respect to different divisions of labour in each country, provide a warning and led to the decision to focus the EQF instead on the classification of outcomes (Bjørnåvold and Coles 2006). The development of mutual trust will be easier for those countries with relatively stable institutional and governance structures for VET, built on social partnership.

As apparent from all the chapters in this book, there are distinct differences in understandings of some of the key terms underpinning VET systems though agreement on terminology is of fundamental importance to the development of ZMTs. The EQF is a 'translation device' intended to facilitate understanding of the relative value of qualifications in terms of three main criteria: *knowledge, skill* and *competence*, yet each is understood differently in different countries. Tendentious translation has the potential for distorting what is meant in a particular national context. An example is the translation of *knowledge* in English as *Kenntnis* in German, which refers to context-specific and non-systematic knowledge, rather than as *Wissen* or systematic knowledge, which also plays an important role within German VET (Hanf 2007). The three continental countries in this research project make use of multi-dimensional conceptions of competence, encompassing the integration of systematic and contingent knowledge into practice together with social and personal qualities, which themselves tend to be thought of in occupational rather than task terms (Brockmann *et al.* 2008c, 2009b). England by contrast makes use of a narrow functionalist and behaviourist conception of competence, built around occupational standards which are, in effect, bundles of task descriptions – discrete and capable of combination into different qualification packages (Delamare Le Deist and Winterton 2005; Winterton *et al.* 2005). Attitudes too are an explicit element in the Dutch definition of competence, reflected in *savoir-être* in France and social and personal *Kompetenzen* in Germany. In England, in contrast, though there is increasing focus on 'soft skills', these are only weakly analogical with attitudes, *savoir-être* and *Kompetenzen*. In its almost exclusive focus on skills, the English meaning of competence – described at length in Chapters 6 and 10 – is almost incomprehensible in most countries.

The terminological differences are interminable, though agreement on terminology is essential for the establishment of a ZMT. It is precisely this that prompts the need for transnational categories which can be agreed on within a ZMT, a need now aggravated by the fact that each country has developed its own terminology for comparing VET, HE and General Education. Indeed, as a first step in allocating qualifications to a supra-sectoral NQF, countries have separately developed a meta-vocabulary, further complicating the issue of terminology. From a transnational perspective, in contrast, the deep knowledge associated with *savoir* (see Chapter 3), could be combined in the European framework with the broad multi-dimensional notion of competence found in the Dutch (see Chapter 5) or German systems (see Chapter 4) and the English 'skills' could be replaced by 'know-how' in a European meta-vocabulary. Similarly learning outcomes could be defined as standards, just as 'occupational capacity' could be used to describe the breadth of a qualification. More problematic is a term such as 'occupation', given that few countries could emulate the rock of the *Beruf* described in Chapter 4. Nevertheless as a definite division of labour in society, an occupation can be well understood across countries.

Conclusions

There remain a number of different and not necessarily mutually exclusive ways in which equivalence between qualifications can be established across Europe. Perhaps the most effective is through regulation, which can considerably facilitate comparability of qualifications. This is nowhere more evident than with nursing, covered by the European Qualifications (Health and Social Care Professions) Regulations of 2007 relating to 'access to, the training for, the pursuit of, and the award and recognition of HE diplomas, formal qualifications, or experience in the professions of dentistry, medicine, midwifery, nursing and pharmacy and their specialities' (OPSI 2007: 1), and social work. The qualification is a mandatory requirement for nurse registration and regulations include inputs in the form of content of curricula and length of vocational education, as well as outputs in the form of 'competences'. Thus nursing, with its common ethical and professional tradition transcending national boundaries, can, despite the differences identified in Chapter 8, be regarded now as a European occupation.

Lorry driving too is subject to regulation, covered by European Directive 2003/59/EC 'Initial Qualification and Periodic Training for Drivers of Road Vehicles for the Carriage of Goods or Passengers', which stipulates a particular period of training dependent upon the age of the driver and size of the vehicle. European qualifications relating to lorry drivers thereby exhibit a similar incorporation of inputs and outputs as for nursing. An important rationale for regulation and licence to practise of both nursing and lorry driving is the critical importance of health and safety to the occupations. Health and safety is, however, a very significant issue in many other occupations, thus suggesting the possibility of similar Directives introduced as health and safety measures, for instance to cover bricklaying and other construction occupations.

Unlike these regulations, the EQF is not explicitly attached to any curriculum or pedagogic processes. Nor does it represent regulation as such, though the framework will encompass qualifications for regulated occupations and those which, under national regulations, act as a licence to practise of some kind, however loose. For example, in England gas fitters cannot practise without a qualification and in many countries, including Germany and the Netherlands, it is increasingly difficult to work in many occupations and industries such as construction without a recognized qualification stemming from a programme of vocational education.

Where qualifications are regulated or act as a licence to practise, then the establishment of ZMTs can well be envisaged. But, in these cases the respective qualifications are part of the VET system. Indeed, it is difficult to imagine transnational trust being established concerning qualifications that are not grounded in one way or another in the VET system, or at least partly so. For example, in the Netherlands, where VET qualifications are used as standards for the accreditation of prior learning (APL) procedures, it is not required that a qualification be fully acquired through a process of VET learning. The need to refer to VET-based qualifications is evident too from the work of the National Recognition Information Centre (NARIC), the British-based National Agency responsible for providing equivalency and benchmarking services to individuals, to help them work and study anywhere, and to organizations (educational and training institutions, government departments, professional bodies and companies) to improve their understanding of overseas qualifications and skills and of their own systems and procedures when dealing with international applications. In its advice on establishing skills and qualifications frameworks and on vocational, academic and professional skills and qualifications, NARIC invariably refers both to inputs – for instance the VET and curriculum typically associated with an occupation – and learning outcomes, such as knowledge, skills and competences acquired.

Although APL has been introduced in many countries in Europe, essentially severing the link between formal education and qualifications, the latter are commonly linked to some kind of VET programme, with general education forming a crucial element for competence development. The EQF too is fully engaged with the European policy of lifelong vocational and professional education, thus covering without distinction qualifications in both initial and continuing education (EC 2006a). Indeed it seeks to provide a comprehensive framework aiming at transcending the borders and establishing parity of esteem between vocational and general education. However, it goes further in – following European terminology and recommendations – aiming at qualifications that recognize learning acquired through 'formal', 'informal' and 'non formal' processes. It thus breaks with the traditional 'input–output' approach (number of years of study, number of hours of VET (inputs) and, for example, an exam pass mark signifying a level of knowledge (outputs)) but goes beyond this by suggesting that it can be used with qualifications gained through APEL. This would, however, imply, first, that learning outcomes are applied in the Anglo-Saxon sense and not in the much more universally understood sense of standards and, second, that qualifications outside the recognized system of VET are included. One can only envisage that this could open up a can of worms, opening the door to qualifications with little or no credibility or educational validity and for which little trust can be established, especially where there are no objective criteria and procedures in place to guarantee quality.

The EQF has features of a 'Reforming Framework', designed to reform existing qualification structures and even of a 'Transformational Framework' by instituting a process of transforming or creating national frameworks (NQFs) which will be based on learning outcomes (Raffe 2009: 35). Both the EQF and NQFs are similar in the sense that they use a grid of vertical and horizontal classifications of qualifications in terms of cognitive characteristics and levels within an academic hierarchy. Comparisons between two national qualifications are made by locating two or more qualifications or qualification classifications within the EQF grid and, if the location coincides, they are deemed equivalent. Nevertheless, just aligning NQFs to the EQF remains a political process, which may or may not be realizable and does not have any significant bearing on the labour market. The danger is that, where NQFs are exclusive, they will be very difficult to align and, where they are inclusive, they will not be trusted. The whole exercise therefore, given that it rests on the OMC, may as a result simply serve to reinforce national differences and distrust rather than furthering European co-operation. It has, however, considerably enhanced – and will continue to enhance – our understanding of different qualification systems and the degree to which qualifications can be regarded as equivalent.

Note

1   EQAVET is a community of practice bringing together Member States, Social Partners and the European Commission to promote European collaboration in developing and improving quality assurance in VET by using the European Quality Assurance Reference Framework. It is seen as a kind of guarantee that the processes leading to a qualification (in the NQFs and EQF) meet more or less the same quality standards.

10

INTERPRETIVE DICTIONARY: COMPETENCE, QUALIFICATION, EDUCATION, KNOWLEDGE

Michaela Brockmann, Linda Clarke,
Christopher Winch, Georg Hanf,
Philippe Méhaut and Anneke Westerhuis

Introduction

This interpretive dictionary of vocational education and training (VET) terms is intended to focus on the different dimensions of usage of key terms, bearing in mind that our interest lies in the nature of qualifications within an occupational context, that is in *occupational qualifications*. The dictionary is based on usage in England, France, Germany and the Netherlands, drawing on examples from lorry driving, bricklaying, software engineering and nursing.

The term 'occupation' is systematically ambiguous, so it is important to clarify the way in which it is used in this dictionary. Occupations may be considered from the point of view of the organization of labour at the plant or enterprise level or they may be considered from the perspective of VET. Germany marks this distinction as between an '*Erwerbsberuf*', which is related to the plant or enterprise, and an '*Ausbildungsberuf*' which is specified by the VET system. In this project we approach occupations from the point of view of VET, so look at the equivalent of an '*Ausbildungsberuf*' in each country, although, as apparent from Chapters 7 and 8, occupations are structured very differently in different countries according to the VET systems in place and the assumptions that underpin them. Our broad aim is to shed light on the central concepts that underpin the four VET systems studied, in particular those associated with the four distinct occupations. This means that we are not so much interested in core definitions but with the role that these concepts play within different parts of each system.

The dictionary is put together in the following way. Under a set of five categorial concepts – Education, Qualification, Knowledge, Competence and Skill – we distinguish between different dimensions of use in all four languages (English, French, Dutch and German) including:

- *Official definitions or accounts*, such as those offered by the European Centre for the Development of Vocational Training (CEDEFOP), the European Union (EU) or government regulations in individual countries.
- *Everyday usages within VET institutions*, workplaces or in the vernacular, which may well diverge from official usage. These are the particular conceptions associated with the categorial concepts, each of which may well be contested. Where there are contradictions or tensions within either official or vernacular usage or between them, this is made clear.
- *Usage of associated terms* within the broader category, such as 'skill' or '*Fähigkeit*' within the category of 'competence'.

Where possible, descriptions of the contexts of usage are given through inset case studies and examples of actual usage by different individuals with different roles within the system, in particular related to the English system. French, German and Dutch examples could only have been inserted in their respective language; to have translated them into English would have defeated the purpose of illustrating actual usage which is different within each language.

Section 1: Education

The *concept* of education refers to a process to be found in any human society of preparing the young for adult life and preparing adults for different phases of life. In contrast, particular *conceptions* of education refer to the different instances of education in this general sense, such as the English conception of liberal education or the German conception of education as *Bildung*. Different European countries have different conceptions of education and sometimes more than one is operative within the same country, serving the needs of different individuals or the needs of the same individual at different phases of life (for example *Bildung* and *Ausbildung* in German).

General education

There is no extant official definition of this term that we have been able to find.

Interpretation

English: this term is usually reserved for the continuing academic education that accompanies a programme of VET.

French: two notions are in play in France, as indeed in Germany and the Netherlands, distinguishing the two realms of education: academic education which is characteristic of non-vocational learning (the academic baccalaureate as opposed to the vocational baccalaureate); and, within vocational education, 'academic' subjects, which have a triple value – as part of civic education, as a contribution to eventual career change, and as a bridge between vocational and academic education.

German: *Allgemeinbildung* refers to the academic basic core of *Bildung* which also includes the acquisition of numeracy and literacy, as well as a basic stock of common knowledge (*Grundbildung*; English: Grounding).

Dutch: *algemeen vormend onderwijs* (AVO) refers to the school types in secondary general education in terms of subjects, including: foreign languages, history, geography, and so on, as opposed to VET. Apart from numeracy and literacy in Dutch and English, general education subjects are not standard in VET curricula.

Liberal education

Artes Liberales was the medieval and earlier nomenclature for the *Trivium and Quadrivium* (*artes triviales* and *artes quadriviales*: grammar, rhetoric, dialectics, arithmetic, geometry, music and astronomy), the education and training deemed suitable for free persons (Latin *liber*: free), as distinct from the *artes illiberales* for the less (or not) free, now broadly termed VET. Seneca writes in his 88th letter: *Quare liberalia studia dicta sunt vides: quia homine libero digna sunt.* (Hence you see why the liberal arts are so called: they are studies worthy of a free-born man) (Mehl 1994: 301)

Interpretation

This is primarily a conception of general education which has its home within the English context, although there are analogies in French, German and Dutch:

English: in English this refers to a grammar school or public school academic education with a traditional curriculum, organized around different subjects but conceptualized as forms of knowledge, as in Hirst's (1974) typology which, however, excludes the foreign and classical languages usually considered to be a part of liberal education. In VET curricula, liberal education is usually organized, not as forms of knowledge, but as *subjects*.

French: education in French is concerned primarily with the development of *savoir* or systematic subject-based knowledge, though it can also refer to character development, as exemplified in Rousseau's *Emile ou de l'Education* [1762] (1968). The term 'education' (and education system), emphasizing personal development, is often contrasted with that of 'vocation' (and the vocational education system) which places more emphasis on useable knowledge. The term 'formation' is coming more and more into use in the VET context as well as in general education, perhaps explained by a tension between a holistic conception of education, principally stemming from post-war education reforms, and a more utilitarian conception focused on the relationship *formation* – employment. Unlike in England, initial *formation* remains largely integrated into the education system, as also reflected in the aspect of *compétence*, which stresses the need to be able to work in complex and changing situations.

German: the German term *Bildung* includes the English term *liberal education*, but rather more than that, although it should be noted that the nearest equivalent is *Allgemeinbildung* (English: General Education). *Bildung* relates mainly to school education and is described by Pöppel and Rekus (2001) in terms of: *Unterricht* (academic education); and *Erziehung* (character formation), which can be found as an aim in the English system but is not usually understood as liberal education. The German usage of *Bildung* also includes adult personal development as an unfinished and unfinishable process, concerned with the development of a person's unique individuality (Benner 2003). This conception, which further depends on *Allgemeinbildung*, is known as *allgemeine Menschenbildung*. Unlike the English notion of *lifelong learning*, which is closely associated with continuing vocational education and training (CVET), it has character development and self-discovery at its core. *Lernfelder* (learning fields) should be distinguished from traditional academic subjects.

Dutch: there is no Dutch equivalent of the term *liberal education* as distinguished from *general education*. In the Anglo-Saxon tradition, *liberal education* is 'a philosophy of education that empowers individuals with broad knowledge and transferable skills, and a strong sense of value, ethics, and civic engagement' (source: Association of American Colleges and Universities, AACU). A proxy term is *klassieke opvoeding* (classical education), a historic term referring to the Aristotelian philosophy of education in which education's aim is to abolish the shortcomings of Nature. In contrast to the dominant utilitarian concept of education, *klassieke opvoeding* does not ground the relevance of subjects (*humaniora*) in their use for work and society, but in their contribution to character formation (the Dutch term *opvoeding* is equivalent to the German term *Erziehung*). In this it contrasts with Rousseau's concept of character-building by the development of the self through learning by experience.

Vocational education

Definitions (CEDEFOP 2008: 202)

English: education and training that aims to equip people with knowledge, know-how, skills and/or competences required in particular occupations or more broadly on the labour market.

French: *formation et enseignement professionnels* (*FEP*): education and training that has for its objective the acquisition of knowledge (*savoir*), know-how (*savoir-faire*), skills (*aptitudes*) and/or competences (*compétences*) required in specific occupations (*métiers*) or more generally on the labour market.

German: *Berufsbildung/berufliche Bildung*: education and training provision imparting the knowledge (*Kenntnisse*), know-how, skills (*Fähigkeiten*) and/or competences (*Kompetenzen*) necessary for specific occupational activities or more generally on the labour market.

Definition in the Dutch context

Dutch: *Beroepsonderwijs*. The term *Beroepsonderwijs* is used in the context of secondary vocational education, leading to an official state-regulated diploma.

Interpretation

English: the term *vocational education* is used in English usually in conjunction with and often synonymously with *training*. Training is the inculcation of *know-how* through the practice of routine or regularized activities which do, nevertheless, involve some exercise of judgement. Episodes of training can constitute part of a process of education. The French *formation* and German *Ausbildung* are commonly translated as 'vocational education' but mean more than training in the English sense.

French: *formation* refers to the process of induction into and development within an occupation (*métier*), involving both initial and continuing VET, and the development of *compétence* as well as civic education. *Compétence* itself encompasses the application of *savoir, connaissance, savoir-faire* and *savoir-être* to the occupational activity. Vocational education follows the tracks of the system which are oriented to vocational activity, that is, to the labour market. 'Continuing' vocational education designates all those VET activities (including explicitly educational ones) that apply to individuals who have left school education and initial VET, even if their goals are not necessarily vocational. For example, adults following literacy courses are in continuing education, as are those who have retired and who are following an art history course at university. 'Continuing' education is most often designated as continuing *vocational* education, to emphasize its vocational aspect, but also the personal status and the financial arrangements that cover this type of education.

German: *Berufsbildung/berufliche Bildung* involves an element of *Bildung*, but is oriented towards the development of occupational capacity (*berufliche Handlungsfähigkeit*), which also involves the underpinning and theoretical knowledge required to practise an occupation (see *Wissen, Savoir, Kenntnis, Connaissance*, respectively), in addition to continuing general education (*allgemeine Bildung*) and moral and civic education (see *personale, soziale Kompetenzen*).

Dutch: according to the 1996 Dutch Law on Vocational Education and Adult Education, the aim of *Beroepsonderwijs* is theoretical and practical preparation for the execution of occupations that require a vocational qualification. *Beroepsonderwijs* also stimulates the general education and individual development of its students and contributes to social behaviour. Higher education (HE) is not included in *Beroepsonderwijs*.

Vocational education is commonly divided into initial VET (IVET), referring to introduction to an occupation, and continuing VET (CVET), referring to the acquisition of skill and knowledge when an employee has completed IVET and is engaged in work.

CVET

Definitions

English: Adult Continuing Education, which is a form of general education, encompasses both liberal and more functional forms of adult learning.

> **Box 10.1 Occupational differences between IVET and CVET in England**
>
> The nursing diploma in England is primarily based on initial VET. However, about 15% of students in nursing schools are there under the heading of CVET, such as for example, care assistants who benefit from funding from their employing hospitals.
>
> The licence for LGV driving in England is administered by the Ministry of Work and is part of CVET, targeted primarily at adult wage earners or at the unemployed. An equivalent labour market-based qualification also exists in France alongside the VET-based French CAP for drivers. The latter is within the national education system (in a *lycée professionnel* or an apprentice training/*formation* centre) and is mainly targeted at young people leaving the school system.

French: *formation continue*. This term encompasses both of what in German are termed '*Weiterbildung*' and '*Fortbildung*' (see below).

German: *Weiterbildung/Fortbildung*. *Weiterbildung* is any kind of continuing education after completion of school education and IVET, including general and political education as well as VET known as *Fortbildung* (which is divided into training, career development and re-training).

Dutch: *beroepsgerichte scholing* as opposed to *scholing*. While *scholing* also encompasses non-vocational education and training for adults, *beroepsgerichte scholing* refers to all types (formal, non-formal) and all kinds (*Weiterbildung* as well as *Fortbildung*) of VET.

Apprenticeship

Official definitions (CEDEFOP 2008: 29, 30)

English: systematic, long-term training alternating periods in a school or training centre and at the workplace; the apprentice is *contractually linked* to the employer and receives remuneration (wage or allowance). The employer assumes responsibility for providing the trainee with training leading to a specific occupation.

Comment: strictly speaking, apprenticeship does not require 'alternance' between workplace and school/training centre. This happens to be its contemporary form.

French: *Apprentissage*: a mode of VET of long duration, alternating between effective periods in the school (*école*) or a training centre and the place of work. The apprentice (*apprenti(e)*) is contractually bound to the employer and receives a remuneration (wage or compensation). The employer is responsible for providing the apprentice with the VET (*formation*) issuing from a defined occupation (*métier*).

German: apart from the traditional craft (*Handwerk*) areas where the word *Lehrlingsausbildung* is still used, the term 'apprentice' (*Lehrling*) has been outmoded in the Federal Republic since the Vocational Training Act (*Berufsbildungsgesetz*) of 1970, though it was retained in east Germany till 1990. As a result there are two definitions of the term, the latter now being the official one:

• *Lehrlingsausbildung/Lehre*. Systematically constructed long-term VET (*Ausbildung*), alternating between the classroom (*Bildungseinrichtung*) or training centre (*Ausbildungszentrum*) and the firm (*Betrieb*). The apprentice (*Lehrling*) signs an agreement with the employer (*Arbeitgeber*) and receives remuneration (wage or compensation). The employer is responsible for the trainee obtaining a training (*Ausbildung*) which qualifies for a definite occupation (*Beruf*).

• *Berufsausbildung* in the Dual System. Systematically organized long-term VET (2–3.5 years) combining different learning venues, the company, the part-time vocational college (*Berufschule*) and – in certain occupations – the intercompany training centre (*Überbetriegliche Berufsbildungsstätte*). This alternation between different learning locations can be organized on a weekly, monthly or yearly basis. The trainee (*Auszubildende/r*) signs a contract with an employer and receives remuneration (*Lehrlingsvergütung*). The employer is responsible for providing proper training, qualifying the apprentice for a certain occupation (*Beruf*).

Interpretation

English: apprenticeship is a general term that covers a wide variety of institutions and practices. Its practical basis is the need for skills in professions, crafts and trades to be passed from generation to generation. Its moral rationale rests on the need for the values and outlooks of occupations to be passed on. Typically, apprenticeship has involved a close relationship between the *apprentice*, or aspiring entrant into a craft, and the *master*, who is not only skilled in the craft but a custodian of its values and traditions and, importantly, a teacher of those skills and values to the rising generation. Apprenticeship was, in the Middle Ages, the mode of reproduction for those crafts that were practised by associations of tradesmen known as guilds. Apprenticeship continues to exist in some sectors, such as Construction and Engineering, as an institution which involves a young person employed by a firm but undertaking a restricted, though increasing, range of tasks while also receiving training and instruction.

The term 'Apprenticeship' has acquired a distinct meaning when used with a capital letter, as a scheme with government subsidies whereby an employer undertakes to provide an employment place and to provide a structured package which usually includes a work-based NVQ (National Vocational Qualification), a Technical Certificate and Functional Skills (including IT, literacy, numeracy and communication skills). However, the elements of this package do not need to be undertaken in strict sequence so they do not result in *competence* in the French or German senses.

French: the term *Apprentissage* refers to one of the tracks within VET which is distinguished from the school-based track through the labour contract between the apprentice and the firm. *De facto*, the apprenticeship encompasses a tripartite relationship between the firm, the apprentice and the training centre (*centre de formation d'apprentissage*) The term can also mean 'the cumulative process of learning' as in '*l'apprentissage de la lecture*' (learning to read). The context determines which sense of '*apprentissage*' is referred to.

German: German distinguishes between the traditional (time-served) form of apprenticeship which involves the young person becoming an apprentice or *Lehrling*, with the modern, standards-based form within the Dual System, for which the term is a trainee or *Auszubildende/r* (*Azubi* popularly). This reflects the fact that the Dual System is not simply a modern version of the Guild System, but that there is a legal status on both sides: the *Ausbildende* (the one who has obligations to provide vocational education) and the *Auszubildende* (the one who has to be educated).

Dutch: *Leerlingwezen* is a historic concept in the Netherlands since the introduction of the new law on VET and Adult Education in 1996. In 1996 the apprenticeship and the school-based systems were merged. As a result, Dutch VET is now offered by large-scale Regional Colleges in two equivalent tracks: dual (originally the apprenticeship system) and school-based. The formal difference between the two tracks has been limited to: 1) the distribution of the time dedicated to learning at school and to learning in the workplace, and 2) the status of the trainee (trainees in dual tracks have dual status in being students as well as employees).

Box 10.2 Apprenticeship in England

I was an apprentice. The qualification had to increase, but we were very much part of a team and that has been lost. Now placements are short and this cannot happen so easily. People are failing to understand what nursing is all about. A lot of the soft skills which involve communication and caring are being passed to health care assistants. You learned about the job that way. We've gone too far into education and people are not now functioning enough on the wards.

(Nursing sister)

You know, the three-year, so many hours in a college, that type of learning – it's about giving more opportunity to some, so we do the traditional apprenticeships and take on adult trainees and qualify them and mentor them and then qualify them in the workplace. The problem is they haven't got the underpinning theory knowledge of that element of the jobs which they're doing.

(Training Manager, Building firm)

Box 10.3 Apprenticeship in France

The bricklayer CAP in France can be followed either full time (the school-based route) or through an apprenticeship. In this latter case, the apprentice alternates, in various configurations, between the workplace and a training institute. These students have the same obligations as those following the school route in terms of the competences that they are expected to acquire and will receive the same qualification. Apprenticeship is typical of so-called 'manual' occupations at the initial vocational education level; it tends to remain at this basic level, whereas apprenticeship in non-manual occupations progresses to higher levels including university. Currently only a (very) small minority of apprentices prepare for the DUT in software engineering. However, they can be in the majority in other vocational routes, following a two-year post *baccalauréat* programme and even bachelor and masters programmes.

Professional education

Definitions

There is no official definition of professional education though CEDEFOP (2008: 154) defines a regulated profession as: a professional activity or group of professional activities, access to which and the practise of which is directly or indirectly subject to legislative, regulatory or administrative provisions concerning the possession of specific professional qualifications. The distinction between a profession and other occupations exists in all four countries but has a different legal status in each. In addition, the distinction between professions and other occupations, both legally and in vocational and social contexts, varies. However, professional education almost invariably takes place under the auspices of, or accredited by, a HE institution and involves learning a body of declarative (including theoretical) knowledge, which is to be employed in professional judgement and action. Learning to do this usually takes place in a simulated workshop/clinical/legal environment and in controlled probationary operational contexts. Almost invariably, there is a regulatory body, dominated by senior members of the profession, which regulates professional education, entry and exit into and from the profession. It can be seen that professional education shares some of the traits of vocational education in the broader sense.

English: professional education is the education needed for entry into a profession, a legally distinct type of occupation in the UK. Almost invariably professional education takes place under the auspices of a HE institution for at least part of the time, for instance in a medical school for doctors. Like continental forms of vocational education, it involves academic instruction in the relevant theoretical knowledge, simulated activities, observation and controlled practice in operational conditions. In recent years it has tended to incorporate 'learning to learn' and 'social skills' elements, to take account of changing needs within the profession. Some parts of professional education may be undertaken on an *apprenticeship* basis (for example pupillage in a law firm). The term 'vocational education' is not usually applied to professional education.

French: as the notion of a profession refers to any regulated occupation in France, the vocational/professional contrast is not very clear. This unclear boundary between vocational and professional is embodied by the French term *formation professionnelle*, which is commonly used both for IVET and CVET. A 'professional' is a qualified agent, master of an occupation, who has the competences required for that occupation and who usually has a formal qualification to signify these competences. Vocational education, or better vocational learning, has as its aim to prepare practitioners of whatever kind. Whilst the term 'profession' also refers to a regulated occupation such as nursing, nursing education is based on vocational education in the health sector, just as bricklaying education is based on secondary vocational education.

German: there is no equivalent term for 'professional education' in the German context. However, there are special forms of education and examinations for medical doctors, lawyers and teachers, who all undergo a two-step education – within the university and in the field of practice – with a state examination for the latter two. It could be argued that nurses are undertaking professional education since their VET takes place in the *Schulen des Gesundheitswesens* (schools of the health sector), under the auspices of professional bodies. The introduction of the Bachelor degree triggered discussion on the extent to which universities are providing or should provide vocational education. As a reaction to the Bachelor, the Chambers pushed the title 'bachelor professional' for their advanced VET qualifications. But this is not generally accepted.

Dutch: there is no Dutch equivalent for the English term 'professional education'. The Dutch term *Beroepsonderwijs* encompasses both VET at secondary level and HE at Bachelor (BA) level, in Dutch: *middelbaar beroepsonderwijs* (secondary level) and *hoger beroepsonderwijs* (tertiary level). Although the term *professional* is usually associated with graduates from HE (BA level), there is no legal or formal distinction between professions and other occupations. The introduction of the BA–MA structure into the binary tertiary education system is a cause for much linguistic confusion in the Netherlands. The BA–MA structure encompasses non-academic HE institutions (*hoger beroepsonderwijs*) as well as universities. The non-academic HE institutions in particular, faced with the dilemma of identifying either with *Beroepsonderwijs* or HE, sought a new international profile. The association for HE institutions (*Hoger Beroeponderwijs Raad*) has chosen to translate *hoger beroepsonderwijs* as 'Universities of Applied Sciences'.

Terms used in teaching and learning

Unterricht (German) is the formal process of *instruction* (English), particularly as this relates to academic matter (*Wissen*). It involves the teacher and the student in a structured interaction concerning the subject matter, which depends not only on the teacher's expertise but also the student's commitment and motivation. *Unterricht* thus refers to formal, institutional education, but is more restricted in scope than *Bildung*.

Erziehung (German); *Upbringing, Character Formation* (English). This term refers both to child-rearing and character-forming activities and processes, which together result in the development of a person's individuality. Such a process is incomplete without *Unterricht*, usually in a school situation. *Erziehung*, along with *Unterricht* are essential components of *Bildung*.

Dutch: the Dutch language distinguishes *Onderwijs* and *Opvoeding*. The meaning of *Onderwijs* is equivalent to the German term '*Unterrricht*' and *Opvoeding* to the German '*Erziehung*'.

Training

Official definition

Despite its inadequacy, training is identified with vocational education (CEDEFOP 2008), reflecting the lack of distinction that exists in English between 'training' and 'non-professional vocational education'. For instance, the French term refers to '*formation professionnelle*' (vocational education or vocational training) and hence to sites of formal learning. 'Training' in English also has a more specific usage.

Interpretation

English: *training* refers to a process of *instruction* and *practice* that results in the confident carrying out of practical activities (know-how). Training is used in order for tasks to be mastered. Thus a bricklaying job may need a discrete range of tasks to be mastered. In the NVQ system, a list of tasks to be mastered through a process of training will be drawn up from an occupational analysis. Although suited to routine and semi-routine activities, training need not be confined to these and can be used to contribute to processes requiring complex judgement. In this respect, it differs from *drilling* or *conditioning*. German: *abrichten*, French: *dresser*.

French: the word *training* has no equivalent in French, apart from the English usage, employed most often to refer to sports training. The contrast between 'training' and *formation professionnelle* is more between an emphasis on, on the one hand, learning on the job (which resonates with the English concept of training) or even 'sitting with Nelly' and, on the other hand, learning experiences that amount to more than either imitation or formal learning (in a classroom or workshop with a teacher/trainer).

German: the terms in German usage that come closest to 'training' are *anlernen* or *einarbeiten*. *Anlernen* signifies the development of *Fertigkeiten* through training which may take between three months and two years to acquire (English: trainee/German: *Anlernling*). It involves instruction in declarative knowledge or training which takes place as an episode of learning over a short period for

---

Box 10.4 Lorry driving training in England

It is fairly detailed: personal details, licence, passports. Our own drivers pick up recruits and drivers tell them about the company, but we need to select the drivers who do this. (They) need a C+E licence – this is the minimum. Then we do health and safety: manual handling, for example, this is the proper way of bending down; risk assessment – they are obliged to do their own risk assessment; think of the consequences of what you are doing; report near misses so that the business manager can see if there's a pattern; the Working Time Directive, tachographs. Then we move on to the vehicle; they learn about the onboard computer.

(Business manager, Logistics firm)

---

particular activities. Through it, the status of *Angelernte/r* is acquired; below three months the term used is *Einarbeitung*, with no change in status. Another term applied is *Unterweisung*, which is used for short-term instruction on safety issues.

Dutch: the word 'training' is also used in the Dutch language and is commonly associated with short, practice-oriented, non-formal courses, including day courses (skill training, memory training, etc.). Training is also used to characterize exercises for sport (football training) and practical additional elements of formal education courses (homework training).

Civic and citizenship education

There is no official definition of these terms, although they form an integral component in VET programmes in most of the countries studied.

Interpretation

English: the distinction between civic and citizenship education is usually drawn in terms of democracy. One can have civic education for participation in an authoritarian society, but citizenship requires democracy. Confusingly however, the term 'civics' has traditionally been used for the element of citizenship education that became mandatory in vocational education programmes after the 1944 Education Act. Since the lapsing of those provisions, citizenship education plays little or no role in English vocational education, although it has now assumed subject status in the school system.

French: in IVET, in order to develop the capacities of the individual as a whole human being (including as a producer and a citizen), academic learning is included. Such elements of learning also have as their objective to limit the severing of links between the academic and vocational strands of education and to facilitate permeability (parity of esteem). Often criticized because they also work as a selection out of and barrier towards qualification, these elements have been heavily revised in order to make them less academic and better integrated into the 'vocational' content. They cover, for example, mathematics, history and geography, together with knowledge of the political and civil organization of society and mastery of a foreign language, and are often described as being part of civil and social education.

German: civic education could be translated into German as *staatsbürgerliche Erziehung*. The principal architect of the Dual System, Georg Kerschensteiner, writing at the turn of the nineteenth century was concerned about the *staatsbürgerliche Erziehung* of German youth. His aim was to integrate the working class into the political system. Today, *Wirtschafts-und Sozialkunde* (economic and social education) form part of the VET school curriculum, covering both civic and citizenship education, and there is *Politische Bildung* (political education) as a part of voluntary continuing education.

Dutch: the qualification files for secondary vocational education distinguish three types of competence to be developed through VET: occupational, civic and career. In contrast to France, academic learning is not regarded as a prerequisite for the development of the individual as a whole human being. Civic competences are defined in terms of behaviour in the public domain, employability and career development, personal health care, participation in policymaking and democratic decision making, and so on.

Section 2: Qualification

Official definitions

CEDEFOP (2008: 144)

The term 'qualification' covers different aspects:

(a) *formal qualification*: the formal outcome (certificate, diploma or title) of an assessment and validation process which is obtained when a competent body determines that an individual has achieved learning outcomes to given standards and/or possesses the necessary competence to do a job in a specific area of work. A qualification confers official recognition of the value of learning outcomes in the labour market and in education and training. A qualification can be a legal entitlement to practice a trade (OECD); and
(b) *job requirements*: the knowledge, aptitudes and skills required to perform the specific tasks attached to a particular work position (ILO).

European Commission (EC), European Qualifications Framework (EQF) Recommendation

A formal outcome of an assessment and validation process which is obtained when a competent body determines that an individual has achieved learning outcomes to given standards.

French: *Certification*: the formal result of a process of evaluation (*évaluation*) and validation (*validation*) obtained when a competent authority establishes that an individual possesses at the end of an apprenticeship (*au terme d'un apprentissage*) the acquisitions (*acquis*) corresponding to a given norm (*norme donnée*).

German: *Qualifikation*: the formal result of processes of review and validation (*Beurteilungs-und Validierungsprozess*), whereby the responsible authority establishes that the learning outcomes (*Lernergebnisse*) of a person correspond to given standards (*Standards*).

Definition in the Dutch context

Dutch: in Dutch secondary vocational education the word 'qualification' is short for 'qualification file', the document containing all competences to be mastered in order to obtain a secondary vocational education diploma. Therefore, 'qualification' and 'secondary vocational education diploma' are often used as synonyms.

Comments

Both CEDEFOP definitions (a and b) exist in all countries. The EC definition reflects the learning outcomes approach of the EQF, that is, qualifications are awarded regardless of the learning process. It therefore neglects qualifications based on input.

Interpretation

In terms of initial *vocational qualifications*, the most important distinction between the English and the 'continental' definitions is that the latter encompasses the notion of occupational capacity or 'competence', developed through a regulated learning process which encompasses the development of the person as a citizen as well as within the occupation. Qualifications are based on a comprehensive notion of occupation and are designed to enable occupational and social mobility. In England, qualifications are more often awarded on the basis of individual skills and relate to specific fragmented tasks as needed by employers.

English: the dominant definition of qualification in the English context is that of formal accreditation for knowledge or – more usually – 'skill'. It does not imply that one has pursued a course of study, as exemplified by the NVQ. Vocational qualifications signify the level of skills achieved; they do not carry labour market rights, which would relate to the second part of the CEDEFOP definition (a) (successful performance in a test or examination). The English notion of skill relates rather to CEDEFOP definition (b). The definition of qualification as completion of a programme exists with regard to HE, as well as certain more traditional vocational qualifications, such as BTEC.

French: French usage of the term *qualification* typifies the labour market facet of the relationship between *formation* and employment, and refers specifically to the

---

Box 10.5 Examples from the research of the use of the term 'qualification' in the English context

Driving Goods Vehicles, which is an NVQ mapped to the driving test. The candidate has to exhibit skills on a laden vehicle in real-life conditions on the job on the road. The Carrying Goods NVQ is about associated skills to do with handling goods and liaising with customers, colleagues and business contacts. These are both at level 2. There are about 140,000 drivers, of whom about 18,000 end up in traffic offices and there is an NVQ level 3 associated with this. Mostly these NVQs are used as part of an apprenticeship qualification, moving, for instance, from a warehousing to a driving job or from one category of licence to another. No standing requirement to have NVQs for any of these jobs.

(Interview Sector Skills Council for Logistics)

Should be linked to licence. T&G [transport and general workers union] would prefer a broader type of training, including a broader understanding of the industry (particularly in view of substantial technological changes), understanding the importance of logistics, where drivers fit into the labour process, fit into supply chains, just-in-time deliveries, etc. (important in terms of integration of different functions, complete restructuring of the industry). We need to educate them on that.

(Interview union official)

---

labour market value of an individual's personal attributes (which can include *formation* and work experience). The term can also refer to the *qualification* for a particular job in the sense of its position in a hierarchy of employment (from 'unskilled' to 'skilled').

'Qualifications' in the sense of the CEDEFOP definition (a), and translated in French as '*certifications*', are referred to by their specific type, that is, *diplôme*, *titre* and *certificat* (similar to the German term *Abschluss*). A qualification in this sense is based upon a broadly conceived occupation and, in most cases, developed in negotiation with the social partners and educationalists. There is some ambiguity as to whether a *diplôme* confers immediate productive capacity or future potential to be developed in the workplace. Part of this ambiguity arises from the fact that in France, Germany and the Netherlands qualifications layered in 'levels' have, in fact, a dual value: within the education system, they allow the pursuit of studies at a higher level; on the labour market, their value exists as a signal of the individual's capability.

In France and the Netherlands, a qualification as an award has traditionally signified that the holder of the qualification has completed a recognized VET course,

> ## Box 10.6 The French software DUT
>
> In France, the holder of the software DUT can directly enter the labour market. His/her diploma does not, however, guarantee grading as a technician unless this grading is agreed within the collective bargaining associated with this particular employment. But this qualification also allows the possibility of further study up to Bachelor or engineer level, and this is nowadays the choice of the great majority of these students.

has acquired a specified range and level of knowledge and skills, and is competent within a specified occupational field. Recently, the link between knowledge acquisition and the granting of awards has been severed (with the introduction of APEL (Accredited Prior Experiential Learning) and competence-based qualification frameworks). However, the principles of traditional qualifications have been retained, notably the comprehensive notion of occupation, the integrative and multi-dimensional nature of competence, and the association with a learning process (through curricula or experiential learning).

German: the German term *Qualifikation* relates to the two CEDEFOP definitions: (a) form and (b) content (similar to the French *qualification*) and signifies both an *Abschluß* (completion of a learning process) and the value of particular competences demanded in the labour market. A qualification in the sense of the CEDEFOP definition (a) is referred to as *Abschluss*, thus emphasizing the link between the granting of the award and the completion of a regulated and recognized course. Vocational qualifications in this sense are based on the *Beruf* principle and, more than in France and the Netherlands, confer occupational capacity within a strongly delineated occupational field with a specified and exclusive set of activities. A qualification is associated with a particular status and social recognition, confers a strong occupational identity, is linked to the collective bargaining system as well as with social welfare and thus has strong labour market currency. To pursue a *Beruf* qualification, the individual needs a typical combination of formal knowledge, skills and experience. The concept of the *Beruf* places the individual capacity to work and act competently in a vocational environment (*berufliche Handlungsfähigkeit*) as the overarching aim of VET. The qualification therefore reflects the holistic and integrated nature of the *Beruf* and is incompatible with full modularization.

German uses *Qualifikation* also for a *Hochschulabschluss* (HE degrees).

Dutch: the term qualification (*kwalificatie*) has two meanings in Dutch VET. Qualification stands for a) learning outcomes that have to be mastered to be entitled to receive a VET diploma and for b) the VET diploma itself. The first meaning refers to the national qualification files containing sections for occupational, career and civic competences, known in the Netherlands as a 'threefold qualification' process. The second meaning refers to the result of the learning process; somebody has obtained a *kwalificatie*/qualification. All IVET national qualifications can be obtained through IVET courses, either in dual track or a school-based track, or via APL (Accredited Prior Learning). In the second meaning, the term refers to all competences.

Licence to practise

In *England*, a certificate is often needed instead of, or in addition to, the qualification, as a precondition to enter the labour market. This is a regulatory mechanism reflecting the weakness of standards in VET. For example, in the construction sector, employees often require a so-called CSCS (Construction Skills Certification Scheme) card to enter building sites. On the continent, the qualification itself commonly serves as a licence to practise, constituting evidence that its holder possesses a set range of competences. Examples of 'licence to practise' that apply in all countries include the nursing registration (with the qualification as a pre-condition for registration) and the driving licence. In *Germany* there are about 40 'crafts' (*Berufe*) which require a certificate (*Anlage A zur Handwerksordnung* annex A to the craft code) and other occupations where the qualification is sufficient for labour market entry.

Regulated professional qualifications can also be regarded as a licence to practise, as defined by European Directive of 2005 (EC 2005b) on the recognition of professional qualifications: 'An occupational activity or group of occupational activities, access to which, and the practice of which (or to one of its forms), is directly or indirectly subject to legislative, regulatory or administrative provisions concerning the possession of specific qualifications.'

Modularization

The type of modularization varies according to the conceptualization of an occupation. In *France* and the *Netherlands*, while VET courses have been modularized and certificates are awarded on completion of individual modules to enable flexible and lifelong learning, the exit qualification is awarded only on successful completion of all relevant modules constituting the qualification. This compares with a more flexible form of modularization in the NVQ system in *England*. Qualifications are awarded on completion of typically narrow sets of fragmented and largely optional modules. While the system does not fully subscribe to the fragmentation model, as NVQs are awarded only for certain combinations of qualifications (Ertl 2002), it is highly flexible and allows for the accumulation of competencies through a variety of modes (including APEL) and within a flexible time frame.

In *Germany*, a degree of modularization was introduced in the early 1990s. More recently, units of assessment taken from qualifications are used as part of an inclusion strategy for those without an apprenticeship contract (*Qualifizierungsbausteine*); the idea is for them to be credited towards a full qualification. Currently, there is a pilot programme testing 14 fully modularized qualifications, each broken down into five to eight modules (*Ausbildungsbausteine*). Apart from that, there are *Zusatzqualifikationen* (supplementary units), which supplement initial qualifications and link them with advanced vocational or HE qualifications. Modularization, as a systematic approach, is highly contested by most stakeholders as it is deemed incompatible with the German principle of *Beruf*.

Learning outcomes

Official definitions

CEDEFOP (2008: 120)

The set of knowledge, skills and/or competences an individual acquired and/or is able to demonstrate after completion of a formal, non-formal or informal learning process.

EC, EQF recommendation

A statement of what a learner knows, understands and is able to do on completion of a learning process. Learning outcomes are defined in terms of knowledge, skills and competence.

German: *Lernergebnisse*: denoting the totality of *Kenntnisse*, *Fähigkeiten* and/or *Kompetenzen* which a person after having gone through (*durchlaufen*) a formal, non-formal or informal learning process (*Lernprozess*) has achieved and/or is in a position to certify (*nachweisen*).

French: *Resultats/Acquis de l'apprentissage*: The ensemble (*ensemble*) of '*savoirs*', '*aptitudes*' and/or '*compétences*' which an individual has acquired and/or is ready (*en mesure*) to demonstrate as issuing from a formal, non-formal or informal apprenticeship (*apprentissage*) process.

Definition in the Dutch context

Dutch: *leerresultaten*. The results of a learning process (in secondary vocational education). The word does not differentiate between results in terms of skills, knowledge and behaviour.

Interpretation

The concept of 'learning outcomes' is used and understood differently in different countries: as output of a learning process (the 'official' EQF definition), as educational standard (waymark of progression through a curriculum), and as lesson objective (the way it is often used within educational institutions).

Learning outcomes in *England*, exemplified in levels 1–3 of the NVQ framework, specify outputs, which are the criteria for assigning a qualification to an individual on the basis of *in situ* performance of a range of tasks based on occupational standards. Outputs (in the form of units of competence and occupational standards) relate to specific tasks which are individually assessed. There is no 'inferential gap' assumed between an item of assessment and the conclusion concerning grasp of the content of the programme of study, but direct inference of task ability based on observation.

Learning outcomes in relation to the *French* and *Dutch* competence-based qualifications represent a hybrid model. Similar to the English NVQ model, competences are derived from a functional analysis of work activities. However, in *France* the unity of tasks constituting an occupation is preserved. The learning outcomes are expressed less in terms of task performance than of general capacities for managing the range of tasks or functions involved and in developing in a professional manner in the performance of these. Crucially, in France and the Netherlands, competences form the basis for curriculum development. Thus, the development of competence is achieved through what is essentially an input-based system. Furthermore, if certain qualifications are today designed on a learning outcomes basis, this is by no means the case with all of them. The software DUT, for example, rests principally on a curriculum and an input design strategy.

The *German* VET system follows the standards-based approach. VET qualifications in the Dual System are based on a set of occupational standards which form a qualification profile. Based on these standards, curricula are developed using a combination of learning outcomes and input. They do not relate to particular tasks, but are designed to develop broad occupational capacity. Assessment is based on sampling across a range of knowledge, know-how and understanding set out in a programme of study in order to draw conclusions about the individual's grasp of its content.

Other terms associated with qualification

Recognition of skills and competences (CEDEFOP 2004: 66)

a) Formal recognition: the process of granting official status to skills and competences either:
   • through the award of certificates or
   • granting of equivalence, credit units, etc.
b) Social recognition: the acknowledgement of the value of skills and/or competences by economic and social stakeholders.

Validation of informal/ non-formal learning (CEDEFOP 2004: 84)

The process of assessing and recognizing a wide range of knowledge, know-how, skills and competences, which people develop throughout their lives within different environments, for example through education, work and leisure activities.

Certification (of skills and competences) (CEDEFOP 2008: 40)

The process of issuing a certificate, diploma or title formally attesting that a set of learning outcomes (knowledge, know-how, skills and/or competences) acquired by an individual have been assessed and validated by a competent body against a predefined standard.

Interpretation

The CEDEFOP definition is unduly restrictive as it limits certification to learning outcomes, whereas it can also relate to standards (Brockmann *et al.* 2008a). Certification validates the outcome of either formal learning or informal/non-formal learning. When validation is undertaken by an authoritative body, such as the state, or social partnership organizations, awarding bodies or recognized bodies in civil society such as Chambers of Commerce, it serves as a guarantee to society that the individual does in fact possess these attributes. For example, in France and the Netherlands VET and HE (BA level) qualifications are the only standards used in APL procedures. So, APL procedures are, in fact, official exam procedures and subject to strict regulations and supervision by the School Inspectorate.

Section 3: Knowledge

Official definition (CEDEFOP 2008: 105f)

The outcome of the assimilation of information through learning. Knowledge is the body of facts, principles, theories and practices that is related to a field of study or work.

Comment

There are numerous definitions of knowledge. Nevertheless, modern conceptions rest broadly on several basic distinctions:

- Aristotle distinguished between theoretical and practical logic. In line with this distinction, modern theoreticians (Alexander *et al.* 1991) distinguish declarative (theoretical) knowledge from procedural (practical) knowledge. Declarative knowledge includes assertions on specific events, facts and empirical generalizations, as well as deeper principles on the nature of reality. Procedural knowledge includes heuristics, methods, plans, practices, procedures, routines, strategies, tactics, techniques and tricks (Ohlsson 1994).
- Between forms of knowledge which represent different ways of learning about the world. Whilst various attempts have been made to compile such lists, the following categories are frequently represented:

a) objective (natural/scientific) knowledge, judged on the basis of certainty;
b) subjective (literary/aesthetic) knowledge, judged on the basis of authenticity;
c) moral (human/normative) knowledge, judged on the basis of collective acceptance (right/wrong); and
d) religious/divine knowledge, judged by reference to a divine authority (God).

This basic understanding of knowledge underpins the questions we ask, the methods we use and the answers we give in our search for knowledge.

*   Knowledge encompasses tacit and explicit knowledge. Tacit knowledge (Polanyi, 1966) is knowledge that learners possess, which influences cognitive processing but which they may not necessarily express or be aware of. Explicit knowledge is knowledge a learner is conscious of, including tacit knowledge that converts into an explicit form by becoming an 'object of thought' (Prawat 1989).

Sources: EC 2006b; CEDEFOP 2008.

Related terms: competence, know-how, learning, learning outcomes, skill (CEDEFOP 2008: 105).

Interpretation

The problems associated with practical knowledge are included in this glossary under the headings of *skill* and *competence*. However, the definition is unsatisfactory in a number of ways. Here we deal with propositional knowledge (knowledge that) and also include an example of practical knowledge in England by way of contrast with theoretical/contingent knowledge.

The official definition given above does not distinguish between knowledge and belief. It is assumed that if someone knows something, that something is true. But one can believe something that is false. In many cases, too, knowledge presupposes that one can give a reason for what one knows. This condition is added to indicate instances where we want to distinguish between true belief and knowledge, that is, where someone believes something that just happens to be true from cases where someone has a reason for holding a true belief.

In addition, whilst French and German distinguish between systematic and non-systematic knowledge, English and Dutch do not. Confusion over this issue has arisen in the EQF documentation. Thus, the English version uses the undiffer-entiated term 'knowledge' as one principal column heading. The German version uses the term '*Kenntnisse*', which refers to non-systematic knowledge in German, while the French version uses the term '*savoir*', which refers to systematic knowledge, and '*connaissances*', which can in some contexts refer to non-systematic knowledge. Since it is clear from examination of the curricula of many, if not all, German vocational programmes that both *Wissen* and *Kenntnisse* are involved, it

Box 10.7 Examples of lorry driving knowledge

There is a legislative requirement to carry out a daily walkaround check, but how much detail depends on the organization. In the UK it is going to be very basic: checking oil, water, wheelnuts, lights . . . not expecting them to check the engine. Potentially the CPC (Certificate of Professional Competence) expects this; in Germany, knowledge of engine mechanics will be expected. But my argument is that you would not need this to be a fuel-efficient driver. A lot is down to practical experience. Too much theory may restrict what they can actually pick up. The danger is that you may confuse the individual; what is the added value when you are just trying to achieve a behavioural shift? Images of a rolled-over vehicle plus practical illustrations of load-shifting behaviour might change behaviour. Training of this kind tends to be one to one. Drivers with 25 years' experience think that they haven't anything to learn, but they think otherwise after a training session; they will be taken over different routes. Too much theory is difficult to teach with diagrams etc. Drivers came into haulage because they don't want an academic path and the risk is that they will become confused.

(*Representative Employers, transport industry*)

is misleading to use one, restrictive, term to indicate the kind of propositional knowledge that is involved in such programmes.

Knowledge is usually conceived of as having three main aspects:

- *propositional knowledge* or *knowledge that* (German: *Wissen*; French: *Savoir*);
- *knowledge how* or practical knowledge (German: *können* for ability to act, *wissen wie* for the ability to give an account of how something is done; French: *savoir-faire* for ability to act, *savoir comment faire* for the ability to give an account of how something is done) and, finally;
- *knowledge by acquaintance* (German verb = *kennen*, substantive = *Kenntnisse*; French verb = *connaître*, substantive = *connaissance*).

For *Germany* there are only two substantives: *Wissen* and *Kenntniss*, though the latter is not usually referred to explicitly in Learning Outcomes and Curricula but is implicitly understood to be an aspect of contingent knowledge (for example 'knows that X is an instance of Y'). (*Kenntnis* is not *Fertigkeit* and vice versa.)

In *Dutch* the distinction between theoretical and practical knowledge is quite common. Although both concepts are not officially defined and often used in combination, the common understanding is that theoretical knowledge is grounded in academic research while practical knowledge has its roots in experiences (see: tacit knowledge). As in German, the Dutch language distinguishes the verbs *weten* (*wissen*, as in *wetenschap* or *Wissenschaft*) and *kennen*. Surprisingly the Dutch language has no noun for *weten*, only for *kennen*: *kennis/Kentniss*, knowledge.

In VET contexts, these distinctions are adhered to. Thus in *England*, the Technical Certificate refers to propositional knowledge underlying the occupation and the NVQ refers to skill or know-how, without distinguishing between contingent and systematic propositional knowledge. In *France*, systematic knowledge has been and continues to be most often associated with formal educational situations and with academic subjects, in contrast to know-how which relates to work situations or to simulatory situations such as training workshops. However, this distinction between contingent and systematic knowledge has been questioned in numerous works of professional pedagogy which show how knowledge in action, that is, concepts exercised in action, can also be seen as an integral part of work situations or experiences. In *Germany*, *Wissen* and *Können* (the constituents of *Fachkompetenz*), as is also the case with *savoir*, are the province of the *Berufschule* or vocational school and constitute at least part of the underpinning knowledge. *Kenntnisse* and *Fertigkeiten* on the other hand, as with *connaissance*, can be developed within workshop and workplace environments.

It should be noted that there is an ambiguity in the English expression 'knows how to', which can mean either 'can do X' or 'knows the way to do X'. German distinguishes between *können* and *wissen wie*, the latter marking the second sense of the English expression. Similarly, in French the distinction is made between *savoir-faire* and *savoir comment faire*. *Declarative knowledge* or *knowledge that* refers to knowing that something is the case or to a collective body of knowledge as in a subject. English does not distinguish explicitly between knowledge of a single fact and *theoretical* or *systematic knowledge* of a subject. *Scientific Knowledge* usually means knowledge of a particular subject such as Biology or Physics.

Dutch: in Dutch VET no formal definition of *kennis* (knowledge) has been given. From their analysis of the types of knowledge to be found in qualification files, Onstenk and Huisman (2007) distinguish three dimensions:

1. Explicit (codified) knowledge versus implicit (tacit) knowledge.
2. Knowledge associated with specific occupational tasks versus a knowledge that can be applied in a great number of occupational settings.
3. Knowledge structured in traditional subjects versus knowledge embedded in occupational contexts.

Subject

No official definition of this term is offered.

Interpretation

English: *subject*; German: *Fach*; French: *sujet* or *matière* (vernacular); Dutch: *vak* or *schoolvak*.

These terms signify the systematic organization of knowledge according to central propositions, central concepts and ways of discovering and validating new claims. For example, history employs central propositions concerning major historical events (for example, the French Revolution, the unification of Germany, the Norman Conquest), central concepts (such as historical documentation, evidence or narrative) and means of discovery and analysis (such as archival research, participant interviews and archaeological excavation). In this sense, subjects are embodiments of systematic knowledge (*Wissen, savoir*). Traditionally, vocational education has been concerned with the application of subject knowledge to practice (for example, mechanics to construction). Subject underpinning has been important to the 'dual value' nature of a qualification in some countries, such as France, as the academic currency can be cashed within the education system as well as the labour market and also confers social status and self-esteem on the individual who possesses it.

Lernfelder (German, literally meaning 'learning field'). This is an example of another way of organizing underpinning knowledge, which is now in widespread use in German VET. It stems from a concern with the better integration of theory and practice and with '*Handlungsorientierung*' (literally 'action orientation'), meaning that teaching and learning in vocational schools are based upon authentic situations in the workplace. This does not necessarily mean that the systematic nature of the knowledge is lost, but that the knowledge in the occupational field is drawn from across different subject boundaries. On the other hand, if the systematization of the knowledge is dependent on being organized into subjects, then there is at least the possibility that occupationally-based propositional knowledge will become more fragmentary and more like *Kenntnis/connaissance* than *Wissen/savoir*.

Box 10.8 Example of theoretical knowledge in English IT

DW rejects the statement (made by HR) that software engineering is not rooted in theory but is about finding practical solutions for customers. He thinks it is rooted in theory; you need to understand the theory to be able to apply it in the real world. Within the firm, there are engineers working on the telecoms network who have no or very little theoretical understanding, and they struggle and don't enjoy the job as much because the way they are finding the fault is by trying and opening the network in as many places as they can (they fiddle around until they find it). Whereas somebody with the theoretical understanding will sit down with the meter and do some tests, and make some informed choices and decisions, and maybe only open the network once, because they know what they're looking for and they know where to look.

(*Head of Apprenticeship, IT Enterprise*)

Box 10.9 Example of contingent knowledge in English lorry driving

. . . legislation, safe loading practices, highway code. A lot of knowledge is required to do the job, particularly where there are enforcement issues. Some say that the responsibility rests with the drivers, but legislation states that companies have a duty of care, so legally it rests with the company as well as the driver. We provide guides to transport managers who will cascade that information. We provide lots of courses, but what about the small operator? He may not even buy updates. There are still people who don't know about the working time directive because they have never been informed about it. There is a requirement to keep up-to-date on a weekly, monthly basis. FTA (Freight Transport Association) will provide the legislative updates. Some specific organisation knowledge is also required, e.g. occasional drivers like scaffolders and such people are also in the scope of the legislation. They are probably more exposed than anyone else. Getting knowledge sometimes just doesn't happen.

(*Representative, employer's association transport industry*)

Section 4: Competence

Official definitions

CEDEFOP (2008: 47)

The ability to apply learning outcomes adequately in a defined context (education, work, personal or professional development).

German: *Kompetenz*.
French: *compétence*.

EU, EQF recommendation

The proven ability to use knowledge, skills and personal, social and/or methodological abilities, in work or study situations and in professional and/or personal development. In the EQF, competence is described in terms of responsibility and autonomy.

French: compétence: established capacity (*capacité avérée*) to utilize *savoirs, aptitudes* and personal, social and/or methodological (*méthodologiques*) *dispositions* in work situations or in study for professional (*professionnel*) and/or personal development. The EQF describes *compétences* in the form of taking responsibility (*prise de responsabilité*) and of autonomy (*autonomie*).

German: *Kompetenz*: proven *Fähigkeit*, to use *Kenntnisse*, *Fertigkeiten* as well as personal, social and/or methodologic (*methodisch*) *Fähigkeiten* in a work or learning situation and for occupational (*berufliche*) and/or personal development (*Entwicklung*). In the EQF *Kompetenz* is described in the sense of taking over (*Übernahme*) responsibility (*Verantwortung*) and autonomy (*Selbstständigkeit*).

Interpretation

Both the CEDEFOP and EC definitions are problematic as neither takes account of distinctions in interpretations across and within different national contexts and terms are translated in the literal sense. The EC definition is highly ambiguous; it contains reference to the comprehensive, integrated concept of competence prevalent in continental European countries, whereas the EQF itself has adopted a narrowed-down version, omitting the social and personal dimensions. The definition of 'competence' as 'responsibility and autonomy' may be interpreted to refer to control and supervision in the workplace, but also to learning situations in the most general sense, since EQF applies to academic as well as vocational qualifications.

The move towards competence-based approaches is generally associated with the greater complexity of tasks in the workplace, accelerating technological and socio-economic change, and the need for lifelong learning. A major distinction is to be made between 1) integrated, multi-dimensional approaches denoting occupational capacity prevalent in many continental countries; and 2) functional, task-based systems dominant in England. This distinction relates to a person-centred, integrative approach to competence on the one hand, and one concerned with the workplace and the labour market on the other. This distinction is not always clear cut, with systems combining aspects of either approach. For example, the French and Dutch systems are explicitly outcomes-based, while the outputs are also clearly related to the inputs (curriculum, pedagogy). The German notion of competence has both an individual-focused and a workplace-focused facet, reflecting the dualism of the college and the workplace of the German Dual System of apprenticeship.

In a multi-dimensional approach, competence denotes the *potential* of the individual worker to draw on multiple resources, including knowledge, know-how and social and personal qualities to deal with complex and unpredictable tasks and situations. The development of competence through curriculum-based IVET involves occupational knowledge and practical know-how as well as social and civic dimensions, in order to develop trainees for a specific (comprehensively defined) occupational field and as citizens in wider society. Competence is conceived as disposition, highlighting the focus on the whole person developing ways of responding to occupational demands. Learning is conceived as broad-based and open-ended, enabling workers to cope with the demands of fast-changing environments. Didactically, competence is developed increasingly through self-directed learning within authentic work situations.

By contrast, in a task-based approach, individual competencies are identified on the basis of a detailed analysis of tasks and activities in the workplace. This approach focuses on *what is required by the job*, that is, the outcome rather than the potential of labour, and is exemplified in the English NVQ system. The task-based system of specifying knowledge and skills for a specified list of tasks is potentially in conflict with the integrative conception of competence which relies on a broad-based and open-ended approach to learning. The outcomes-based approaches in France and the Netherlands differ from the English one in that they incorporate to some extent both conceptions of competence. Thus, while competences are task-based, a comprehensive notion of occupation is retained. Competence-based qualification frameworks and APEL have been introduced to enhance transparency, flexibility and adaptability of qualifications.

In *England*, the integrative conception of competence has been absent from the policy debate (although examples were found of how it is applied in practical contexts, see Box 10.10). The dominant definition is that of the NVQ model which is defined as a competence-based qualifications system. NVQs consist of units of competence, based on occupational standards (elements of competence with associated performance criteria) relating to individual tasks as identified through an analysis of job functions. This conception of competence is concerned with the performance of prescribed tasks to a defined standard, and thus with the output of labour rather than with individual capacity. It denotes the performance of *skills* with minimal underpinning knowledge. Competences are narrowly defined, and are cumulative rather than integrative, constituting the *skills* deemed necessary for a particular job. A defining characteristic is the separation of qualifications from learning processes. Being assessment-led, NVQs are not commonly linked to curricula and more often rely on the accreditation of skills commonly learned on the job, underpinned by a belief that knowledge needed for the execution of tasks is acquired through experience in the workplace.

A further and increasingly common conception of competence is that of discrete abilities (cognitive, social and personal), widely applied in Human Resource Management (HRM) and Human Resource Development (HRD) policies, including recruitment, selection and staff development. These were previously (and often still are) referred to as *soft skills* and include abilities related to communication and team-working, problem-solving, decision-making and leadership. They are reminiscent of the continental notions of *Fähigkeiten*, *savoir-être* and *attitude*, but differ from them in that they are not conceived as part of a comprehensive notion of competence.

French: competence in the workplace relies on the integration of *savoir* (knowledge), *savoir-faire* (know-how) and *savoir-être* (social and personal qualities and attributes) in a given work situation. This conception has become progressively more central to the design of professional qualifications. It is echoed in HRD and the recognition of the importance of CVET and personal development in the workplace, involving continuous experiential learning based on reflected experience.

Box 10.10 Understandings of competence in the English context

The task-specific meaning of competence was strongly reflected in day-to-day usage of the term in both lorry driving and bricklaying, reflecting the NVQ definition and signifying the ability to perform a task 'to the standard required'. In relation to bricklaying, the further education (FE) college head explained that the term was in fact only used in relation to assessment (of performance). Competence was seen as the application of skill in practice. Knowledge was seen as important only to the extent that it was necessary to carry out the task. More important than knowledge was having the right 'attitude' in terms of certain normative behaviours, such as an attitude of compliance in lorry driving: 'having been taught the skill, they can then be totally incompetent at doing it . . . because they do not follow rules'.

(*Head of training company in lorry driving*)

The following quotation illustrates the focus of competence on required behaviour, rather than independent professional judgement:

A lot of this is down to practical experience. Too much theory may restrict what they can actually pick up. The danger is that you may confuse the individual – what is the added value when you are just trying to achieve a behavioural shift?

(*Representative of logistics employer association*)

Both nursing and software engineering practice rely on the integration of theoretical knowledge, practical know-how and social and personal competences, although IVET is not structured in terms of competence development and there is no civic dimension. At the same time, aspects of the task-based approach to competence are evident within CVET. For example, the NHS 'Knowledge and Skills Framework' foresees career progression in a very restrictive sense, tightly bound by job descriptions. In both software engineering and nursing competence is understood as performing a task to a certain standard: 'Competence is about what somebody has proven to be able to do; so they can have a Java skill, but the competency is the level to which they can do it'.

(*HR manager in case study company*)

There is no integrative notion of competence in IT. However, there is increased recognition of the importance of social and personal competences in view of the broader and enhanced profile of software engineers which includes project management and customer negotiation. However, in the absence of an integrative conception of competence, these are typically discrete competences, such as communication and interaction with others, ability to lead or motivate others.

The competence-based qualification register reflects the concern with greater practice orientation in VET. Qualifications are developed for an occupation and/or for a family of jobs/occupations on the basis of competences identified through an analysis of tasks in the workplace. Through the adoption of APEL, individual competences have been disassociated from formal learning processes. However, it is the same classification of competences that underpins assessment in the grid for APEL, on the one hand, and in that for formal VET on the other. Thus, the French approach differs from the English NVQ system in important ways and may still be termed an 'occupational model'. Competences are based on a comprehensive notion of occupation; they are integrative and no single competence can be disassociated from the whole; they are multi-dimensional, relating to *savoir* (knowledge), *savoir-faire* (practical know-how) and *savoir-être* (social and personal qualities and attributes); and they form the basis for curricula which include occupational as well as general and civic education.

German: *Handlungskompetenz*, or competence of action-taking, has been the defining principle of the German Dual System since the late 1980s and refers to the development of the individual. It denotes the ability and readiness of the individual to act responsibly and independently in situations both within the occupational field and within wider society. *Handlungskompetenz* as developed in framework curricula for (part-time) vocational colleges encompasses the dimensions of *Fachkompetenz* (occupational competence), *Sozialkompetenz* (social competence), *Personalkompetenz* (personal competence), *Methodenkompetenz* (procedural competence) and *Lernkompetenz* (learner competence). This concept of *Handlungskompetenz* is based on the integration of *Wissen* (knowledge), *Können* (know-how) and social and personal attributes in order to deal with complex tasks.

Berufliche Handlungsfähigkeit refers to competence in the workplace. The underlying concept is the notion of 'complete action' (*vollständige Handlung*), which includes the planning, execution and controlling of tasks. The training regulations specify *Fertigkeiten* (practical skills), *Kenntnisse* (non-systematic knowledge) and *Fähigkeiten* (abilities to carry out tasks) to be developed in the workplace.

Recent reforms have sought to diminish the dualism of vocational college and workplace, promoting the better integration of theory and practice (therefore of *Wissen* rather than *Kenntnisse*). Learning in colleges in reconstructed or simulated work situations (based on complete action) is designed to enable trainees to work across work processes and to engage in continuous (experiential) learning, based on foundational knowledge of underlying principles, in order to solve unpredictable tasks in fast-changing environments. Similarly, knowledge is no longer structured into subjects, but in so-called *Lernfelder* (learning fields) (see above). Traditional subjects are converted into a cross-curricular structure, which combines the knowledge and know-how relevant to particular situations.

Dutch: competence in the workplace denotes the ability to integrate *knowledge*, practical *know-how* and *attitudes* (*houdingen*) to solve specific tasks in a given work situation. Competence has also been defined more broadly as 'the ability to

Box 10.11 The French bricklayer (*maçon*) and nurse (*infirmière*)

For *maçons*, there are four broad areas of activity (*fonctions*): preparation, organization and execution; implementation of new projects or renovations; equipment maintenance; and communication. Each of these is linked to one or more activity, broken down into detailed tasks. Each activity specifies the resources required, the level of autonomy and responsibility involved, and the expected outcome. In the work-in-progress on nurses' qualifications, there is now a description of the occupation (*métier*) that cites relevant legislation, since nursing is a regulated occupation, and refers to nine activities, themselves detailed into '*opérations*', or tasks, and a schedule of situations, methods, outcomes and resources.

Based on these activities, *compétences* are identified and included in a qualification framework that teases out what the individual should be able to do, under what conditions, and the criteria by which s/he is to be assessed. For *maçons*, 'making sense of technical documents' supposes that the individual is able to relate information from written documents to plans and charts, and vice versa, to read documentation, and to locate a particular operation in the overall planning stage – that is, to be able to read maps, specifications and planning documentation. The criterion by which this is assessed is the accuracy of response. The pairing of activity and *compétences* has been fleshed out by a list of 'related expertise' or 'related knowledge' (*savoirs associés* and *connaissances associées*, respectively). In the case of *maçons*, 'related expertise' is organized under seven headings that cross-cut the *compétences*. These include, for example, organizing building operations, technical communication and quality control. Under each heading is a schedule of 'knowledge, principles and concepts' along with the extent to which these need to be mastered. For example, under the heading 'Materials' are listed familiarity with materials groups, such as stone, wood or plaster, and with the specific materials used in building, such as concrete, or specific features, such as lintels, beams and shafts. Expertise boundaries relate to the ability to identify, understand and suggest a material, use technical documentation, and cite provisions for use of the material in question. Here, too, the knowledge and expertise can be seen as underlying *compétences* and the efficient execution of *fonctions*.

successfully meet complex demands in a particular context through the mobilization of psychosocial prerequisites'.

In the competence-based qualifications framework, competences are derived from an analysis of core tasks with associated work processes. As in France, competences are integrative and based on a comprehensive notion of occupation.

They are multi-dimensional with each competence defined in terms of *knowledge*, *skills* and *attitude*. Competences form the basis for curriculum development by individual schools. Competence is developed through a comprehensive IVET programme, with qualifications comprising occupational, career, civic and learning-to-learn competences.

Reflecting the conflict between the two conceptions of competences, in the workplace and more broadly, there is a tension between what are relatively narrowly defined outcomes-based competences and the idea of self-directed learning in schools (reflecting a conflict between the different stakeholders). Based on constructivist learning theory, self-directed learning is thought to enable continuous learning and lifelong careers, built upon broad, fluid notions of occupations. There is a further tension between competence-based learning and the restricted capacity of schools to provide relevant courses.

Section 5: Skill

Official definitions

CEDEFOP (2008: 164)

The ability to perform tasks and to solve problems.

French: *aptitudes professionnelles/capacités professionnelles* (professional aptitudes and capacities). *Capacité de réaliser des tâches et résoudre des problèmes* (capacity to realize tasks and resolve problems).

German: specific occupational (*berufliche*) *Fähigkeiten* and/or *Fach-/Sachkenntnisse* (subject or object knowledge). *Bezeichnet die Fähigkeit, berufliche Aufgaben durchzuführen und Probleme zu lösen* (connotes the ability to carry out occupational tasks and to resolve problems).

Definition in the Dutch context

Dutch: *vaardigheid* or *beroepsvaardigheid*. In contrast to the CEDEFOP definition, the Dutch word '*vaardigheid*' does not refer to experience or knowledge, but solely to the physical or mental abilities to perform an activity, any activity, varying from: *vaardigheid* in playing the organ; *vaardigheid* in speaking English; to *vaardigheid* in using a hammer. Knowledge is not explicitly included in *vaardigheid*, only in explicit references like *cognitieve vaardgheden*.

EC, EQF recommendation

The ability to apply knowledge and use know-how to complete tasks and solve problems. In the EQF, skills are described as cognitive (use of logical, intuitive and creative thinking) and practical (involving manual dexterity and the use of methods, materials, tools and instruments).

French: *aptitude*: capacity to apply *connaissances* and to utilize *un savoir-faire* for realizing tasks (*tâches*) and resolving problems. The EQF describes *aptitudes* as being cognitive (using logical, intuitive and creative thought) and practical.

German: *Fertigkeiten*: the ability (*Fähigkeit*) to apply knowledge (*Kenntnisse*) and to employ (*einzusetzen*) know-how to carry out tasks (*Aufgaben*) and resolve problems. In the EQF, *Fertigkeiten* are described as cognitive (logical, intuitive and creative thought) and practical (dexterity (*Geschicklichkeit*)) and utilization (*Verwendung*) of methods, materials, tools (*Werkzeugen*) and instruments).

Know-how (CEDEFOP 2008: 104)

Practical knowledge or expertise
    French: *savoir-faire*: *compétence, expérience* in the exercise of an activity.
    German: *das Wissen*, how one practically realizes a thing (*Sache*).

Definition in the Dutch context

Dutch: Knowing (*Weten*) how you carry out a task.

Interpretation

The CEDEFOP and EC definitions are confusing, and the distinctions made between skill and competence are blurred. The translations into French and German are problematic and convey nothing about the differences in interpretations. There is no equivalent in the other languages for the English notion of 'skill', which is firmly associated with the historical concern with the labour market in England. The contrasting German notions (*Fertigkeiten*, *Fähigkeiten*) are associated with the integrative approach to competence within a comprehensively-defined occupational field, while the French notion of *aptitude* explicitly refers to the use of knowledge in practical activities without necessarily relating aptitude to a broad occupational field. The notion of know-how is not an official term in English VET, while the French notion of *savoir-faire* is associated with the integrative approach of competence (the German equivalent is *Können*).

    English: skills: the concept of *skills* relates to individual tasks or jobs and typifies the English VET and labour market systems. The concern in England with the output of labour can be traced back to Adam Smith and the fragmentation of the labour process into specialized tasks. The notion of *skills* can be found to originate in the craft-based system of apprenticeship, with an apprentice working alongside a master craftsman, and learning to carry out relevant tasks on-the-job, with minimal underpinning knowledge, so that *skills* can be seen as individual attributes. Consequently, occupational ability is thought of as a bundle of skills rather than as broad occupational capacity. In the labour market, individual *skills* and work experience are commonly valued over comprehensive qualifications. Furthermore, and in contrast to the continental conception of competence, *skills* do not rely on

Box 10.12 Understandings of skills in the English context

In all four occupations studied, 'skills' are understood as the abilities to do the job, while competence denotes the ability to perform a task to the standard required.

In both bricklaying and LGV driving, skills are highly specialized and narrowly defined, with a strong demarcation between different occupations. Thus, for lorry driving, skills are confined to driving the vehicle and basic maintenance. The emphasis is on required behaviour and compliance rather than a broad range of skills:

a lot of discretion is being taken away from the driver, they are being tracked, and traffic office designs the route, using for example only left turns

(*Trade union representative*)

Drivers just follow orders and don't need to do much planning

(*Employers' association representative*)

In both lorry driving and bricklaying, there is extensive on-the-job learning and accreditation of existing skills, typically involving – in the case of the bricklayer – mixing mortar and laying bricks. Knowledge is deemed important only to the extent that it is necessary to underpin skills:

Skills are appropriate to what people need to know. They probably don't contain as much, they are probably narrower now than they used to be . . . It's not a bad thing that people learn what they do rather than what they don't do . . . If things don't have a use, we don't learn it.

(*Representative of Sector Skills Council for Construction*)

In nursing, skills include both 'technical' and social skills (or 'attitude') and, together with knowledge, are required for competence in the workplace. The Knowledge and Skills Framework lists the knowledge and skills required in relation to specific tasks and posts. While the range is broader than those typified by the NVQ system, it reflects the labour market orientation of the English system.

the integration of knowledge and social and personal qualities, but typically denote the performing of tasks without the reflective use of knowledge.

French: *savoir-faire* may be translated as know-how (or practical knowledge) and denotes the ability to perform a task in a specific environment, through the integration with *savoir* and *savoir-être* as captured by the notion of competence (see above). In contrast to the English term *skills*, *savoir-faire* cannot be disassociated

---

Box 10.13 Understanding of *savoir-faire* in the French context

One of the competences specified in the driving qualification is 'to take charge of and deliver the load'. The general practical knowledge and techniques associated with this competence are: to take and carry out instructions; to use the different functions and equipments of the vehicle; to put into effect a loading plan; to make written comments, use signs and body language appropriately and to apply security protocols. This practical knowledge presupposes associated knowledge like, for example, calculating areas of surfaces and volumes, or recognizing the forces which act on masses in movement.

---

from *savoir* and *savoir-être*. Tasks are solved through the reflective use of knowledge and by drawing on and developing social and personal competences.

German: *Fertigkeiten* denote the functional skills necessary to perform a task. However, the term cannot be disassociated from *Kenntnisse* (non-systematic knowledge) and *Fähigkeiten* (methodological, social and personal abilities), which are integral elements of *Berufliche Handlungsfähigkeit*, that is competence as achieved in the workplace element of the Dual System. Tasks are solved through the reflective use of knowledge and by drawing on and developing social and personal competences.

Können denotes the practical knowledge necessary to carry out a task through the integration with *Wissen*, *Kenntnisse* and social and personal abilities as captured by the notion of *Handlungskompetenz*, which relates to the development of the person and thus the college-based element of competence. It is similar to the notion of *savoir-faire* and may be translated as know-how.

Box 10.14 Understanding of *vaardigheden* in the Dutch context

An explanation of *vaardigheden* given by one of the Knowledge Centres was: the ability to perform activities, to combine thinking and doing, having learned to apply knowledge while performing a task (GOC 2010). In general, *vaardigheden* refers to somebody's manual, mental and verbal abilities in a specific setting, such as: vaardigheden in driving, music making, communication, using specific tools, handling tensions between social and cultural differences, analytical skills and so on.

Dutch: the concept of *vaardigheden* is embedded in the definition of competence. In the Dutch understanding, competences are expressed in knowledge, skills and attitudes (*kennis, vaardigheden* and *houdingen*). However, in the context of competence, there are no national definitions for *kennis, vaardigheden* and *houdingen*. Occupation-based tasks are performed through the integration of *vaardigheden* with knowledge and attitude. In contrast to the English term 'skills', *vaardigheden* cannot be disassociated from knowledge and attitude in the context of VET.

Savoir-être, *attitude,* Fähigkeit

Savoir-être and *attitude* are fluid and all-encompassing notions commonly used to refer at one and the same time to 1) personal attributes, including individual life experience, and 2) discrete abilities (similar to the second conception of competence in England). There are no official definitions for either term.

French: *savoir-être* denotes generic/abstract abilities, including social competencies, such as communication and negotiation (the German *Sozialkompetenz*), and personal qualities, including personal attributes and experience (the German *Personal-kompetenz*). In the workplace, *savoir-être* is integrated with *savoir* and *savoir-faire* to underpin competence.

German: *Fähigkeit*: until 2005, training regulations referred merely to knowledge and skills, even though new regulations introduced since the late 1980s have adhered to the concept of autonomous planning, performing and controlling – directed at the ability to carry out complete action and work across processes. The term *Fähigkeit* was integrated into the Vocational Training Act in 2005 and is associated with *berufliche Handlungsfähigkeit*, the workplace-oriented facet of competence, which refers to the abilities to be developed through the company part of the VET programme. Thus, *Fähigkeiten* are specified in the training regulations along with *Kenntnisse* (work-related non-systematic knowledge) and *Fertigkeiten* (skills). *Fähigkeiten* capture 'extra-functional skills' corresponding to *Methoden-, Sozial-* and *Personalkompetenz* in the school framework curricula. The term '*Fähigkeit*' in the singular also has a general use, meaning the 'integrated totality of

---

Box 10.15 Understanding of *savoir-être* **in the French context**

In the case of an LGV driver, organizational and social aptitudes associated with dealing with a client are: punctuality, discretion, evidence of a commercial sense, rigour in procedures, communicating in a clear and concise manner. For the bricklayer, effective communication with the gang leader, the customer, other specialists is required, as well as autonomy for some tasks.

action–competence' as in *'berufliche Handlungsfähigkeit'* and should be distinguished from the *Fähigkeiten* that appear in the training regulations.

Dutch: *attitude* (*houding*): in the Netherlands, competence is based on knowledge, know-how and *attitude*. *Attitude* refers to the social dimension of behaviour and includes generic/abstract abilities and personal attributes. It is broader than the French term s*avoir-être*, including normative behaviour based on the ethical and social values associated with an occupation. In an even broader interpretation, *attitude* refers to somebody's posture towards the ethical and social values associated with an occupation.

BIBLIOGRAPHY

Abelshauser, W. (2004) *Deutsche Wirtschaftsgeschichte seit 1945*, München: C.H. Beck Verlag.

ACOA (1999) *Een wending naar kerncompetenties*, 's-Hertogenbosch: ACOA.

Alexander, P.A., Schallert, D.L. and Hare, V.C. (1991) 'Coming to terms – How researchers in learning and literacy talk about knowledge', *Review of Educational Research*, 61 (3): 315–43.

Allais, S., Raffe, D. and Young, M.F.D. (2009) *Researching NQFs: Some Conceptual Issues*, Geneva: ILO.

Arrighi, J.J. and Brochier, D. (2005) '1995–2003 L'apprentissage tiré vers le haut', *Bref Céreq*, No. 217, Marseille: Céreq.

Ashton, D. and Green A. (1996) *Education, Training and the Global Economy*, Cheltenham: Edward Elgar.

Astin, A.W. (2003) *Assessment for Excellence: The Philosophy and Practice of Assessment and Evaluation in Higher Education*, Phoenix: The Oryx Press.

Authoring Group Educational Reporting (2008) *Education in Germany 2008 – An Indicator-based Report Including an Analysis of Transitions Subsequent to Lower Secondary Education*, Berlin/Bonn: BMBF.

Backes-Gellner, U. (1996) *Betriebliche Bildungs-und Wettbewerbsstrategien im deutsch-britischen Vergleich*, München: Mering:

Bader, R. and Müller, M. (2002) 'Leitziel der Berufsbildung: Handlungskompetenz: Anregungen zur Ausdifferenzierung des Begriffs', *Die berufsbildende Schule*, 6 (54): 176–82.

Baethge, M. and Baethge-Kinsky, V. (1998) 'Jenseits von Beruf und Beruflichkeit? – Neue Formen von Arbeitsorganisation und Beschäftigung und ihre Bedeutung für eine zentrale Kategorie gesellschaftlicher Integration', *MittAB*, 3: 461–72.

Baethge, M., Solga, H. and Wieck, M. (2007) *Berufsbildung im Umbruch. Signale eines überfälligen Aufbruchs*, Berlin: Gutachten zur beruflichen Bildung in Deutschland im Auftrag der Friedrich-Ebert-Stiftung.

Beck, U., Brater, M. and Daheim, H. (1980) *Soziologie der Arbeit und der Berufe – Grundlagen, Problemfelder, Forschungsergebnisse*, Reinbek bei Hamburg: Rowohlt.

Benner, D. (2003) *Wilhelm von Humboldt's Bildungstheorie*, Weinheim and Munich: Juventa.

Bertrand, O. and Merle, V. (1993) 'Comparabilité et reconnaissance des qualifications en Europe, Instruments et enjeux', *Formation Emploi*, 43: 41–56.

Biemans, H., Nieuwenhuis, L., Poell, R., Mulder, M. and Wesselink, R. (2004) 'Competence-based VET in the Netherlands: background and pitfalls', *Journal of Vocational Education and Training*, 56 (4): 523–38.

Biernacki, R. (1995) *The Fabrication of Labor: Germany and Britain 1640–1914*, Berkeley: University of California Press.

Birenbaum, M. (2003) 'New Insights into Learning and Teaching and Their Implications for Assessment', in M. Segers, F. Dochy & E. Cascallar (eds) *Optimising New Modes of Assessment: In Search of Qualities and Standards*, Dordrecht, The Netherlands: Kluwer Academic Publishers.

Bjørnåvold, J. and Coles, M. (2006) *Governing Education and Training: The Case of Qualifications Frameworks*. Draft paper, November, Brussels: European Commission.

—— (2008) 'Gérer l'éducation et la formation: l'exemple des cadres de certifications', *Revue européenne de formation professionnelle*, 42–43: 227–65.

Bjørnåvold, J. and Pevec Grm, S. (2010) *The Development of National Qualifications Frameworks in Europe*, Thessaloniki: CEDEFOP.

Blackman, B. (2007) Regulating the situation for migrants in the British construction industry, *CLR News*, European Institute for Construction Labour Research, 4: 12–16.

Blankertz, H. (1968) 'Zum Begriff des Berufs in unserer Zeit', in H. Blankertz (ed.) *Arbeitslehre in der Hauptschule*, Essen.

Bloom B. S. (1956) *Taxonomy of Educational Objectives, Handbook I: The Cognitive Domain*, New York: David McKay Co Inc.

Blossfeld, H.-P. and Stockmann, R. (1999) 'The German Dual System in Comparative Perspective', *International Journal of Sociology*, 28 (4): 3–28.

Bohlinger, S. (2008) 'Competences as the Core Element of the European Qualifications Framework', *European Journal of Vocational Training*, 42/43 (3/1): 96–112.

Boon, J. and van der Klink, M. (2002) 'Competencies: The Triumph of a Fuzzy Concept', Academy of Human Resource Development Annual Conference, Honolulu, HA, 27 February–3 March, in *Proceedings*, Vol. 1: 327–334.

Boreham, N. (2002) 'Work Process Knowledge, Curriculum Control and the Work-based Route to Vocational Qualifications', *British Journal of Educational Studies*, 50 (2): 225–37.

Boreham N., Samurçay, R. and Fischer, M. (eds) (2002) *Work Process Knowledge*, London: Routledge.

Bosch, G. and Charest, J. (eds) (2008) *Vocational Training in the 21st Century: A Comparative Perspective on Systems and Innovations in Ten Countries*, London: Routledge.

Bouder, A. (2008) *Européanisation de la certification: Un passé éclectique, un avenir incertain*, Marseille: Céreq.

Bouder, A. and Kirsch, J.L. (2008) 'Drawing up European Competence Standards, Some Thoughts about the Experience Gained in France', *Training and Employment*, No. 78, Marseille: Céreq.

Bouix, B. (1997) 'Le système de négociation et de construction des diplômes technologiques et professionnelles en France', in M. Möbus and M. Verdier (eds) *Les diplômes professionnels en Allemagne et en France, conception et jeux d'acteurs*, Paris: L'harmattan.

Bouteiller, D. and Gilbert, P. (2005) 'Regards croisés sur les compétences', *Relations Industrielles*, 40 (1): 3–28.

Bradshaw, A. (2001) *The Nurse Apprentice, 1860–1977*, Aldershot: Ashgate.

Braverman, H. (1974) *Labour and Monopoly Capital: The Degradation of Work in the Twentieth Century*, New York: Monthly Review Press.

Brockmann, M., Clarke, L. and Winch, C. (2008a) 'Can Performance-related Outcomes have Standards?' *Journal of European Industrial Training*, 32 (2/3): 99–113.

—— (2008b) 'Knowledge, Skills, Competence: European Divergences in Vocational Education and Training – the English, German and Dutch cases', *Oxford Review of Education*, 34 (5): 547–67.

Brockmann, M., Clarke, L., Méhaut, P. and Winch, C. (2008c) 'Competence-based Vocational Education and Training (VET): The Cases of England and France in a European Perspective', *Vocations and Learning*, 1: 227–44.

Brockmann, M., Clarke, L. and Winch, C. (2009a) *Cross-national Equivalence of Vocational Qualifications, Final Report and Documentation*, unpublished report for the Nuffield Foundation, London: Kings College London.

—— (2009b) 'Competence and Competency in the EQF and in European VET Systems', *Journal of European Industrial Training*, 33 (8/9): 767–99.

—— (2009c) *Bricklaying Country Report England*. Findings from the Leonardo-da-Vinci Project 'Bricklaying qualifications, work and VET in Europe. www.bricklayer-llp.eu (accessed 29 March 2010).

—— (2009d) 'Cross-national Equivalence of Vocational Skills and Qualifications – The Case of England', unpublished report for the Nuffield Foundation, London: Kings College London.

—— (2010a) 'The Apprenticeship Framework in England: A New Beginning or a Continuing Sham?' *Journal of Education and Work*, 23 (2): 111–27.

—— (2010b) 'Bricklaying Qualifications, Work and VET in Europe', in *CLR News*, European Institute for Construction Labour Research, 1: 7–42.

Brown, P., Green, A. and Lauder, H. (2001) *High Skills: Globalisation, Competitiveness and Skill Formation*, Oxford: Oxford University Press.

Brown, P., Lauder, H. and Ashton, D. (2008) *Education, Globalisation and the Knowledge Economy – A Commentary by the Teaching and Learning Research Programme*, London: Teaching and Learning Research Programme (TLRP), Institute of Education, University of London.

Brucy, G. (1998) *Histoire des diplômes de l'enseignement technique et professionnel (1880–1965)*, Paris: Belin.

—— (2008) 'La certification: quelques points d'histoire', in F. Maillard (ed.) *Des diplômes aux certifications professionnelles, nouvelles normes et nouveaux enjeux*, Rennes: Presses Universitaires.

Bundesinstitut für Berufsbildung (BIBB) (2007) *Verordnung über die Berufsausbildung zum Mathematisch-technischen Softwareentwickler*. Online. Available www2.bibb.de/tools/aab/aab_start.php?brf = 261007&s (accessed 13 May 2010).

—— (2009) *Datenreport zum Berufsbildungsbericht 2009*, Bonn: BIBB.

Bundesministerium für Bildung und Forschung (2008) *Berufsbildungsbericht 2008*, Bonn/Berlin: BMBF.

Bundesregierung (2009) *Eckpunkte zur, Verbesserung der Feststellung und Anerkennung von im Ausland erworbenen beruflichen Qualifikationen und Berufsabschlüssen*. Bonn/ Berlin. Online. Available www.bmbf.de/press/2747.php (accessed 1 November 2010).

Busemeyer, M.R. (2009) *Die Europäisierung der deutschen Berufsbildungspolitik: Sachzwang oder Interessenpolitik?*, Bonn. Online. Available http://library.fes.de/pdf-files/id/ipa/06512.pdf (accessed 27 October 2010).

Business Enterprise and Regulatory Reform (BERR) Department (2008) *Construction Statistics Annual 2008*, London: BERR.

Campinos-Dubernet, M. (1995) 'Baccalauréat professionnel: une innovation?', *Formation Emploi*, 49: 3–30.

CBS (2009) *Jaarboek onderwijs in cijfers*, Den Haag: CBS, Table 4.1.10: 190.

CEDEFOP (2008) *Terminology of European Education and Training Policy – A Selection of 100 Key Terms*, Thessaloniki: Cedefop. Online. Available www.cedefop.europa.eu/EN/Files/4064_en.pdf (accessed 17 June 2010).

CEN (European Committee for Standardisation) (2006) *European ICT Skills Meta-Framework: State-of-the-Art Review, Clarification of the Realities, and Recommendations for Next Steps*, Brussels: CEN.

CGP (Commissariat général du plan) (1978) *La qualification du travail, de quoi parles-t-on?*, Paris: La documentation française.

Chan, P., Clarke, L. and Dainty, A. (2010) 'The Dynamics of Migrant Employment in Construction: Can Supply of Skilled Labour Ever Match Demand?' in M. Ruhs and B. Anderson (eds) *Labour Shortages, Immigration and Public Policy*, Oxford: Oxford University Press.

Clarke, L. (2005) 'From Craft to Qualified Building Labour in Britain: A Comparative Approach', *Labor History*, 46 (4): 473–94.

Clarke, L., Cremers, J. and Janssen, J. (2007) 'The Transformation of Employment Relations or "Undeclared Labour"', paper presented at IIRA conference, Manchester, September 2007.

Clarke, L. and Herrmann, G. (2004a) 'The Institutionalisation of Skill in Britain and Germany: Examples from the Construction Sector' in C. Warhurst, Irena Grugulis and E. Keep (eds) *The Skills that Matter*, Basingstoke: Palgrave.

—— (2004b) 'Cost vs. Production: Disparities in Social Housing Construction in Britain and Germany' *Construction Management and Economics*, 22: 521–32.

Clarke, L. and Wall, C. (1996) *Skills and the Construction Process: A Comparative Study of Vocational Training and Quality in Social Housebuilding*, Bristol: Policy Press in association with Joseph Rowntree Foundation.

—— (2000) 'Craft versus Industry: The Division of Labour in European Housing Construction', *Construction Management and Economics*, 18: 689–98.

Clarke, L. and Winch, C. (2004) 'Apprenticeship and Applied Theoretical Knowledge', *Educational Philosophy and Theory*, 36 (5): 509–21.

—— (2006) 'A European Skills Framework? – But What are Skills? Anglo-Saxon versus German Concepts', *Journal of Education and Work*, 19 (3): 255–69.

—— (eds) (2007) *Vocational Education: International Approaches, Developments and Systems*, Abingdon: Routledge.

Coles, M. (2007) *Qualifications Frameworks in Europe: Platforms for Qualifications, Integration and Reform*, Brussels: EU, Education and Culture DG.

Coles, M. and Oates, T. (2004) *European Reference Levels for Education and Training – An Important Parameter for Promoting Credit Transfer and Mutual Trust. Final Report*, London: Qualifications and Curriculum Authority.

—— (2005) *European Reference Levels for Education and Training: Promoting Credit Transfer and Mutual Trust*. Study commissioned to the Qualifications and Curriculum Authority, Luxembourg: Office for Official Publications of the European Communities.

Commissie van Onderzoek Lager Nijverheidsonderwijs (1948) Rapport, 's-Gravenhage: SDU.

Construction Industry Joint Council (CIJC) (2003) *Working Rule Agreement for the Construction Industry*, London: Construction Industry Joint Council.

Construction Industry Training Board (CITB) (2006) *National Occupational Standards and Recommended Qualification Structures for Trowel Occupations (Construction)*, Bircham Newton: CITB.

ConstructionSkills (2008) *Training and the Built Environment*, Bircham Newton: ConstructionSkills.

Coördinatiepunt (2009) *Niveau MBO; een analyse van niveauaanduidingen in de kwalificatiestructuur van het mbo*, Zoetermeer: Het Coördinatiepunt.

Cort, P. (2008a) 'The EC Discourse on Vocational Training. How a "Common Vocational Training Policy" Turned into a Lifelong Learning Strategy', *Vocations and Learning*, Vol. 2, No. 2, December, 87–107.

—— (2008b) 'VET Policy Formation and Discourse in the EU: A Mobile Workforce for a European Labour Market?', in Vibe Aarkrog and Christian Helms Jørgensen (eds) *Divergence and Convergence in Education and Work*, Bern: Peter Lang.

Crahay, M. (2006) 'Dangers, incertitudes et incomplétude de la logique de la compétence en éducation', *Revue française de pédagogie*, 154: 97–110.

Creemers, B.P.M. and Kyriakides, L.(2008) *The Dynamics of Educational Effectiveness. A Contribution to Policy, Practice and Theory in Contemporary Schools*, Abingdon: Routledge.

Creemers, B.P.M. and Reezigt, G.J. (1996) 'School-level Conditions Affecting the Effectiveness of Instruction', *School Effectiveness and School Improvement*, 7 (3): 197–228.

Culpepper, P.D. and Finegold, D.(1999) *The German Skills Machine: Sustaining Comparative Advantage in a Global Economy*, New York: Berghahn Books.

Deakin S. (2007) 'Does the "Personal Employment Contract" Provide a Basis for the Reunification of Employment Law?', *Industrial Law Journal*, 36 (1): 68–83.

Dearden, R. (1979) 'The Assessment of Learning', *British Journal of Educational Studies*, 27 (2): 111–24.

Deissinger, T. (1995) 'Das Konzept der "Qualifizierungsstile" als kategoriale Basis idealtypischer Ordnungsschemata zur Charakterisierung und Unterscheidung von "Berufsbildungssystemen"', *Zeitschrift für Berufs-und Wirtschaftspädagogik*, 91 (4): 367–87.

Deissinger, Th. (2001) 'Zum Problem der historisch-kulturellen Bedingtheit von Berufsbildungssystemen. Gibt es eine "Vorbildfunktion" des deutschen Dualen Systems im europäischen Kontext?', in T. Deißinger (ed.) *Berufliche Bildung zwischen nationaler Tradition und globaler Entwicklung. Beiträge zur vergleichenden Berufsbildungsforschung*, Baden-Baden: Nomos.

Delamare Le Deist, F. and Winterton, J. (2005) 'What is Competence?' in *Human Resource Development International*, 8 (1): 27–46.

Department of Health (2004) *The NHS Knowledge and Skills Framework (NHS KSF) and the Development Review Process*. Online. Available www.dh.gov.uk/en/Publicationsandstatistics/ Publications/PublicationsPolicyAndGuidance/DH_4090843 (accessed 10 October 2007).

—— (2007) *Implementation of European Directive 2005/36/EC for Health and Social Care Professions in the UK*. Online. Available http://webarchive.nationalarchives.gov.uk/ +/www.dh.gov.uk/en/Consultations/Responsestoconsultations/DH_080250 (accessed 5 February 2009).

Doolittle, P.E. and Camp, W.G. (1999) 'Constructivism: the Career and Technical Education Perspective', in *Journal of Vocational and Technical Education*, Fall, 16/1: 5–16.

Drexel, I. (2006) 'Europäische Berufsbildungspolitik: Deregulierung, neoliberale Reregulierung und die Folgen – für Alternativen zu EQR und ECVET' in P. Grollmann, G. Spöttl and F. Rauner (eds) *Europäisierung beruflicher Bildung – eine Gestaltungsaufgabe*, Hamburg: LIT-Verlag.

Dubois, D.D. and Rothwell, W.J. (2004) *Competency-based Human Resource Management*, Palo Alto: Davies-Black Publishing.

Dupray, A., Guitton, C. and Monchatre, S. (eds) (2003) *Réfléchir la compétence, Approches sociologiques, juridiques, économiques d'une pratique gestionnaire*, Toulouse: Octares.

Durkheim, E. (1902 [1972]) *Emile Durkheim: Selected Writings*, Cambridge: Cambridge University Press.

Eckert, H. (1999) 'L'émergence d'un ouvrier bachelier, les bac pro entre déclassement et recomposition de la catégorie ouvrière', *Formation Emploi*, Avril: 227–53.

EdExcel (2003) *BTEC National Diploma in Construction, Unit One: Health, Safety and Welfare in Construction and the Built Environment*, London: EdExcel.

Eraut, M. (1994) *Developing Professional Knowledge and Competence*, Falmer: Routledge.

Erpenbeck, J. (2005) *Positionspapier für BIBB Workshop zum 1. EQF Entwurf vom 16.11.2005*. Unpublished paper. Bonn: BIBB.

Ertl, H. (2002) 'The Concept of Modularisation in Vocational Education and Training: the Debate in Germany and its Implication', *Oxford Review of Education*, 28 (1): 53–73.

—— (2003) 'Tradition and Reform: Modernising the German Dual System of Vocational Education', in G. Hayward and S. James (eds) *Balancing the Skills Equation. Key Issues and Challenges for Policy and Practice*. Bristol: The Policy Press.

—— (2006) 'European Union Policies in Education and Training; the Lisbon Agenda as a Turning Point?', *Comparative Education*, 42 (1): 5–27.

Ertl, H. and Phillips, D. (2003) 'Introduction', in D. Phillips and H. Ertl (eds) *Implementing European Union Education and Training Policy; A Comparative Study of Issues in Four Member States*, Dordrecht/London: Kluwer Academic.

Ertl, H. and Sloane, P.F.E. (2005) *Kompetenzerwerb und Kompetenzbegriff in der Berufsbildung in internationaler Perspektive*, Paderborn: Eusl.

E-Skills (2005) *Information and Communication Technologies and Contact Centres – S/NVQ Qualification Structure*. Online. Available www.e-skills.com/public/File/QS%20for%20IT,%20CT%20and%20CC%20V2.0rebrand.pdf (accessed 3 June 2007).

Etzioni, A. (1969) *The Semi-professions and their Organisation: Teachers, Nurses and Social Workers*, New York: Free Press.

European Commission (EC) (2002) *The Copenhagen Declaration*. Online. Available http://ec.europa.eu/education/pdf/doc125_en.pdf (accessed 29 March 2010).

—— (2005a) 'Vocational qualifications and competences: transparency and recognition. Presentation by Jens Bjørnåvold', Director General for Education and Culture, 24/25 March 2005 in Brussels.

—— (2005b) Directive 2005/36/EC of the European Parliament and of the Council of 7 September 2005 on the recognition of professional qualifications.

—— (2006a) *Proposal for a Recommendation of the European Parliament and of the Council on the Establishment of the European Qualifications Framework for Lifelong Learning*, Brussels: Commission of the European Communities.

—— (2006b) *European Glossary on Education*, Volume 2, Brussels: Eurydice.

—— (2007a) *Employment in Europe*, Luxembourg: Office for Official Publications of the European Communities.

—— (2007b) *Outcome of the Public Consultation on the Commission's Green Paper 'Modernising labour law to meet the challenges of the 21st century'*, Brussels: European Commission.

—— (2008a) *Employment in Europe*, Luxembourg: Office for Official Publications of the European Communities.

—— (2008b) *The European Framework for Lifelong Learning (EQF)*, Luxembourg: Office for Official Publications of the European Communities.

—— (2008c) *Progress Towards the Lisbon Objectives in Education and Training, Indicators and Benchmarks*. Commission Staff Working Document. Online. Available http://ec.europa.eu/education/policies/2010/doc/progress06/report_en.pdf (accessed 29 June 2010).

—— (2009) *European Glossary: Open Method of Coordination*. Online. Available www.europa.eu/cgi-bin/etal.pl (accessed 28 October 2010).

—— (2010) *Europe 2020. A European Strategy for Smart, Sustainable and Inclusive Growth*, Brussels: European Commission.

European Federation of Building and Woodworkers (EFBWW) (2010) *Self-employment and Bogus Self-employment in the European Construction Industry*, Brussels: EFBWW.

European Union (EU) (2010a) *The European Credit System for Vocational Education and Training (ECVET)*. Online. Available http://ec.europa.eu/education/lifelong-learning-policy/doc50_en.htm (accessed 29 June 2010).

—— (2010b) *Frequently Asked Questions about the European Qualifications Framework*. Online. Available http:europa.eu/rapid/pressReleasesAction.do?reference=MEMO/08/265&format=HTML&aged=0&language=EN&guiLanguage=en (accessed 29 June 2010).

Eyraud, F., Marsden, D., and Silvestre, J. (1990) 'Occupational and Internal Labour Markets in Britain and France', *International Labour Review*, 129 (4): 501–17.

Felstead, A. (1998) *Output-related Funding in Vocational Education and Training, a Discussion Paper and Case Studies*, Thessaloniki: CEDEFOP.

Finch, C.R. and Crunkilton, J.R. (1999) *Curriculum Development in Vocational and Technical Education: Planning, Content, and Implementation* (5th ed.), Boston: Allyn and Bacon.

Finegold, D. and Soskice, D. (1988) 'The Failure of Training in Britain: Analysis and Prescription', *Oxford Review of Economic Policy*, 4: 21–53.

Gallie D. (2007) *Employment Regimes and the Quality of Work*, Oxford: Oxford University Press.

Gautié, J. (2000) *Déstabilisation des marchés internes et gestion des âges sur le marché du travail*, Document de travail no. 15. Paris: Centre d'études de l'emploi.

Gerrish, K., McManus, M. and Ashworth, P. (2003) 'Creating What Sort of Professional? Master's Level Nurse Education as a Professionalising Strategy', *Nursing Inquiry*, 10 (2): 103–12.

Gonon, P. (2009) *The Quest for Modern Vocational Education – Georg Kerschensteiner between Dewey, Weber and Simmel*, Bern: Peter Lang.

Goudswaard, N.B. (1981) *Vijfenzestig jaren nijverheidonderwijs*, Assen: van Gorcum.

Green, A. (1990) *Education and State Formation*, London: Macmillan.

Green, A., Wolf, A. and Leney, T. (1999) *Convergence and Divergence in European Education and Training Systems*, London: Institute of Education.

Greinert, W.-D. (2004) 'European Vocational Training Systems: The Theoretical Context of their Historical Development' in G. Hanf and W.-D. Greinert (eds) *Towards a History of Vocational Education and Training in Europe in a Comparative Perspective*. Cedefop Panorama series 103, Luxembourg: Office for Official Publications of the European Communities.

Grollmann, P., Tutschner, R. and Wittig, W. (2007) 'Structuring IT Qualifications: Lessons from the German Case', *Journal of European Industrial Training*, 31 (7): 514–29.

Guergoat-Larivière, M. (2008) *Politique européenne d'éducation et de formation: quels enjeux dans l'Europe élargie*, Bordeaux: Université de la Formation.

Halfpap, K. (2000) 'Curriculumentwicklung im Rahmen der dualen Berufsausbildung in Deutschland', *European Journal of Vocational Training*, 21: 37–44.

Hall, A. (2007) '*Berufswechsel von dual ausgebildeten Fachkräften*', Berufsbildung in Wissenschaft und Praxis, 4.

Hall, P.A. and Soskice, D.W. (eds) (2001) *Varieties of Capitalism: The Institutional Foundations of Comparative Advantage*, New York, Oxford: Oxford University Press.

Hampson, I. and Junor, A. (2010) 'Contesting Competence as Australia Enters Another Round of Training Reform'. Paper Prepared for the 28th *International Labour Process Conference*, Rutgers: State University of New Jersey.

Hanf, G. (2007) *Quick Scan Report on the Terminological and Conceptual Framework for German VET*. Online. Available www.kcl.ac.uk/content/1/c6/01/57/15/GermanyQuickScan Nov07.pdf (accessed 18 October 2010).

—— (2009) 'Cross-national Equivalence of Vocational Skills and Qualifications – The Case of Germany', unpublished report for the Nuffield Foundation, London: Kings College London.

Hanfling, O. (2000) *The Philosophy of Ordinary Language*, London: Routledge.

Hantrais, L. (2007) *Social Policy in the European Union*, Basingstoke: Palgrave.

Harney, K. (1998) 'Beruf ist Lebensperspektive', *Der berufliche Bildungsweg*, 3: 2–4.

Harney, K., Geselbracht, S. and Weichet, M. (1999) 'Der Beruf als Input der Weiterbildung', in K. Harney and H.-E. Tenorth (eds) *Beruf und Berufsbildung. Situation, Reformperspektiven, Gestaltungsmöglichkeiten*, Basel: Weinheim.

Harney, K. and Kissmann, G. (2000) 'Maßstabsbildung, lokale Anpassung und hochschulischer Raumgewinn: Europa als Umwelt der beruflichen Ausbildung in Deutschland', in Jahrbuch *Arbeit, Bildung, Kultur*, Forschungsinstitut für Arbeiterbildung, 18: 43–68.

Harney, K. and vom Hau, M. (2010) *The Institutional Logics of Human Capital: Historical Analysis of Vocational Education in Germany*. FIAB-Arbeitspapier, Recklinghausen: 14 FIAB Verlag.

Hartmann, H. (1968) 'Arbeit, Beruf, Profession', *Soziale Welt*, 19: 197–212.

Heijke, H. (2008) *Werken aan heterogeen menselijk kapitaal*, Maastricht: Universiteit Maastricht.

Heyes, J. and Rainbird, H. (2009) 'Vocational Education and Training', in M. Gold (ed.) *Employment Policy in the European Union: Origins, Themes and Prospects*, Basingstoke: Palgrave.

Hillmert, St. and Jacob, M. (2008) *Multiple Episodes: Training Careers in a Learning Society*.GLOBALIFE Working paper 64, Bamberg: University of Bamberg.

Hirst, P. (1974) *Knowledge and the Curriculum*, London: Routledge.

HMSO (2009) *Twenty-Twenty Vision*, London: United Kingdom Commission on Education and Skills (UKCES).

HMSO/DCSF (2009) *Trends in Education and Skills*. Online. Available www.dcsf.gov.uk/trends/index.cfm?fuseaction=home.showChart&cid=4&iid=27&chid=106 (accessed 15 January 2010).

Hofheinz, P. (2010) *EU 2010: Why Skills are Key for Europe's Future. Lisbon Council Policy Brief*, Brussels: the Lisbon Council.

Hövels, B., Jager, A. and Vermulst, R. (2009) *Een kwantitatief onderzoek bij deelnemers*, Nijmegen: Kenniscentrum Beroepsonderwijs Arbeidsmarkt.

Hövels, B.W.M., Nieuwenhuis, A.F.M., Kraayvanger, G. and le Rütte, R. (1995) *Landelijke kwalificatiestructuur in ontwikkeling*, Leiden: Adviesraad voor het Onderwijs.

Hövels, B., Visser K. and Schuit, H. (2006) *Over Hamers en vasthouden gesproken; vijfentwintig jaar middelbaar beroepsonderwijs in Nederland*, 's-Hertogenbosch: ACOA.

Hyland, T. (2008) 'Reductionist Trends in Education and Training for Work: Skills, Competences and Work-Based Learning', in Kraus, K., Gonon, P., Oelkers, J. and Stolz, S. (eds) *Work, Education and Employability*, Bern: Peter Lang.

Innovation Circle on Vocational Education and Training (IKBB) (2007) *Ten Guidelines for the Modernization and Structural Improvement of Vocational Education and Training*, Bonn: Federal Ministry of Education and Research, BMBF

d'Iribarne, A. (1996) 'Une lecture des paradigmes du Livre Blanc sur l'éducation et la formation: éléments pour un débat', *Revue européenne de formation professionnelle*, 8–9: 24–32.

Jessup, G. (ed.) (1991a) *Outcomes: NVQs and the Emerging Model of Education and Training*, Brighton: Falmer.

—— (1991b) 'Implications for Individuals: the Autonomous Learner' in Jessup, G. (ed) *Outcomes: NVQs and the Emerging Model of Education and Training*, Brighton: Falmer.

Jobert, A. (2000) *Les espaces de la négociation collective, branches et territoires*, Toulouse: Octares.

Jobert, A. and Tallard, M. (1995) 'Diplômes et certification de branche dans les conventions collectives', *Formation Emploi*, 52: 131–50.

Kanter Moss, R. (1989) *When Giants Learn to Dance: Mastering the Challenge of Strategy, Management and Careers in the 1990s*, New York: Simon and Schuster.

Karagiannis, S. (2008) 'A Study of the EU's Structural Indicators using Panel and Data Analysis', *International Research Journal of Finance and Economics*, 13: 192–205.

Keep, E. (2007) 'The Multiple Paradoxes of State Power in the English Education and Training System', in Clarke and Winch (eds) *Vocational Education: International Approaches, Developments and Systems*, Oxford: Routledge.

Keep, E. and Brown, E. (2004) 'Paradoxes, Pitfalls and the Prospects for a Dynamic VET System', in W. Nijhof and W. van Esch (eds) *Unraveling Policy, Power, Process and Performance*, 's-Hertogenbosch: CINOP.

Keller, B. and Sörries, B. (1999) 'The New European Social Dialogue: Old Wine in New Bottles?' *Journal of European Social Policy*, 9/2: 111–25.

Kirpal, S. (2003) *Nurses in Europe: Work Identities of Nurses across 4 European Countries*, Bremen: ITB, University of Bremen.

—— (2004) *Work Identities in Europe: Continuity and Change*, Final Report of the 5th EU Framework Project FAME, Bremen: ITB, University of Bremen.

Kirsch, J.L. (2005) *Formation générale, formation professionnelle, vieille question et nouveaux débats*, Net.Doc no. 14, Mars, Marseille: Céreq.

KMK (1999, 2007) Sekretariat der Ständigen Konferenz der Kultusminister der Länder in der Bundesrepublik Deutschland (eds) *Handreichungen für die Erarbeitung von Rahmenlehrplänen der Kultusministerkonferenz für den berufsbezogenen Unterricht in der Berufsschule und ihre Abstimmung mit Ausbildungsordnungen des Bundes für anerkannte Ausbildungsberufe*. Online. Available www.kmk.org (accessed 1 October 2010).

Konsortium Bildungsberichterstattung (2006) *Bildung in Deutschland. Ein indikatorengestützter Bericht mit einer Analyse zu Bildung und Migration*, Bielefeld: Bundesministerium für Bildung und Forschung.

Kraus, Katrin (2006) *Vom Beruf zur Employability? Zur Theorie einer Pädagogik des Erwerbs*, Wiesbaden: VS-Verlag.

—— (2007) 'Die "berufliche Ordnung" im Spannungsfeld von nationaler Tradition und europäischer Integration', *Zeitschrift für Pädagogik*, 53 (3): 381–97.

Kraus, K., Gonon, P., Oelkers, J. and Stolz, S. (2008) 'Work, education and employability', in P. Gonon, K. Kraus, J. Oelkers and S. Stolz (eds) *Work, Education and Employability*, Bern: Peter Lang.

Kremer, H.-H. and Sloane, P.F.E. (2000) 'Lernfeldkonzept – Erste Umsetzungserfahrungen und Konsequenzen für die Implementation', in R. Bader, R. and P.F.E. Sloane (eds) *Lernen in Lernfelder. Theoretische Analysen und Gestaltungsansätze zum Lernfeldkonzept*, Markt Schwaben: Eusl-Verlag.

Kuhn, M. (ed.) (2007) *New Society Models for a New Millennium, The Learning Society in Europe and Beyond*, New York: Peter Lang.

Kurtz, Th. (2005) *Die Berufsform der Gesellschaft*, Weilerswist: Velbrück Wissenschaft.

Kutscha, G. (2000) *Pluralisierung der Berufsbildung als Innovationsstrategie – Modernisierung der Qualifikationsentwicklung im Spannungsfeld von Regulierung und Deregulierung*.

—— (2008) *Beruflichkeit als regulatives Prinzip flexibler Kompetenzentwicklung – Thesen aus berufsbildungstheoretischer Sicht*. Online: Available www.bwpat.de/ausgabe14/kutscha_bwpat14.pdf (accessed 20 September 2010).

Labruyère, C. and Teissier, J. (2008) 'Points de vue interprofessionnels: convergences et divergences sur les certification, leur construction et leur reconnaissance', in F. Maillard (ed.) *Des diplômes aux formation professionnelles, nouvelles normes et nouveaux enjeux*, Rennes: Presses Universitaires.

Laffan, B. and Shaw, C. (2005) *Classifying and Mapping the OMC in Different Policy Area*, Newgov. Online. Available www.eu-newgov.org (accessed 29 June 2010).

Lambeth College (2006) *General Prospectus 2006/7*, London: Lambeth College.

Lane, C. and Bachmann, R. (2000) *Trust within and between Organisations: Conceptual Issues and Empirical Applications*, Oxford: Oxford University Press.

Lee, D. (1979) 'Craft Unions and the Force of Tradition', *British Journal of Industrial Relations*, 17 (1): 34–49.

Leitch Review of Skills (2006) *Prosperity for all in the Global Economy: World Class Skills*, Final Report, December, London: HM Treasury.

Leney, T. and Green, A. (2005) *Achieving the Lisbon Goal: The Contribution of VET*, European *Journal of Education*, 40 (3): September, 261–78.

Leskien, A. (2008) 'Flexibilisierung als Chance zur Stärkung des Berufsprinzips nutzen', interview in *Berufsbildung in Wissenschaft und Praxis*, 4: 5.

Lewis, P. and Ryan, P. (2009) 'The Role of Inspection in the Public Services: the Case of the UK Training Market', *Public Administration*, 87/4: 791–817.

Lorig, B. and Schreiber, D. (2007) 'Ausgestaltung kompetenzbasierter Ausbildungsord-nungen. Grundlage für Kompetenzmessung und Kompetenzbewertung', *Berufsbildung in Wissenschaft und Praxis*, 6: 5–9.

Maillard, F. (2005a) *Pour un regard sociologique sur la formation et les diplômes, mémoire pour l'habilitation à diriger des recherches*, Université de Picardie, Amiens.

—— (2005b) 'L'ambivalence de la politique éducative, le CAP entre déclin et relance', *Formation Emploi*, 89: 65–78.

—— (2008a) 'De la démocratisation de l'enseignement et de la formation à la certification généralisée', in F. Maillard (ed.) *Des diplômes aux formation professionnelles, nouvelles normes et nouveaux enjeux*, Rennes: Presses Universitaires.

—— (ed.) (2008b) *Des diplômes aux formation professionnelles, nouvelles normes et nouveaux enjeux*, Rennes: Presses Universitaires.

Mansfield, B. and Mitchell, L. (1996) *The Competent Workforce*, London: Gower Press.

Markowitsch, J. and Luomi-Messerer, K. (2008) 'Développement et interprétation des descripteurs du cadre européen des certifications', *Revue européenne de formation professionnelle*, 42–43: 38–65.

Marks, A. and Scholarios, D. (2008) 'Choreographing a System: Skill and Employability in Software Work', *Economic and Industrial Democracy*, 29 (1): 96–124.

Marsden, D. (1990) 'Occupational and Internal Labour Markets in Britain, France, Italy and West Germany', in R. Brunetta and C. Dell'Aringa (eds) *Labour Relations and Economic Performance*, London: Macmillan.

—— (1999) *A Theory of Employment Systems*, Oxford: Oxford University Press.

—— (2007) 'Labour Market Segmentation in Britain: The Decline of Occupational Labour Markets and the Spread of Entry Tournaments', *Économies et Sociétés*, 28 (6): 965–98.

MBO Raad (2009) *Derde Benchmark Middelbaar beroepsonderwijs*, De Bilt: MBO Raad.

McGuiness, S. (2006) 'Over-education in the Labour Market', *Journal of Economic Surveys*, 20 (3): 387–418.

Méhaut, P. (2009) '*Cross-national equivalence of vocational skills and qualifications – The case of France*', unpublished report for the Nuffield Foundation, London: Kings College London.

Méhaut, P. (1997) 'Le diplôme, une norme multivalente?' in M. Möbus and E. Verdier (eds) *Les diplômes professionnels en France et en Allemagne, conceptions et jeux d'acteurs*, Paris: L'harmattan.

—— (2004) 'Competencies Based Management: What Consequences for the Labour Markets?' *Economia et Lavoro*, 38 (1): 165–80.

Méhaut, P. and Hervy-Guillaume, D. (2009) *Bricklaying Country Report France*. Findings from the Leonardo-da-Vinci Project 'Bricklaying qualifications, work and VET in Europe'. www.bricklayer-llp.eu (accessed 27 April 2010).

Méhaut, P. and Winch, C. (2009) 'Le cadre européen des certifications: quelles stratégies nationales d'adaptation ?' *Formation Emploi*, 108: 97–112.

Mehl, J. (1994) 'Language, class, and mimic satire', *The Sixteenth Century Journal*, vol. 25, no. 2, Summer, 289–305.

Merrienboer, J. van, Klink, M. van der and Hendriks, M. (2002). *Competenties van complicaties tot compromis. Over schijfjes en begrenzers*, Den Haag: Onderwijsraad.

Migration Advisory Committee (MAC) (2008) *Skilled Shortage Sensible: The Recommended Shortage Occupation Lists for the UK and Scotland*, Croydon: the Home Office.

Ministerie van Onderwijs en Wetenschap (1986) *Beroepsprofiel-en leerplanontwikkeling beroepsonderwijs*, Zoetermeer: Ministerie van OCW.

Möbus, M. and Verdier, E. (1997) *Les diplômes professionnels en Allemagne et en France, conception et jeux d'acteurs*, Paris: L'harmattan.

Mulder, M. (2001) *Competentieontwikkeling in organisaties. Perspectieven en praktijk*, 's-Hertogenbosch: Elsevier Bedrijfsinformatie.

—— (2007) 'Competence – the Essence and Use of the Concept in ICVT', *European Journal of Vocational Training*, 40: 5–21.

Müller, W. and Gangl, M. (eds) (2003) *Transitions from Education to Work in Europe*, Oxford: Oxford University Press.

Müller, W. and Wolbers, M.H.J. (2003) 'Educational Attainment in the European Union: Recent Trends in Qualification Patterns', in W. Müller and M. Gangl (eds) *Transitions from Education to Work in Europe*, Oxford: Oxford University Press.

National Joint Council for the Building Industry (NJCBI) (1991) *Working Rule Agreement*, London: NJCBI.

Naville, P. (1956) *Essai sur la Qualification du Travail*, Paris: M. Rivière.

Nerland, M. (2008) 'Knowledge Cultures and the Shaping of Work-based Learning: The Case of Computer Engineering', *Vocations and Learning*, 1: 49–69.

Nijhof, W. (2008) *Naar 'nieuwe' examenvormen in het mbo?*, Amsterdam: Max Goote Kenniscentrum.

Oakeshott, M. (1962) 'Rationalism in Politics', in *Rationalism in Politics and other Essays*, London: Methuen.

Oates, T. (2004) 'The Role of Outcomes-based National Qualifications in the Development of an Effective Vocational Education and Training System; the Case of England and Wales', *Policy Futures in Education*, 2 (1): 53–71.

OECD (2010) *Education at a Glance 2010*, OECD Indicators, Paris: OECD.

Office of Public Sector Information (OPSI) (2007) *Statutory Instruments Health Care and Associated Professions: The European Qualifications Regulations 2007, No 3101*, 1st November. OPSI. Online. Available www.opsi.gov.uk/si/si2007/uksi_20073101_en_1 (accessed 18 October 2010).

Ohlsson, S. (1994) 'Declarative and Procedural Knowledge', in *The International Encyclopedia of Education*, Oxford: Pergamon, Vol. 3: 1432–34.

Onderwijsraad (1998) *Een leven lang leren in het bijzonder in de bve-sector*, Den Haag: Onderwijsraad.

—— (2000) *Jaarverslag 2000*, Den Haag: Onderwijsraad.

—— (2009) *Middelbaar en hoger onderwijs voor Volwassenen*, Den Haag: Onderwijsraad.

Onstenk, J. (1997) *Lerend leren werken. Brede vakbekwaamheid en de integratie van werken en innoveren*, Delft: Eburon.

Onstenk, J. and Huisman, J. (2007) 'The Meaning of Knowledge in Competence Based Education', paper presented at the Education Sociology Conference, Lunteren, November 2007.

Oxford Dictionary (1980) *The Shorter Oxford English Dictionary on Historical Principles*, Oxford: Clarendon Press.

Pépin, L. (2006) *The History of European Cooperation in Education and Training: Europe in the Making – An Example*, Luxembourg: European Commission.

Pierson, P. (2004) *Politics in Time: History, Institutions, and Social Analysis*, Princeton: Princeton University Press.

Piore, M. and Sabel, C. (1984) *The Second Industrial Divide*, New York: Basic Books.

Polanyi, M. (1966) *The Tacit Dimension*, London: Routledge.

Pöppel, K.G. and Rekus, J. (2001) *Neues schulpädagogisches Wörterbuch*, Weinheim, München: Juventa-Verlag.

Prawat, R.S. (1989) 'Promoting Access to Knowledge, Strategy, and Disposition in Students: A Research Synthesis', *Review of Education*, 59 (1): 1–41.

Prokou, E. (2008) 'The Emphasis on Employability and the Changing Role of the University in Europe', *Higher Education in Europe*, 33 (4): 387–94.

Qualifications and Curriculum Authority (QCA) (2005) *The National Curriculum*, London: HMSO.

Raffe, D. (2009) 'Towards a Dynamic Model of National Qualification Frameworks' in Allais, Raffe and Young, *Researching NQFs: Some Conceptual Issues*, Geneva: ILO.

Raggatt, P. and Williams, S. (1999) *Government, Markets and Vocational Qualifications: An Anatomy of Policy*, Buckingham: Open University Press.

Rainbird, H. (1993) 'Vocational Education and Training', in M. Gold (ed.) *The Social Dimension: Employment Policy in the European Community*, Basingstoke: Macmillan.

Rauner, F. (2004) *Praktisches Wissen und berufliche Handlungskompetenz. ITB Forschungsberichte [Research Reports]14/2004* [Practical knowledge and occupational action competence], Bremen: University of Bremen.

—— (2006) 'Berufliche Bildung – die europäische Perspektive', in P. Grollmann, G. Spöttl and F. Rauner (eds) *Europäisierung Beruflicher Bildung – eine Gestaltungsaufgabe*, Hamburg: Lit Verlag.

—— (2007) 'Vocational Education and Training – A European Perspective', in A. Brown, S. Kirpal and F. Rauner (eds) *Identities at Work*, Dordrecht: Springer.

Reinberg, A. and Hummel, M. (2007) *Qualifikationsspezifische Arbeitslosigkeit im Jahr 2005 und die Einführung der Hartz-IV-Reform – empirische Befunde und methodische Probleme*. IAB-Forschungsbericht, 09/2007), Nürnberg: IAB.

Reuling, J. (1998) 'The German "Berufsprinzip" as a model for regulating training content and qualification standards', in W.J. Nijhof and J.N. Streumer (eds) *Key Qualifications in Work and Education*, Dordrecht: Kluwer.

Reynolds, R. and Cuttance, P. (eds) (1992) *School Effectiveness: Research, Policy and Practice*, London: Cassell.

Robichon, M. (2001) 'De l'analyse des emplois à la formation professionnelle des adultes', in *Les travaux prospectifs sur les besoins en qualification en France et en Allemagne*, document no. 122, Juin, Paris: Ministère de l'éducation.

Rope, F. and Tanguy, L. (eds) (1994) *Savoir et compétences, de l'usage de ces notions dans l'école et l'entreprise*, Paris: L'harmattan.

Roth, H. (1971) *Pädagogische Anthropologie. Bd. II. Entwicklung und Erziehung. Grundlagen einer Entwicklungspädagogik*, Hannover: Schroedel.

Rousseau, J.-J. [1762] (1968) *Emile ou de l'Education*, Paris: Flammarion.

Ruhs, M. and Anderson, B. (eds) (2010) *Who Needs Migrant Workers? Labour Shortages, Immigration and Public Policy*, Oxford: Oxford University Press.

Rychen, D.S. and Salganic, L.H. (2003) 'A Holistic Model of Competence', in D.S. Rychen and L.H. Salganic (eds) *Key Competencies for a Successful Life and a Well-functioning Society*, Göttingen: Hogrefe and Huber.

Ryle, G. (1946) 'Knowing How and Knowing That', *Proceedings of the Aristotelian Society*, 56: 1–16.

—— (1949) *The Concept of Mind*, London: Hutchinson.

Samurçay, R. and Pastré, P. (eds) (2004) *Recherches en didactique professionnelle*, Toulouse: Octares.

SCEREN/CNDP (2006) *The Common Base of Knowledge and Skills: Decree of 11 July 2006*, Ministère education nationale enseignement supérieur recherché, Paris: CNDP.

Seibert, H. (2007) *IAB Kurzbericht*, Issue 1, 19.1.2007. Online. Available http://doku. iab.de/kurzber/2007/kb0107.pdf (accessed 15 September 2010).

Sellin, B. (1999) 'Les programmes d'éducation et de formation professionnelle de la CE et de l'UE de 1975 à 1999-ébauche d'un bilan historique critique', *Formation Professionnelle*, 18: 17–28.

—— (2008) 'La proposition d'un cadre européen des certifications: possibilité et limites de sa transposition dans la réalité', *Revue européenne de formation professionnelle*, 42–43: 4–21.

SER (1958) *Advies de aanpassing van de vakopleiding aan de automatisering*, Den Haag: SER.

—— (1996) *Arbeidsmarkt, informatietechnologie en internationalisering*, CED-rapport, Den Haag: SER.

—— (1997) *Versterking secundair beroepsonderwijs, Advies Versterking secundair beroepsonderwijs, uitgebracht aan de Staatssecretaris van Sociale Zaken en Werkgelegenheid*. Publicatienummer 34, Den Haag: SER.

Sheer, B. and Wong, F.K.Y. (2008) 'The Development of Advanced Nursing Practice Globally'. *Journal of Nursing Scholarship*, 40 (3): 204–11.

Simon, G. (2001) L'apprentissage, Nouveaux territoires, nouveaux usages, *Bref Céreq*, No. 175, Marseille: Céreq.

Skills for Health (2007) *What are National Occupational Standards and National Workforce Competences?*. Online. Available www.skillsforhealth.org.uk/ (accessed 3 May 2007).

Sloane, P.F.E. (2001) 'Lernfelder als curriculare Vorgaben', in Bonz, B. (ed.) *Didaktik beruflicher Bildung*, Baltmannsweiler: Schneider-Verlag.

Smith, A. (1776) *The Wealth of Nations*, Indianapolis: Liberty Fund.

Smollett T. (1979 (1748)) *The Adventures of Roderick Random*, Oxford: Oxford University Press.

Soskice, D. (1999) 'Divergent Production Regimes: Coordinated and Uncoordinated Market Economies in the 1980s and 1990s', in H. Kitschelt, P. Lange, G. Marks and J.D. Stephens (eds) *Continuity and Change in Contemporary Capitalism*, Cambridge: Cambridge University Press.

Spitzer, A. and Perrenoud, B. (2006) 'Reforms in Nursing Education across Western Europe: From Agenda to Practice', *Journal of Professional Nursing*, 22 (3): 150–61.

Steedman, H. (1992) *Mathematics in Vocational Youth Training for the Building Trades in Britain, France and Germany*, NIESR discussion paper No. 9. London.

Steedman, H. and Wagner, K. (2007) 'The Impact of National Qualifications Systems on Companies' Recruitment Practices – An Anglo-German Comparison', *Zeitschrift fuer Arbeitsmarktforschung (ZAF)*, 40 (2/3): 235–49.

Steedman, H., Wagner, K. and Foreman, J. (2003) *The Impact on Firms of ICT Skill-supply Strategies: An Anglo-German Comparison*, London: Centre for Economic Performance, London School of Economics.

Stender, J. (2006) *Berufsbildung in der Bundesrepublik Deutschland, Teil 1: Strukturprobleme und Ordnungsprinzipien des dualen Systems*, Stuttgart: S. Hirzel Verlag.

Streeck, Wolfgang (2009) *Re-forming Capitalism: Institutional Change in the German Political Economy*, New York: Oxford University Press.

Streeck, W. and Hilbert, J. (1991) 'Organised Interests and Vocational Training in the West German Construction Industry', in H. Rainbird and G. Syben (eds) *Restructuring a Traditional Industry*, New York: Berg.

Sturt, G. (1926, 1976) *The Wheelwright's Shop*, Cambridge: Cambridge University Press.

Sultana, R.G. (2008) *Competence and Competence Frameworks in Career Guidance: Complex and Contested Concept*. Online. Available www.um.edu.mt/~data/assets/pdf_file/0015/60414/Competence_IJEVG.pdf (accessed 2 October 2009).

—— (2009) 'Competence and competence frameworks in career guidance: complex and contested concepts', *International Journal for Educational and Vocational Guidance*, 9: 15–30.

Syben, G. (2009) *Sectoral Qualifications Framework for the Construction Industry in Europe*, Final Report of the Working Group, Bremen: BAQ ForschungsInstitut.

Tanguy, L. (2004) 'La fabrication des nomenclatures de formation initiale et leur inférence sur la notion de qualification', in D. Meda and F. Venat (eds) *Le Travail non qualifié: permanences et paradoxes*, Paris: La Découverte.

—— (2008) 'La fabrication d'un bien universel', in Brucy, G., Caillaud, P., Quenson, E. and Tanguy, L. (eds) *Former pour Réformer*, Paris: La découverte.

Temple, P. (2004) What is the knowledge society? – *EUEREK Working Paper*. Online. Available www.euerek.info/Public.../knowledge%20soc%20sep04.doc (accessed 13 May 2010).

Thelen, K. and Busemeyer, M. (2008) *From Collectivism towards Segmentalism: Institutional Change in German Vocational Training*, Cologne: Max Planck Institute for the Study of Societies Discussion Paper 08/13.

Training and Development Agency for Schools (TDA) (2007) *Professional Standards for Teachers: Why Sit Still in Your Career?*, London: TDA.

Trampusch, Ch. (2009) 'Europeanization and Institutional Change in Vocational Education and Training in Austria and Germany', *Governance: An International Journal of Policy, Administration and Institutions*, 22 (3): 369–95.

Treaty of Maastricht (1992) *Provisions Amending the Treaty Establishing the European Economic Community with a View to Establishing the European Community*. Online. Available www.eurotreaties.com/maastrichtec.pdf (accessed 27 September 2010).

Treaty of Rome (1957). Online. Available www.eurotreaties.com/rometreaty.pdf (accessed 27 September 2010).

Uhly, A. and Troltsch, K. (2009) 'Duale Berufsausbildung in der Dienstleistungs-und Wissensökonomie', *Zeitschrift für Berufs-und Wirtschaftspädagogik*, 105 (1): 17–32.

van den Berg, J. and Doets, C. (eds) (2005) *Een dag zonder leren is een verloren dag. Onderzoek proeftuinen 2004–2005*, 's-Hertogenbosch: CINOP.

van der Meijden, A., Westerhuis, A., Huisman, J. and Neuvel, J. (2009) *Beroepsonderwijs in verandering: op weg naar competentiegercith onderwijs. De vierde meting van de cgo-monitor*, Amsterdam/'s-Hertogenbosch: ecbo.

van Middelaar, L. (2009) *De passage naar Europa. Geschiedenis van een begin*, Groningen: Historische Uitgeverij.

van Zolingen, S.J. (1995) *Gevraagd: sleutelkwalificaties,een studie naar sleutelkwalificaties voor het middelbaar beroepsonderwijs*, Nijmegen: KUN.

Verdier, E. (2008) 'L'éducation et la formation tout au long de la vie: une orientation européenne, des régimes d'action publique et des modèles nationaux en évolution', *Éducation et Société*, 40: 195–225.

Villemer, R. (1947) *Organisation industrielle: principes et applications*, Paris: Soc. D'Editions Françaises et internationales.

Vinokur, A. (1995) 'Réflexions sur l'économie du diplôme', *Formation Emploi*, 52: 151–83.

VNO-NCW and MKB Nederland (2008) *Brief aan de vaste commissie voor Onderwijs, Cultuur en Wetenschappen van de Tweede Kamer der Staten Generaal betreffende de ronde tafel conferentie over Competentiegericht Onderwijs*, Den Haag.

Vocational Training Act (*Berufsbildungsgesetz*), as of 23 March 2005; Federal Law Gazette [BGBl. I].

Voß, G. and Pongratz, H.J. (1998) 'Der Arbeitskraftunternehmer. Eine neue Grundform der Ware Arbeitskraft?' *Kölner Zeitschrift für Soziologie und Sozialpsychologie*, 50 (1): 131–58.

Warhurst, C., Lockyer, C. and Dutton, E. (2006) 'IT Jobs: Opportunities for All?', *New Technology, Work and Employment*, 21 (1): 75–88.

Weber, M. (1980) *Wirtschaft und Gesellschaft. Grundriß der Verstehenden Soziologie. 5. Auflage (Studienausgabe)*, Tübingen: von Johannes Winckelmann.

Westerhuis, A. (2007) 'The Role of the State in Vocational Education: A Political Analysis of the History of Vocational Education in the Netherlands', in L. Clarke and C. Winch (eds) *Vocational Education: International Approaches, Developments and Systems*, London: Routledge.

—— (2009a) 'Cross-national Equivalence of Vocational Skills and Qualifications – The Dutch Case', unpublished report for the Nuffield Foundation, London: Kings College London.

—— (2009b) 'VET Research in Relation to VET Policy, Planning and Practice', in F. Rauner and R. Maclean (eds) *Handbook of Technical and Vocational Education and Training Research*, Dordrecht: Springer.

Williams, M. (2000) *Wealth without Nations*, London: Athol Books.

Winch, C. (2006) Georg Kerschensteiner. Founding the German Dual System, *Oxford Review of Education*, 32 (3): 381–96.

—— (2009) 'Gilbert Ryle on Knowing How and the Possibility of Vocational Education', *Journal of Applied Philosophy*, 26 (1): 88–101.

Winch, C. and Clarke, L. (2003) 'Front-loaded Vocational Education versus Lifelong Learning', *Oxford Review of Education*, 29 (2): 239–52.

Winterton, J., Delamare le Deist, F. and Stringfellow, E. (2005) *Typology of Knowledge, Skills and Competences: Clarification of the Concept and Prototype*, Thessaloniki: CEDEFOP.

Yam, B.M. (2004) 'From Vocation to Profession: The Quest for Professionalization of Nursing', *British Journal of Nursing*, 13 (16): 978–82.

Young, M.F.D. (2009) 'Alternative Educational Futures for a Knowledge Society', Keynote Speech given at the European Educational Research Association Conference *EERA*, Vienna, 2009.

Websites

GOC (2010) www.goc.nl/defenities-bij-opleiden.aspx

TDA (2009) www.tda.gov.uk/upload/resources/pdf/s/standards_a4.pdf

The Data Service (2010) www.thedataservice.org.uk/statistics/statisticalfirstrelease/sfr_archive/lscsfr20022008/

INDEX